12.50
biol
T

GEORGE GAYLORD SIMPSON

Splendid Isolation

THE CURIOUS HISTORY OF
SOUTH AMERICAN MAMMALS

NEW HAVEN AND LONDON, YALE UNIVERSITY PRESS, 1980

Designed by Sally Harris
and set in VIP Garamond type.
Printed in the United States of America by
The Murray Printing Co., Westford, Mass.

Published in Great Britain, Europe, Africa, and
Asia (except Japan) by Yale University Press,
Ltd., London. Distributed in Australia and
New Zealand by Book & Film Services, Artarmon,
N.S.W., Australia; and in Japan by Harper & Row,
Publishers, Tokyo Office.

Library of Congress Cataloging in Publication Data

Simpson, George Gaylord, 1902–
   Splendid isolation. The curious history of
South American mammals.

   Includes bibliographical references and index.
   1. Mammals—South America—Evolution.   2. Mammals,
Fossil.   I. Title.
QL725.A1S58   599'.03'8098   79-17630
ISBN 0–300–02434–7

After two long sea voyages and some adventures, tribulations, and efforts ashore, I first set foot on Patagonian soil on Sunday, 28 September 1930. I had been fascinated by South America and its animals since childhood. While training for and entering the profession of paleontology, I had become aware that fossil mammals in Patagonia had been found by Charles Darwin nearly a century earlier and that extensive collections of them had been made since then. Yet much still remained to be done, and I became convinced that an earnest young paleomammalogist could find few, if any, more interesting things to do than to study the early mammals preserved as fossils in South America. The best way to start, after learning what had already been published about them, was to go to Patagonia, to study at first hand the successive strata in which early mammals were preserved, to collect as many as I could, to restudy the great collections already in Argentinian and some other museums, and to go on from there with my own researches and with following the continuing work of others.

Thus started a commitment to a lifetime of work and study, especially on the early mammals of South America but also on the whole history of mammals on that continent. During the fifty years that have elapsed since I definitely started such studies I have had to do many other things as well, but this subject was never far from my mind. Now I am summing up what is known about the history of South American land mammals, what I think about various, sometimes disputed points in that history, and what I find of special importance and interest in it.

This is not a book written particularly for my colleagues, although they will find some interest in it. I have not assumed any previous technical or detailed knowledge of the subject by any reader. At times close attention may be required, but I believe that any literate adult with a real interest in South America, in animals, or in evolution can read this account with pleasure and profit.

References given at the end of each chapter are extremely far from being exhaustive. In general they should be helpful to anyone who wants to read further, and incidentally they may help a student to get started toward more detailed publications. A few references are to technical papers to substantiate some particular point beyond more general or background works. In quoting from foreign language sources I have used my own translations.

All the text figures have been drawn anew for this work by Judy Spencer, most of them in a technique that I find interesting, attractive, and apt and that is quite unusual in this field. In the illustration of fossil and some recent mammals, we have used all the available information from many sources (see the appendix for a note on the restoration of extinct animals). Restorations made under the direction of W. B. Scott, mostly by Bruce Horsfall, have been especially helpful but in no case have they simply been copied.

So many people in South America, North America, and Europe have contributed to my knowledge of this subject and aided me in concrete and direct ways that to name them all is impossible and to select a few may seem invidious. None of them is forgotten and I hope that none will feel so if I just salute the memory of such past friends as Carlos Ameghino and Lucas Kraglievich, both of whom facilitated and enriched my study of the great Ameghino collection in Buenos Aires, and Angel Cabrera, who did the same for study in La Plata. I hesitate to proceed to salute even the oldest and best of friends happily still living, but I am sure that I will not offend others, mostly younger, if I name only Justino Hernández, my indefatigable field assistant in Patagonia, Rosendo Pascual, the leading present Argentinian paleomammalogist, Carlos de Paula Couto, the leading Brazilian paleomammalogist, Bryan Patterson, an outstanding North American authority on this subject, and Robert Hoffstetter, an outstanding French authority on it. So many mammalogists, both paleo- and neo-, are now working in this field that, although I believe this book is well up to date as of February 1979, it will be out of date as to some details and new finds by the time it has been edited, indexed, manufactured, and issued.

The difficult task of transcribing the manuscript from my rough, extensively interlined and revised handscript to legible typescript was performed mainly by Renée Johnson, in lesser part also by my wife Anne Roe and by Carol Nowotny-Young. My wife has also read and usefully criticized the whole work and aided and abetted me in more ways than I can say.

Yale University Press has again been cordial and efficient, and Ellen Graham has again been an excellent editor. Barbara Palmer helped ably with the copy editing and the book has been designed for the Press by Sally Harris. Cynthia J. Plastino ably assisted in preparation of the index.

G. G. S.

Tucson, Arizona
8 February 1979

CHAPTER 1

Why, What, and How

Why should someone write a book about the history of mammals in South America, and why should you and others read it? There are several good answers.

For a start, there are many strange mammals now in South America, fascinating to almost everyone: opossums, armadillos, tree sloths, anteaters, monkeys in great varieties, capybaras (the largest rodents now on earth), wild guinea pigs, tucu-tucus, and many other native rodents strange to us, jaguars and rather weird maned wolves, tapirs, peccaries, llamas and other humpless camels, such peculiar deer as the pudu and the huemul—to name just a few. Here is indeed an interesting mixture of creatures, and it takes only a modicum of human curiosity to want to know their history and to learn, as far as possible, how that mixture arose.

It is a mixture, and that is an essential part of the history. Some of those animals have had ancestors and relatives confined to South America at the beginning of the Age of Mammals and long thereafter, although some (sloths and anteaters, for example) have more recently spread into tropical Central America and a few even into the United States (an opossum and an armadillo). Some, ancestral rodents and monkeys, turned up quite suddenly around the middle of the history; where they came from and how will be discussed in due course. Still others appear rather late in the history as migrants from North America. Some of those, such as the camels, no longer live in North America. Others, such as jaguars and peccaries, are marginal here, and still others, like some rabbits and foxes, are now common on both continents. The tangle is rather complex, and that is part of the interest of the history.

1

The history becomes even more complex and more fascinating for another reason. As we look back into it, we find more and more mammals of groups entirely extinct such as lived nowhere else on earth. As men never saw them, they were not named until scientists who make that their business invented names for them, names strangely assorted as to origin but often coined from Greek: astrapotheres, "lightning mammals" (they were big and probably noisy, so they reminded Hermann Burmeister of thunder and lightning); pyrotheres, "fire mammals" (Florentino Ameghino called them that probably because their remains have been found in volcanic ashes); toxodonts, "bow tooths" (among Darwin's discoveries, so called by Richard Owen because their upper molar teeth are arched like bows); *Thylacosmilus,* "pouch-saber" (an odd combination coined by Elmer Riggs because they were marsupials, hence presumably had pouches like kangaroos, and had saberlike upper canine teeth)—and literally hundreds more. Just here the point is that the wholly extinct native mammals of South America were even more weird, wonderful, and numerous than those still living there.

Important beyond its sheer wonder is the fact that this history, to which Charles Darwin contributed a bit, provided some of the clues that led him to his understanding of the origin of species. Here it continues to play an incomparable role not just in demonstrating that evolution really did occur but in the more arduous, longer, still incomplete task of learning how and, in a causal sense, why it occurred. Some of the principles and causes of evolution can be observed in nature and studied experimentally in laboratories, but evolution involves time in the tens, hundreds, and thousands of millions of years. We cannot observe that directly in our lifetime or prolong our experiments to such lengths. But we can follow evolution at work for tens of millions of years in the history of South American mammals, and here it turns out that we have been provided with an almost ideal natural experiment.

It has been learned, as will be discussed in later chapters, that during most of the Age of Mammals, the Cenozoic in geological terms, South America was an island continent. Its land mammals then evolved in almost complete isolation, as in an experiment with a closed population. To make the experiment even more instructive, the isolation was not quite complete, and while it continued two alien groups of mammals were nevertheless introduced, as might be done to study perturbation in a laboratory experiment. Finally, to top the experiment off the isolation ended, and there was extensive mixture and interaction between what had previously been two quite different populations, each with its own ecological variety and balance. Thus, we can also hope to follow the evolutionary factors in such an event under almost ideal conditions. The ecological mix in South America had changed, evolved, throughout the long history. Here toward the end it was most radically modified or remodeled.

Enough is known about this history to follow its broad sweep in many respects and to see considerable detail. Yet it is part of the fascination of the subject that many things about it are still uncertain and others still quite unknown. Within the scope of the grand history there are mystery stories the ends of which have not yet been read, although we can expect to find that those ends in many if not all cases have been written in the record of the rocks and their contained fossils. It is one of the exciting elements in this history, as it is in any pursuit of human knowledge, that not all is yet known.

So much at present for the why and some of the what of this book. Now must be considered how the subject, details of which could and do fill whole libraries, is to be presented in a single book. There have been several useful summaries of the history of South American mammals at shorter than book length and now inevitably more or less out of date. One of the best and most recent, published in 1972, carries on a long tradition of cooperation between Argentinian and North American paleontologists, here respectively Rosendo Pascual and Bryan Patterson. The present author has published several periodically, most recently in 1969. The great Argentinian paleontologist Florentino Ameghino in 1906 published in French a book-length discussion of the whole history of South American mammals as then known and interpreted by him. That could not serve as a model for later histories because it was at least as argumentative as expository and because much of its theoretical basis soon had to be discarded, for reasons that will be given in the next chapter.

Now a valued classic is *A History of Land Mammals in the Western Hemisphere* by Princeton professor W. B. Scott, published in 1913 and then in a completely rewritten and updated version in 1937. That book gave top billing to North American fossil mammals, which then were and now to less extent still are better known than those of South America, but it did summarize the South American history as well as possible in the early 1910s and in the late 1930s. After several introductory chapters, Scott's plan was first to discuss the succession of faunas briefly, then to consider in some detail each of the major groups of mammals, and finally to devote a chapter to the then somewhat chaotic subject of modes and causes in evolution. The updated version followed almost the same plan but placed more emphasis on the geology of the rocks in which the fossil mammals were found. A peculiarity of Scott's approach was that throughout and in both versions he followed time sequences in reverse order, from the present into the increasingly remote past.

The present book must include the same main topics as Scott's and, more briefly, some others. Specifically, it must include consideration both of successive faunas as whole animal communities and of the roles, characteristics, and individual histories of each of the main groups of mammals involved. The organization, approach, and style, however, are here quite unlike Scott's. For one thing, what most people think of as the normal time sequence will be followed: from early to late, or from the oldest known South American fossil mammals to the mammals now living on that continent. The histories of particular groups of mammals and of whole faunas will be interwoven to some extent, with the two more interrelated and balanced than in Scott or most other previous studies.

An additional "why" for this book is that knowledge of the history of mammals in South America has itself an interesting history. To discuss all of the human history of the discovery and interpretation of the records of the natural history, the fossils of mammals involved in the latter history, would require more than one book as long as this one. Here just the next chapter will be devoted to some of the comparatively early steps in the human history of the subject, those steps that seem to me to have been of special interest in laying the broad foundation on which later scholarship was based. The results of labors by the later scholars, roughly from the 1920s into the late 1970s, form the main subject matter of all chapters after the second.

For the benefit of students and other readers who want to go more deeply into some aspects of this history, and sometimes to document sources for this text, references to a few previous publications will be given as appropriate at the ends of chapters.

References

The chapter references in this book are not meant to be research bibliographies. References to the major bibliographies useful for detailed research are added to this list.

Ameghino, F. 1906. Les formations sédimentaires du Crétacé supérieur et du Tertiaire de Patagonie avec un parallèle entre leurs faunes mammalogiques et celles de l'ancien continent. *Anales del Museo Nacional de Buenos Aires,* 14: 1–568.

Patterson, B., and R. Pascual. 1972. The fossil mammal fauna of South America. In *Evolution, mammals, and southern continents,* ed. A. Keast, F. C. Erk, and B. Glass, pp. 247–309. Albany: State University of New York Press.

Scott, W. B. 1913, 1937. *A history of land mammals in the Western Hemisphere.* New York: Macmillan.

Simpson, G. G. 1969. South American mammals. In *Biogeography and ecology in South America,* ed. E. J. Fittkau, J. Illies, J. Klinge, G. H. Schwalbe, and H. Sioli, pp. 879–909. The Hague: W. Junk.

Research Bibliographies

Allison, H. J.; J. A. Bacskai; B. Bradnikov; C. L. Camp; E. Fulton; M. Green; J. T. Gregory; H. McGinnis; K. Munthe; R. H. Nichols; D. N. Taylor; V. L. Vanderhoof; and S. P. Welles. 1940–1973. *Bibliography of fossil vertebrates.* 9 vols. Geological Society of America, Special Papers 27 and 42, Memoirs 37, 57, 84, 92, 117, 134, and 141. (Authorship changed with most volumes, and names are here in alphabetical order. Camp was senior author of all but the last volume, of which Gregory was senior author, and the whole series is known as the "Camp bibliographies." The publications covered are of dates 1928–1972.)

Charles, R., and J. Ostrom, eds. 1973–1974. Bibliography of vertebrate paleontology. 3 issues. London: Geosystems. (This was an unsuccessful attempt to carry on the Camp bibliographies in computerized form.)

Romer, A. S.; N. E. Wright; T. Edinger; and R. Van Frank. 1962. *Bibliography of fossil vertebrates exclusive of North America, 1509–1927*. 2 vols. Geological Society of America, Memoir 87.

CHAPTER 2

Retrospect on Fundamentals

In 1833 Charles Darwin, an active and enthusiastic young man of twenty-four years, was sailing in the British naval surveying vessel *Beagle* along the coast of what is now Argentina. He made several excursions ashore, where he was fascinated by the many species of living birds and mammals. One of the birds, an ostrichlike rhea, was destined to bear his name; its original name, *Rhea darwini,* has been changed by the vagaries of technical nomenclature, but it is still popularly known as Darwin's rhea. At several localities he found the partially petrified teeth and bones of prehistoric mammals. He was amazed to observe that while some of them were more or less nearly related to living South American mammals others were remarkably different. In his great book, now generally known as *The Voyage of the Beagle* but first published in 1839 as *Journal of Researches into the Geology and Natural History of the Various Countries Visited by H.M.S. Beagle under the Command of Captain Fitzroy, R.N., from 1832 to 1836,* Darwin discussed these peculiar observations at some length, in part as follows:

> If we divide America, not by the Isthmus of Panama, but by the southern part of Mexico, in lat. 20°, where the great table-land presents an obstacle to the migration of species . . . we shall then have two zoological provinces strongly contrasted with each other. Some few species alone have passed the barrier, and may be considered as wanderers, such as the puma, opossum, kinkajou, and peccari. The mammalogy of South America is characterized by possessing several species of the genera of llama, cavy (and allied animals), tapir,

7

peccari, opossum, anteater, sloth, and armadillo. . . . North America, on the other hand, is characterized by its numerous rodents, and by four genera of solid horned ruminants, of which section the southern half does not possess a single species.

This distinction of the two zoological provinces does not appear always to have existed. At the present day the order of Edentata is much more strongly developed in South America, than in any other part of the world: and concluding from the fossil remains, which were discovered [by Darwin himself] at Bahia Blanca, such must have been the case during the former epoch. In America, north of Mexico, not one of this order is now found: yet, as is well known, the gigantic [extinct] megalonyx . . . has been found only in that country. . . .

Of the Pachydermata four or five species are now found in America; but, as in the case of the Edentata, none are peculiar to the continent north of Mexico; and one alone seems to exist there as a wanderer. Yet the account of the multitude of bones of the mastodon and elephant, which have been discovered in the salt-licks of North America, is familiar to every one. . . . In [the vicinity of Quito] three species of mastodon have been discovered. . . .

It is interesting thus to discover an epoch anterior to the division, as far at least as two important orders among the mammalia are concerned, of the continent into two separate zoological provinces. [Darwin 1839, pp. 152–154]

When Darwin wrote, most of the known fossil mammals from both South and North America had lived relatively late in earth history and in mammalian faunal history: all but a few in the Pleistocene or most recent Ice Age, which ended only some 10,000 years ago. Darwin's discovery that the Pleistocene mammals of North and South America were in some respects more alike than are the now living mammals was a vital clue to an extraordinary event. Now, almost a century and a half after Darwin's discoveries, that event is known as the Great American Interchange and is still the subject of lively, occasionally even almost acrimonious, discussion. It will provide a dramatic climax in the present work.

Among the fossil localities found by Darwin was one then already and now still called Monte Hermoso, "handsome hill." Fifty-four years later, it was visited by Florentino Ameghino, a thirty-three-year-old Argentinian who had become in his own way a devoted follower of Darwin. Florentino and his younger brother Carlos, sons of Italian immigrants, grew up in Luján, a town on the pampa not far from Buenos Aires. Prehistoric mammals had already long been known from that vicinity. Those bones so fascinated the Ameghino boys that they determined to spend their lives probing such marvels and mysteries. So on the fourth of March 1887 Florentino sat on Monte Hermoso and wrote (in Spanish):

> Monte Hermoso! On the whole all that is handsome about it is its name. It is a series of semimobile dunes, some thirty-odd meters high, on the highest of which is a lighthouse intended to prevent as far as possible the wrecks that so often happen along that coast. It is an arid and solitary place, scorched by the sun and swept by the winds which lash the face with the burning sand, without water and without pasturage, or, if there is some, hard and prickly as upholsterers' needles. . . .
>
> But this place, isolated from any center of civilization, stuck away in a region all but uninhabitable, is for the naturalist, if not a handsome hill, a golden hill, a hill of life unknown until now, dead, if you like, but coming alive before our eyes under the blows of a pick against the hillside.
>
> Monte Hermoso some day will have its monograph, but it would be selfish if in the meantime I were to keep to myself alone the summing up of the discoveries that I have made there and of the considerations so strongly brought to my mind both by the remains dug up there and by the sight of the strata in which they were buried. . . .
>
> It seems that almost all of the fossil mammals of Monte Hermoso are species and even frequently genera hitherto unknown, very distinct from those we know as coming from the Pampean formation. . . . They form a real transitional fauna whose types, although different, resemble on one hand

those from the lower Pampean of Buenos Aires and La Plata,
and on the other hand those from the much older deposit
. . . of the Paraná. . . . [Ameghino 1916, pp. 331–333]

Although the ages of these faunas in modern terms had not yet
been established, Florentino Ameghino's remarks here take us
back of Darwin's and into a different part of an extraordinary
history. Darwin had noted the marked distinction of the recent
faunas of North and South America and their partial mingling in a
previous epoch, the Pleistocene represented by the Pampean in
Argentina. Now Ameghino was starting to push the story farther
back, into an earlier stage, into pre-Pleistocene ages when the
faunas of the northern and southern continents were even more
distinct than they are today.

It had also been known since Darwin's visit to Argentina that
fossil mammals occurred in the bleak southern reaches of that
country called Patagonia, but before 1887 there had been little
serious investigation of them. Now in the same year as Florentino's trip to Monte Hermoso his brother Carlos went off alone to
Patagonia in search of fossil mammals. He worked there with
astonishing success almost steadily until 1903, sixteen years of
hard, slogging, lonely work in what was then one of the most
desolate regions on earth.

Florentino had done little collecting himself before 1887 and
thereafter he did almost none. In the brothers' busiest years he
worked hard for the barest support of them both, for most of that
time in the city of La Plata. There he also labored day and night
studying, describing, and interpreting the collections that poured
in, almost all from Carlos, who was an experienced collector even
before he went to Patagonia.

There was a certain provinciality in Florentino's outlook and
work, and some critics have assumed that he was a rather naive,
poorly educated, self-taught researcher, an *autodidáctico* in the
rather pejorative Argentine term. His formal schooling indeed
was not impressive, but like all really successful scientists he never
stopped learning and his horizons were far wider than the pampas.
While still in his twenties but already the author of a number of

scientific studies, he spent three years in France. There he met many prominent scientists and worked especially with Paul Gervais, one of the greatest nineteenth-century paleontologists. He married a French girl, née Léontine Poirier, and thereafter with her help he published some of his most important work in polished French, which had a wider world audience than Spanish. He kept in touch by correspondence with most of the leading paleontologists of the late 1800s and early 1900s and honored many of them with names of fossil mammals such as *Edvardocopeia, Guilielmoscottia, Henricosbornia,* and *Othnielmarshia* for North American paleontologists; *Asmithwoodwardia, Guilielmofloweria, Oldfieldthomasia, Ricardolydekkeria, Ricardowenia,* and *Thomashuxleya* for some in Great Britain; *Albertogaudrya, Amilnedwardsia, Edvardotrouessartia, Henricofilholia,* and *Paulogervaisia,* French; *Carolozittelia, Ernestokokenia,* and *Maxschlosseria,* German.

There are several reasons for introducing that list of odd and rather difficult names at this point. One reason is that they are a roster of great contemporaries of the Ameghinos, who were familiar with their work: Cope (1840–1897), Scott (1858–1947), Osborn (1857–1930), Marsh (1831–1899), Smith Woodward (1864–1944), Flower (1831–1899), Thomas (1858–1929), Lydekker (1849–1915), Owen (1804–1892), Huxley (1825–1895), Gaudry (1827–1908), Milne-Edwards (1835–1900), Trouessart (1842–1927), Filhol (1843–1902), Gervais (1816–1879), Zittel (1839–1904), Koken (1860–1912), and Schlosser (1854–1932) are all revered in the history of science. Florentino also named a genus for his collaborating brother: *Caroloameghinia*. Carlos's dates were 1865–1936. There is a slight question about the date of Florentino's birth, but it was probably 1854. He died in 1911.

A second reason for this list is that all the animals to which these names were given lived in what are now called the Casamayoran, Mustersan, or Deseadan land mammal ages. Those were, at the time of the Ameghinos, the three oldest mammalian faunas known from South America, and only one older (the Riochican, about which more later) has been found since then. (There are a few even older scraps now known, but they do not as yet merit designation as a fauna.) Carlos Ameghino discovered the first two faunas and was the first to characterize the third and to collect a real sample of its fauna. Those discoveries carried the history of South American mammals back tens of millions of years earlier than the previously known Montehermosan and Pampean. It was also Carlos in the field and Florentino in the study who filled in most of the vast time span between the Deseadan and the Montehermosan.

Thus one can say in retrospect that by the time of Florentino Ameghino's death in 1911 much of the essential framework for a history of South American mammals had been attained. Some readjustment, much filling in of detail, and a nearly complete change in faunal nomenclature were still necessary and are not yet completed, but the basic groundwork for the sequence of faunas had been put well in hand. Nevertheless, some essential broad readjustments of Florentino's conclusions had to be made before there was an overall groundwork on which later conceptions of the faunal history could be soundly based.

One of the readjustments had to do with the time scale. With minor exceptions and toward the end of their work, the Ameghinos had the sequence of the faunas then known correct, but not the correlation or comparison of relative times with those on other continents. In every case the Ameghinos' final judgment made the relative ages of their faunas older than they are now known to be. For example, they considered the first three faunas definitely established by them, those now known as Casamayoran, Mustersan, and Deseadan, to be Cretaceous in age. It is now clear that they are all some millions of years younger, Eocene to Oligocene. (The significance of the terms involved will be discussed later.) Really precise relative dating and dating in terms of years before present have been a long, hard problem, work on which is still going forward, but it is clear that the Ameghinos' dates were all much too early.

The second major readjustment has to do with the relationships of the Ameghinos' fossil mammals. Here, too, some of the details are still in question, but it is clear that in many cases Florentino was radically mistaken about the affinities and the lines of descent illustrated by the fossils brought to him by Carlos. In that respect Florentino was neither stupid nor ignorant. He was caught in what may in retrospect be seen as a sort of then almost unavoidable booby trap: the phenomenon of evolutionary convergence, which still is a source of disquiet and precaution to paleontologists and other biologists. When different lineages of animals are evolving separately but in similar environments and in adaptation to similar ways of life they commonly also become similar in the structure of the functional part involved. That is especially likely to occur when the groups involved are in different geographic regions separated by barriers to expansion and migration. If the lineages involved had different ancestries and were not closely related, this phenomenon of convergence certainly rarely, probably never, resulted in fully detailed similarity, but the resemblance is often close enough to deceive the unwary. Florentino Ameghino had little reason to be wary, and that was particularly unfortunate because it finally turned out that various South American mammals through the ages had been convergent toward, rather than specially related to, those of other continents in unusually numerous instances and sometimes to extraordinary degrees.

In the following pages we will find many examples of convergence, but one may be briefly particularized here as evidence of how insidious was the trap into which Ameghino fell. He had numerous fossils of mammals that were plainly predaceous, doglike carnivores. He concluded that they were closely related, some of them indeed ancestral, to living members of the dog family, Canidae, and other widespread living carnivores. In fact those animals, which we call Borhyaenidae, one of the names given to them by Ameghino, were only convergent toward the Canidae and had no ancestral or other special relationship to the latter. Ameghino also saw resemblances between the Borhyaenidae and American opossums, and he concluded that the ancestors of the Borhyaenidae were early, primitive opossums. All students of these matters now agree that in this respect Ameghino was essentially correct. Thus in this case, and in many others, Ameghino, faced by real resemblances of a group of his fossils to two other groups of mammals, interpreted these resemblances as representing special relationship to both of the latter groups and was radically mistaken as to one relationship but essentially right as to the other.

Ameghino's belief that so many of his fossil groups were ancestral to others to which they were in fact only convergent was combined by him with his overestimates of the ages of his fossils to produce a stunning conclusion: that practically all the known fossil and now living groups of mammals (including mankind) originated in Argentina and that their descendants subsequently occupied the rest of the world.

The reorientation, or perhaps one should more fairly say continued orientation, necessary as a basis for the history of South American mammals was the work of many hands and was only gradually achieved. Indeed it is still under way, but now not at such broadly basic levels. One of the early steps must be credited to another Argentinian, one of Swiss origin: Santiago Roth. He also grossly overestimated the ages of early mammalian faunas, and much of his exchange of polemics with Ameghino did little credit to either side, but he made one great step forward. In a paper published in 1903, while the Ameghinos were still fully engaged with such matters, he held that the great majority of extinct South American hoofed mammals, ungulates, belonged to a group confined as far as then known to that continent and, contrary to Ameghino's opinion, were not ancestral to any ungulates known on any other continent. That is still considered essentially correct, and the group, which will occupy much of this book, is still known by the name that Roth gave it: Notoungulata, "southern ungulates."

The next major step forward in the basic reorientation was marked by the beginning of direct collaboration between South and North American paleontologists, a friendly association that came to include many from both continents and that continues at the present time. In the 1890s William Berryman Scott, then already a leading student of North American fossil mammals (he was born in 1858), became interested in what the Ameghinos were finding. With the support of a wealthy New Yorker, he arranged for Princeton University, where he spent virtually all of his long adult life, to send an expedition to collect fossils in Patagonia. That expedition was led by John Bell Hatcher, an able North American fossil collector, and worked seasonally from 1896 to 1899. The rich collections were described, illustrated, and discussed from 1905 to 1932 in a series of sumptuous publications, those on the fossil mammals by Scott and his colleague at Princeton, William John Sinclair.

Scott did not himself visit Patagonia or collect any South American fossils, but in 1900 he visited La Plata and Buenos Aires, where he studied and photographed many of the Ameghinos' fossils. He also won and treasured the friendship of Florentino, about whom he wrote many years later in his autobiography:

> The only medium of communication that I had with [Florentino] Ameghino was bad French, which he spoke very fluently, but pronounced as though it were Spanish. Gradually, however, we reached a basis of mutual understanding, and could communicate with each other readily. Every afternoon, at half-past four or five, he would appear with a tray for making tea [surely so-called Paraguay tea, *yerba mate,* not "tea" in the English sense]; I could not bear to dull his enthusiasm by telling him how greatly I disliked that beverage and solemnly imbibed two large cups. During the tea-drinking we discussed the problems of paleontology and squabbled with the most perfect amiability, for we never agreed about anything and yet we never lost our tempers and always kept the discussion on a purely objective plane. . . .
>
> I went to La Plata decidedly prejudiced against [Florentino Ameghino] but a brief acquaintance removed that prejudice entirely. Not only did his heroic devotion compel respect, but I came to value his work as I had not done before. [Scott 1939, p. 251]

The year after Scott's visit, Ameghino named one of his beloved fossils *Guilielmoscottia.*

Most of the fossil mammals collected by Hatcher and his associates belonged to the fauna now called Santacrucian. On these

Scott reported to the Sixth International Congress of Zoology in 1904 (published in 1905): "On looking over a series of representative Santa-Cruz mammals, we are immediately struck by the strangeness of the assemblage; not a single genus of these mammals occurs in any part of the northern hemisphere and, what is more surprising, the difference from the northern faunas is not only one of families and genera, but of orders."

Those words by his friend were a death knell for Ameghino's theory of the Argentine origin of so many groups of mammals in the rest of the world. Ameghino did not abandon his theory in the few years of life remaining to him, but other paleontologists found that the extraordinary, unique nature of so many South American mammals made them, and Ameghino's own work on them, still more valuable and interesting.

Hatcher and his associates also made a large collection of fossil invertebrates, mostly shells, from marine strata lying below the Santa Cruz beds from which their fossil mammals came. Those marine fossils provided another deathblow to the Ameghinian system, for they provided conclusive evidence of the fact, previously suspected, that Ameghino's claimed dates for his faunas were indeed much too old. When studied by Arnold Edward Ortmann, a German paleontologist then temporarily at Princeton, these marine fossils indicated a probable early Miocene age, and in any case certainly tens of millions of years later than the early Eocene age ascribed to them by Ameghino. As the Santa Cruz mammals were later than those marine animals, they, too, could not possibly be of Eocene age.

It may here be explained why the relative dating of South American fossil mammalian faunas has been such a difficult problem. The time-honored and still useful method of relative dating of rocks from one region or continent to another has been by resemblance or difference of fossil faunas. For example, when fossil mammals from certain strata in the Bighorn Basin of Wyoming are compared with those of some strata in the London and Paris basins of Europe, it is found that a number of those from the two continents are closely related, in some cases almost identical.

As mammalian faunas on those continents changed rather rapidly in time, it is evident that the strata here in question are of nearly if not quite the same age. But that method would not work for South American mammalian faunas for the reason that Scott emphasized: many of them had practically no true affinity with those of other continents. However, as Ortmann found, the method did work, not precisely but nearly enough to be useful, for at least one South American marine fauna which resembled those of other continents closely enough to indicate an approximate age. That provided a maximum approximate age for the great Santacrucian mammalian fauna, and from that datum point some extrapolation could be made to other mammalian faunas without so crucial a relationship to marine beds. Now other methods of dating have been devised and are being applied in South America in conjunction with faunal comparisons. More will be said about that later.

Here it appears that the most fundamental requisites for study of the history of South American mammals had been acquired with one exception: a reasonable explanation for the evident peculiarity of so many of the faunas involved. The general explanation in broadest outline now seems obvious. It was implicit in early work by Scott and some others, but it was not clearly stated by Scott, at least, for some time, and then only with some cautious qualifications and restrictions. The final contribution at this level of basic foundation laying may be credited to a great French paleontologist who, like Scott, never collected a South American mammal and indeed, unlike Scott, never even visited that continent. He was (Jean) Albert Gaudry, who during the later years of his life became fascinated by the discoveries made by the Ameghinos. He asked a young friend, André Tournouër, who had been working in Argentina, to go to Patagonia and collect fossils for "the honor of French science." Tournouër replied, "I will go to Patagonia; the Paris Museum shall have fossils," and it did. Tournouër became a good friend of both Ameghinos, and starting in 1898 he made five expeditions to Patagonia, collecting at localities indicated to him by Carlos. Besides several shorter notes from around 1902, Gaudry based five memoirs, 1904–1909, on the fossils collected by Tournouër. He planned to continue, "If God lends me life," but God did not—Gaudry died in 1908 at the age of eighty-one.

It is worthwhile to interpolate here that, although the Ameghinos reacted adversely to some undue antagonism, they were cordial and helpful to anyone who, like Scott and Tournouër, approached them with friendly courtesy even when in disagreement with them. Thus the Ameghinos themselves made indirect but real contributions to the correction of what in retrospect we see as errors in some of their interpretations.

Although Gaudry wrote two later papers in his series on Patagonian fossils, his most important summing up was published in 1906 as "A Study of Part of the Antarctic World." He then wrote, in French, "We do not have any animal from the Deseadan or the Santacrucian that we might consider as coming from the Northern Hemisphere." Gaudry named the Casamayor and Deseado as geological formations; we now use the terms in the form Casamayoran and Deseadan for geological ages and for the mammalian faunas that lived in South America during these ages. The term Santacrucian, variously spelled, now similarly used, had already been applied by the Ameghinos and was adopted by Gaudry.

Farther along in the same publication Gaudry wrote that "There was a lowering [of the land] in Central America which lasted until the beginning of the Pliocene epoch; then [in the Pliocene] Central America formed a bridge between North and South America, which for a long time had been [separate] continents. But this bridge did not exist in the Santacrucian epoch."

Those statements are clear enough as far as they go, and they did indicate the basis that has been clarified and extended in later studies. It would not be expected, and it did not occur, that Gaudry or anyone else in 1906 could all at once understand all the implications that hindsight can now draw from Gaudry's statement. It was at its date the clearest indication that South America was long an island continent. That was the last of the necessary basic elements for study of the history of South American mammals.

Gaudry believed that the Casamayoran fauna, the oldest then known from South America, was similar to faunas now classified as Paleocene in North America and that there was some connection between the two continents at that time. It now seems clear that there was no such land connection then. Yet the placental mammals as a whole had then diverged less from their considerably more remote common ancestry. It was true that the distinctions between South and North American mammals were not yet quite so obvious or nearly so extreme as they later became.

Gaudry also wrote that "Certain remarks make one think of communication between Patagonia and Australia, without our knowing in what epoch they took place." The particular "remarks" to which Gaudry was referring do not seem to support his suggestion, but as will be discussed here on later pages, the history of marsupials does indicate that there was at a remote time some kind of limited "communication" between South America and Australia. Gaudry further suggested that South America and Australia had at some time been parts of a vast Antarctic continent. The evidence for this thought to be available in 1906 was inadequate or indeed erroneous, but more recent studies do suggest that both South America and Australia had once been if not parts of at least more nearly associated with Antarctica.

Gaudry noted that (placental) rodents first appeared in South America in the Deseadan (still true of known appearances), and after commenting on the differences between the Deseadan fauna and any in the Northern Hemisphere he added in a footnote, "I leave aside the rodents because I don't know where they came from." That remark now seems both wise and amusing because (as will later be discussed) there are now a number of paleontologists who profess to know where the rodents came from but who ardently disagree as to where that was.

Here brief reference may again be made to W. B. Scott. In 1932 he finally completed the great series of studies on Santacrucian mammals with some general remarks on the history of South American faunas. He emphasized their peculiar nature and ascribed this, as everyone does now, to the long isolation of the continent. However, he held that South America had at some time been connected to Africa and to Australia, the latter by way of Antarctica, and had also "almost certainly" had a land connection with North America in the late Cretaceous and "perhaps" also in the Paleocene. There was then, as he noted, no direct mammalian evidence for the latter times. As will be made clear in due course, Scott's final views now seem largely correct, partly prophetic of results of later discoveries and studies, and partly but not egregiously wrong.

References

Ameghino, F. 1916. Monte Hermoso. In *Obras completas y correspondencia científica de Florentino Ameghino,* ed. A. J. Torcelli, 5: 329–336. La Plata: Taller de Impresiones Officiales (written in 1887 but apparently not published elsewhere than in the posthumous collected works).

Darwin, C. (1839), 1952. *Journal of researches into the geology and natural history of the various countries visited by H.M.S. Beagle.* Facsimile reprint of the first edition. New York and London: Hafner.

Gaudry, A. 1906. Fossiles de Patagonie: Etude sur une portion du monde antarctique. *Annales de Paléontologie,* 2: 101–143.

Scott, W. B. 1932. Nature and origin of the Santa Cruz fauna. *Reports of the Princeton University Expeditions to Patagonia,* 7: 193–238.

———. 1939. *Some memories of a paleontologist.* Princeton: Princeton University Press.

CHAPTER 3

Time and Faunas

History implies time, and time is usually thought of as implying dates. At the beginning of a historical account time obviously must be considered, and it enters into this particular history in more than one way. For clarity of the verbal account there are also various terms referring to time that must be used. Those absolutely necessary will be given here at the outset.

The classical approach to geological time, which is still in universal use by paleontologists and other geologists and which has already been used in a limited way in this book, does not in fact involve dates as such or in the ordinary sense. It involves only sequence. It indicates which rocks, which fossils, which faunas are older and which younger than others, but not directly how much older or younger. One of its main bases is the order in which rocks were formed. That order can be perturbed by crustal movements, but it is usually quite simple for a geologist to determine in any one region. For example, if molten rock has intruded into what were fissures in another kind of rock and there solidified, that solidification clearly happened later than the formation of the rock around the intrusion. More important to paleontologists, rocks deposited as sediments—and they are the only ones in which fossils usually occur—are normally laid down one after another. Thus, the strata higher in any undisturbed sequence are always younger.

By studying such sequences in different regions and correlating relative ages from one to another, usually by means of similarities in fossils, a sequential time scale for the whole earth was slowly built up and is now everywhere in use. It divides geological time into eras, periods (subdivisions of eras), and epochs (subdivisions of periods). Those involved in the present history are shown in table 1. Eras earlier than the Mesozoic, Mesozoic periods earlier than the Cretaceous, and Cretaceous epochs earlier than the Senonian are not involved in the history of known South American mammals. Earlier eras are not involved because there were no true mammals before the Mesozoic, and earlier periods and epochs are not involved because, although mammals did exist then and doubtless occurred also in South America, none have yet been found in South America.

For many purposes the sequential time scale is still adequate, but geologists do also want to have a scale of dates in years. Such dates are inherently interesting, and they are also necessary for the study of rates of geological processes and of evolutionary changes. Many attempts to determine such dates, and especially to estimate, at least, the age of the earth, were made in the nineteenth century, but the methods then tried were all extremely inaccurate,

Table 1

Worldwide system of sequential geological time units relevant to this history

Eras	Periods	Epochs	Approximate time (millions of years before present)
Cenozoic	Quaternary	Recent or Holocene	0.01
		Pleistocene	2
	Tertiary	Pliocene	5 ? 7/8
		Miocene	22
		Oligocene	37
		Eocene	55
		Paleocene	65
Mesozoic	Cretaceous	Late Senonian or Maastrichtian	

and it is now known that almost all the results obtained by these were grossly incorrect.

In the present century a number of different, new methods for determining such dates have been discovered and applied. None is yet accurate to within less than a few percentage points, but their combined application has become increasingly definite, and at very worst they produce a certain order of magnitude. Most of these methods depend on radioactivity, paleomagnetism, or both.

Radioactive elements tend spontaneously to break down or "decay" into other elements at determinable and constant rates, rates usually measured in "half-lives," which are the times for the transformation into another element of one-half of the atoms of the radioactive element originally present. When the ratio of a radioactive element in a mineral to a product of its radioactive decay is obtained, the time since the mineral was formed can be calculated from the relevant half-life. The rates of radioactive change can also be estimated in several other ways, notably by the tracks left in a mineral by radioactive fission. Numerous radioactive elements and their products can be used for dating, but for geological purposes the most widely used have been two radioactive isotopes (forms of an element with different masses) of uranium and their respective end results as isotopes of lead: uranium-lead dating. Another widely used method involves radioactive potassium and its end-result argon.

The so-called carbon-14 clock has been more widely publicized because of its applications to human history, but its half-life, less than 8,000 years, is too short for it to be useful for most paleontological purposes. Forms of uranium have more geologically relevant half-lives, up to about 4.5 billion years, but those ratios have lately been found less often obtainable for fossil deposits than potassium-argon, KA, K/A, or K-A, ratios. Potassium-argon dates have recently been obtained for a number of South American mammalian faunas, and this work is continuing. The approximate dates of beginnings of Cenozoic epochs in table 1 are based on the potassium-argon method, which, however, is not so precise that everyone agrees exactly on its results. There is also debate as to just where the epoch boundaries, which are essentially arbitrary, should be drawn. Such dates are sometimes symbolized by Ma, signifying millions of years before the present. By agreement, "present" in this sense is fixed as A.D. 1950, a slightly silly refinement as no known method of geological dating before the Recent could possibly distinguish between years before 1950 and, say, 1980.

A still more recent dating method now being actively pursued in connection with South American fossil mammals involves what is called paleomagnetism. It has been found that many rocks, often including sediments in which remains of ancient mammals were buried, contain minerals that were to some extent magnetized by the earth's magnetic field at the time when the rocks were formed. There are as usual difficulties and complications, but by appropriate methods the direction of that original magnetization can often be determined. Surprisingly enough, as these methods were developed it was found that from time to time the earth's magnetic poles have reversed their positions. That is, at times in the past the end of a compass needle that now points to near the earth's north pole of rotation would have pointed to near the earth's south pole of rotation. Times when the magnetic poles were as they are today are called "normal," and times when they were reversed are called "reversed," which seems logical enough except for the fact that in the past reversal seems to have been more normal, in the sense of usual, than what this usage labels normal. In fact, the times when paleomagnetism was "normal" are technically called anomalies.

There is a big, fairly obvious catch in using paleomagnetism for dating. It does not really measure time. At any past time the magnetic poles were either "normal" or "reversed," and in itself a "normal" 50 million years ago, for example, does not differ from a "normal" 50 years ago. The paleomagnetic episodes become useful for dating only when they are tied in with some independent dating either by radioactivity methods or by fossil sequence or preferably by both. Then a characteristic sequence of magnetic events, usually studied in the form of a pattern of anomalies (times of normal earth magnetism) may be observed, and its anomalies can be numbered and recognized widely, eventually all over the earth. When that stage of dating by the combination of three different methods is reached, the inclusion of paleomagnetism in those methods has great advantages. The changes between normal and reversed surely affected the magnetism of the earth everywhere at once. Thus, when a paleomagnetic anomaly found in South American rocks can be identified as the same as one found in European rocks, the onset of that anomaly can be taken as simultaneous on the two continents. That will permit a correlation of times, rocks, and ages of faunas with precision often quite impossible by faunal methods alone, the faunas of the two continents being too different for that, and sometimes also by radioactivity, appropriate radioactive minerals being absent in one place or another for considerable spans of time. This result has as yet been obtained only for the later fossil mammal–bearing rocks of South America, but work now well started gives promise that is will eventually be extended to earlier rocks and faunas.

Now we must turn to still another system of dating, one devised especially for use in studies of mammalian history like this one. This system is primarily sequential, but in South America it is now in the course of being tied with K-A year dating in Ma's and with correlation of paleomagnetic anomalies. It comprises a sequence of named ages defined by mammalian faunas. In South America it was started by the Ameghinos (see chapter 2), who designated a long sequence of mammalian faunas by a mixed nomenclature. Some of the ages, most of the earlier ones, were called by the names of genera of fossil mammals that lived at those times. Most of the later ages were given adjectival names of localities or regions where fossil-bearing rocks of the given ages occur. A modification and a refinement of the latter system have been developed through the years by combined efforts of South and North American paleontologists.

Regional or provincial "land mammal ages" are defined by their mammalian faunas and are given geographic names ending in -an or -ian in English (-ense in Spanish). The same names are used for the faunas that define them, for the ages thus defined, and for the rocks that were deposited in those ages. (Technically the rocks belong to "stages" rather than to "ages.") There is some slight disagreement as to just which ages should be listed, but the system is now used by all paleontologists dealing with South American fossil mammals. The sequence adopted for the present book and a quite provisional assignment of these ages into epochs (originally named in Europe) are given in table 2. The geographic parts of the names should be pronounced as in Spanish. For example, Lujanian is nearly loo-ha'-nee-an, and Uquian is oo-kee'-an.

The three hiatuses noted are ages for which the South American mammalian fauna is inadequately known or completely unknown at present. It can be expected that further exploration, especially outside of Argentina, will fill in these gaps in knowledge. All the geographic features referred to in these ages are in Argentina, those of the earlier ages in Patagonia and of the others farther

Table 2

South American land mammal ages and their tentative assignment to epochs adopted here

Epoch	Land Mammal Age
Pleistocene	Lujanian
	Ensenadan
	Uquian
Pliocene	Chapadmalalan
	Montehermosan
	Huayquerian
Miocene	Chasicoan
	Friasian
	Santacrucian
Oligocene	Colhuehuapian
	(Hiatus)
	Deseadan
Eocene	(Hiatus)
	Mustersan
	Casamayoran
Paleocene	Riochican
	(Hiatus)

(handwritten margin notes: 2, 7-8, 22, 37, 55, 65)

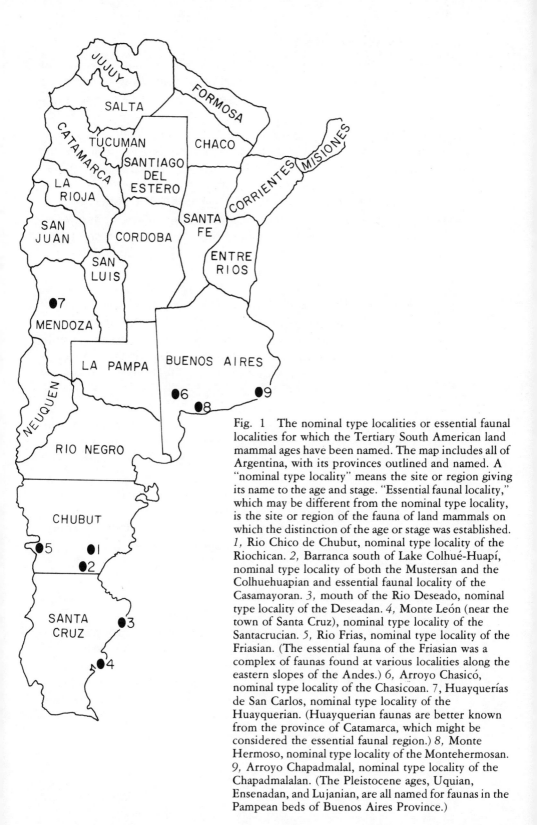

Fig. 1 The nominal type localities or essential faunal localities for which the Tertiary South American land mammal ages have been named. The map includes all of Argentina, with its provinces outlined and named. A "nominal type locality" means the site or region giving its name to the age and stage. "Essential faunal locality," which may be different from the nominal type locality, is the site or region of the fauna of land mammals on which the distinction of the age or stage was established. *1*, Rio Chico de Chubut, nominal type locality of the Riochican. *2*, Barranca south of Lake Colhué-Huapí, nominal type locality of both the Mustersan and the Colhuehuapian and essential faunal locality of the Casamayoran. *3*, mouth of the Rio Deseado, nominal type locality of the Deseadan. *4*, Monte León (near the town of Santa Cruz), nominal type locality of the Santacrucian. *5*, Rio Frias, nominal type locality of the Friasian. (The essential fauna of the Friasian was a complex of faunas found at various localities along the eastern slopes of the Andes.) *6*, Arroyo Chasicó, nominal type locality of the Chasicoan. *7*, Huayquerías de San Carlos, nominal type locality of the Huayquerian. (Huayquerian faunas are better known from the province of Catamarca, which might be considered the essential faunal region.) *8*, Monte Hermoso, nominal type locality of the Montehermosan. *9*, Arroyo Chapadmalal, nominal type locality of the Chapadmalalan. (The Pleistocene ages, Uquian, Ensenadan, and Lujanian, are all named for faunas in the Pampean beds of Buenos Aires Province.)

north. Exploration for fossil mammals in other South American countries has not yet been so intensive, but what has been done, notably in Colombia, Bolivia, and Brazil, indicates that fossil mammalian faunas throughout the continent can readily be placed within the same system. An entirely different set of land mammal ages is used in North America. Until toward the end of the history, approximately from the Montehermosan onward, it is almost impossible to establish equivalences between South American and North American ages by their mammalian faunas alone, but this is now being accomplished by tying in the faunas on each continent with radioactivity Ma's and with numbered paleomagnetic anomalies.

Each age of this system has an appreciable length in geological time. When the hiatuses are filled in, the number of South American Cenozoic ages recognized and separately named will probably be about eighteen to twenty. The time involved is about 65 million years, so the average length of an age will probably be somewhere between 3¼ and 3¾ million years. The length of an age in such a system is somewhat arbitrary; the beginnings and endings of an age are rarely marked by definite geological or evolutionary events. There is some tendency to recognize shorter ages in the later part of the sequence where the amount of information available is usually greater. For example, the three Pleistocene ages in the sequence adopted for this book probably average only about two-thirds of a million years in length, while the two Eocene ages currently recognized may have averaged about 5 million years.

A fauna in terms of these ages is not a single, static thing. There were successive faunas within each age. When the fossil collections are adequate and include earlier and later faunas within one designated age, those faunas generally are distinguishably different in detail even though there is an overall resemblance characteristic of the age as a whole. Early collectors rarely were able to make field records precise enough to serve as a basis for examination of detailed changes within one designated age, but with more modern methods and instrumentation this is becoming increasingly possible. When faunas of about the same age are known from widely separate geographic regions, for example Argentina and

Colombia, there are evident differences in the faunas, just as there are in the now living faunas of different regions in South America. In spite of such local differences, the present fauna of the continent as a whole does have a distinctive overall composition. There is increasing evidence that this has been true of South American faunas throughout the Cenozoic era, Age of Mammals.

References

For general background see the references to Simpson 1969 and to Patterson and Pascual 1972 following chapter 1. The following shorter and more technical papers are examples of results in the current campaign to improve the dating of South American mammalian faunas.

Marshall, L. G.; R. Pascual; G. H. Curtis; and R. E. Drake. 1977. South American geochronology: Radiometric time scale for middle to late Tertiary mammal-bearing horizons in Patagonia. *Science,* 195: 1325–1328.

Marshall, L. G.; R. F. Butler; R. E. Drake; G. H. Curtis; and R. H. Tedford. 1979. Calibration of the Great American Interchange. *Science,* 204: 272–279.

CHAPTER 4

Cast of Characters

The various groups of extinct mammals of South America necessarily go by invented names that are unfamiliar except to
paleomammalogists. Some of these must be listed before they are
used in the narrative text. The list is not meant to be read at this
point, but to serve as a reference and to show how the animals fit
into a general scheme of classification when they are discussed
later. Like almost all modern classifications, the arrangement of
this one follows the old Linnaean system, which is a hierarchy or a
sort of nesting-box arrangement in which each level includes one
or more, sometimes many, groups at the next lower level. The
main levels from higher to lower or larger to smaller are: kingdom,
phylum, class, order, family, genus, and species. The number of
steps may be increased by adding super- above and sub- below any
given level.

This book is about mammals, which are a class, Mammalia, of
the phylum Chordata, in the kingdom Animalia. The reference
classification does not need to go above the level of subclass, and
to keep it within reasonable scope it does not here go below the
level of families. With one exception the families that still survive
have popular as well as technical names, and for them both are
given. The known temporal distribution is given for each family in
terms of land mammal ages. If a family, or higher group, is not
indicated as present in a particular age, that may or may not mean
that it was then absent from South America. For example, it is
fairly certain that there were no rodents in South America in the
Casamayoran or Mustersan ages, and the lack of record there is
taken as reflecting a real absence. On the other hand, the extinct

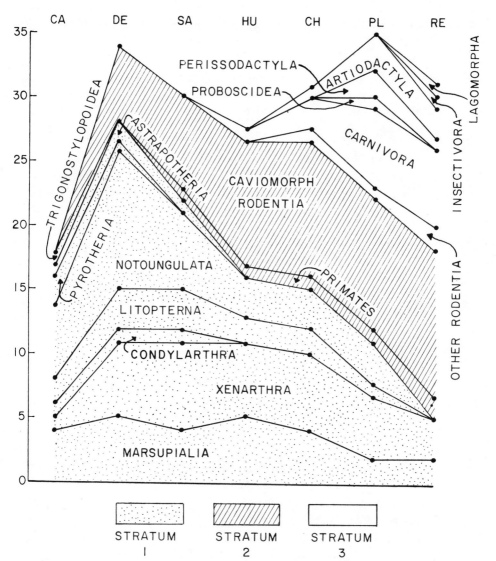

Fig. 2. Orders of land mammals known in South America at some successive ages and numbers of known families in each. The vertical scale measures numbers of known families. The horizontal sequence is that of successive land mammal ages, not scaled in years: *CA,* Casamayoran; *DE,* Deseadan; *SA,* Santacrucian; *HU,* Huayquerian; *CH,* Chapadmalalan; *PL,* Pleistocene (Uquian to Lujanian, combined); *RE,* Recent. The orders are allotted to faunal strata by overlay patterns. Stratum 1 is discussed in chapters 6–10, Stratum 2 in chapters 11–13, and Stratum 3 in chapters 14–16.

family Adianthidae, for example, is also unknown in the Casamayoran and Mustersan, but it is probable that it was then present in South America, and the absence of record is not meaningful.

The classification given here is relatively conservative. Some students would recognize more or in some cases different groups than those named here.

Subclass Metatheria
  Order Marsupialia, marsupials or (usually) pouched mammals [There is good authority for dividing the living marsupials into at least three distinct orders, but the South American marsupials, especially some fossils, do not fit well into that system.]
    Superfamily Didelphoidea
      Family Didelphidae, opossums. Late Cretaceous–Recent.
      Family Borhyaenidae. Riochican-Montehermosan.
      Family Thylacosmilidae. Huayquerian-Chapadmalalan.
    Superfamily Caenolestoidea
      Family Caenolestidae, without a genuine popular name. Casamayoran-Recent.
      Family Polydolopidae. Riochican-Deseadan.
    Superfamily Groeberioidea
      Family Groeberiidae. Deseadan.
    Superfamily Argyrolagoidea
      Family Argyrolagidae. Huayquerian-Uquian.
    Superfamily uncertain
      Family Necrolestidae. Santacrucian.
Subclass Eutheria, placentals
  Order Insectivora
    Superfamily Soricoidea
      Family Soricidae. Recent. [Marginal in South America.]
  Order Primates
    Superfamily Ceboidea

Family Cebidae, New World monkeys. Deseadan-
Recent.
Family Callithricidae, marmosets and tamarins. Recent.
Order Xenarthra
Suborder Cingulata
Family Dasypodidae, armadillos. Riochican-Recent.
Family Palaeopeltidae. ?Mustersan, Deseadan.
Family Glyptodontidae. Mustersan-Lujanian.
Suborder Pilosa
Family Mylodontidae. Deseadan-Lujanian.
Family Megalonychidae. ?Mustersan, Deseadan-Cha-
padmalalan.
Family Megatheriidae. Deseadan-Lujanian.
Family Entelopsidae. Santacrucian.
Family Bradypodidae, tree sloths. Recent.
Suborder Vermilingua
Family Myrmecophagidae, anteaters. Santacrucian-
Recent.
Order Lagomorpha
Family Leporidae, hares and rabbits. Recent.
Order Rodentia
Suborder Sciuromorpha
Family Sciuridae, squirrels. Recent.
Suborder Caviomorpha
Superfamily Erethizontoidea
Family Erethizontidae, New World porcupines.
Deseadan-Recent.
Superfamily Cavioidea
Family Eocardiidae. Deseadan-Friasian.
Family Caviidae, "guinea pigs" (cavies) and many rela-
tives. Friasian-Recent.
Family Hydrochoeridae, capybaras. Chasicoan-Recent.
Superfamily Chinchilloidea
Family Chinchillidae, vizcachas and chinchillas.
Deseadan-Recent.
Family Dasyproctidae, agoutis. Deseadan-Recent.
Family Cuniculidae, pacas. Recent.

Family Dinomyidae, "false paca," pacaranas. Friasian-
Recent.
Superfamily Octodontoidea
Family Octodontidae, degus and relatives. Deseadan-
Recent.
Family Abrocomidae, "chinchilla rats." Huay-
querian-Recent.
Family Echimyidae, "spiny rats" and many relatives.
Deseadan-Recent.
Family Myocastoridae, "nutrias" (coypus). Monte-
hermosan-Recent.
Suborder Myomorpha
Superfamily Muroidea
Family Cricetidae, field mice and many relatives.
Montehermosan-Recent.
Order Carnivora
Superfamily Canoidea
Family Canidae, dogs and relatives. Uquian-Recent.
Family Ursidae, bears. Uquian-Recent.
Family Procyonidae, raccoons, coatis, and kinkajous.
Huayquerian-Recent.
Family Mustelidae, weasels and relatives. Chapad-
malalan-Recent.
Superfamily Feloidea
Family Felidae, cats and relatives. Uquian-Recent.
Order Condylarthra
Family Didolodontidae. Riochican-Friasian.
Order Litopterna
Family Proterotheriidae. Riochican-Chapadmalalan.
Family Macraucheniidae. Riochican-Lujanian.
Family Adianthidae. Deseadan-Santacrucian.
Order Notoungulata
Suborder Notioprogonia
Family Henricosborniidae. Riochican-Casamayoran.
Family Notostylopidae. Riochican? Casamayoran-
Mustersan.
Suborder Typotheria

Family Oldfieldthomasiidae. Riochican-Mustersan.
Family Archaeopithecidae. Casamayoran.
Family Interatheriidae. Riochican-Chasicoan.
Family Mesotheriidae. Friasian-Ensenadan.
Suborder Hegetotheria
Family Archaeohyracidae. Riochican-Deseadan.
Family Hegetotheriidae. Deseadan-Uquian.
Suborder Toxodonta
Family Isotemnidae. Riochican-Deseadan.
Family Notohippidae. Mustersan-Santacrucian.
Family Leontiniidae. Deseadan-Colhuehuapian.
Family Homalodotheriidae. Deseadan-Chasicoan.
Family Toxodontidae. Deseadan-Ensenadan.
Order Pyrotheria
Family Colombitheriidae. Casamayoran?-Mustersan?
Family Pyrotheriidae. Casamayoran-Deseadan.
Order Astrapotheria
Family Astrapotheriidae. Casamayoran-Friasian.
Order Trigonostylopoidea
Family Trigonostylopidae. Riochican-Casamayoran,
Mustersan?
Order Xenungulata
Family Carodniidae. Riochican.
Order Proboscidea
Family Gomphotheriidae. Uquian-Lujanian.
Order Perissodactyla
Suborder Hippomorpha
Family Equidae, horses and their closest relatives.
Uquian-Lujanian. [Also Recent elsewhere.]
Suborder Ceratomorpha
Family Tapiridae, tapirs. Uquian-Recent.
Order Artiodactyla
Suborder Suiformes
Family Tayassuidae, peccaries. Chapadmalalan-
Recent.
Suborder Tylopoda
Family Camelidae, camels (llamas, etc., in South
America). Uquian-Recent.

Suborder Ruminantia
Family Cervidae, deer. Uquian-Recent.

Aquatic and flying mammals have not been listed. The former are not part of the land mammal associations considered in this book, and the latter, bats, although extremely abundant and varied in South American now and doubtless present since early in the Cenozoic, have practically no South American historical record.

CHAPTER 5

Roots

There is an aphorism, sometimes known as "Simpson's Third Law," that no matter what the problem is there is never enough information to solve it definitively. To historians of life that means that there are never enough fossils to answer once and for all the questions that such historians put to them. That is particularly true of questions, to many of us the most interesting ones, that involve origins or what are in a now popular sense the roots of histories. In the present case the first question is, "How did the South American mammalian fauna get started?" A really complete answer might have to begin with the origin of the earth itself, but here we do not need to dig into roots that far back even if we could do so. It would be interesting to start with the origin of mammals as such, and indeed there is much to say on that topic. However, what can now be said about that does not really help with the more specific question of the origins of the South American mammalian faunas and therefore is not included here.

There is still incomplete but reasonably good information about the composition of South American mammalian faunas early in the Cenozoic, Age of Mammals, provided by the Riochican, Casamayoran, and Mustersan faunas, earliest known for the South American Cenozoic. As will be shown, they are very peculiar in some respects, and the reasons for those peculiarities are still in considerable part mysterious. We are at least better off than if we were considering Australia, where there is no direct information at all about early Cenozoic faunas, or Africa, where there is only a little. Here in South America before the Cenozoic we have just a handful of scraps from the late Cretaceous. They do help, but they do not solve the major mysteries.

It was this sort of paucity of information, increasing as one delves farther into time, that led Scott to write faunal history backward (as mentioned in chapter 1), starting with the present fauna, which is known best of all, and then going back through the earlier ones until times are reached for which the faunas are known little, if at all. When Scott originally wrote his history of South American mammals, the Cretaceous scraps and the Riochican fauna were still completely unknown and the Casamayoran and Mustersan faunas were much less well known than they are now. Here the start will be made as near the beginning as there are any really known facts, recognizing that this requires putting up with doubts and mysteries. As the history proceeds some of the uncertainties will disappear, but some will continue right down to the present. It is another aphorism that no one knows everything about anything. That need not dull the pleasure and fascination of the fact that a great deal is known about some things.

So the present positive knowledge of this history starts with that scanty handful of fragments of mammals from late Cretaceous strata. These were found in 1965 and 1967 by a French expedition on the tremendous high Andean plateau of Peru not far from Lake Titicaca and near the small Laguna Umayo. The first specimen found was a fragment of a lower jaw with the posterior half of the first molar and the anterior half of the second molar. Later a small fragment of an upper molar apparently of the same species was found. This animal was with high probability a primitive hoofed mammal, a condylarth rather like the Didolodontidae, the condylarth family known from later faunas. It is not much like anything known from the late Cretaceous of North America but does somewhat resemble some later (Paleocene and Eocene) North American, European, and Asiatic condylarths. The French paleontologist Louis Thaler named it *Perutherium altiplanense*.

The other specimens in this collection are parts of eleven tiny teeth, all more or less broken and incomplete, and two jaw fragments with remains of roots but not crowns of teeth. All of these, as far as identifiable at all, represent primitive opossums, members of the family Didelphidae of the classification in chapter 4. They closely resemble some of the numerous opossums known from the late Cretaceous of North America, to such an extent that their describer, Bernard Sigé of Montpellier, France, has referred the most characteristic fragments to a genus, *Alphadon,* better known from the North American Cretaceous. Another interesting fact about this exiguous sample of so old a fauna is that these small tooth fragments show that there was at least one other fairly distinct opossum present. Thus some differentiation of the Didelphidae, later and still today varied and characteristic in South America, was already under way.

Surely some other kinds of mammals were already there in South America in Cretaceous times, but that is all we really know at present: a very primitive hoofed mammal, ungulate, that could be in or near the ancestry of the many and varied later South American ungulates, and some very primitive opossums, marsupials, that could be in or near the ancestry of the many and varied later South American marsupials. From what we do know of later faunas, it would have been expected that mammals like these would occur in the Cretaceous of South America, and the confirmation is welcome as far as it goes.

The next oldest mammals are those of Riochican age, more or less late Paleocene, perhaps some 55 to 60 million years ago. The first scraps of Riochican mammals were found long ago by Santiago Roth, the paleontologist mentioned in chapter 2 as having recognized and named the great group Notoungulata. Neither he nor at the time anyone else recognized the significance of what we now know were the first Riochican mammals to be found. In 1930 two petroleum geologists, A. Piatnitzky and J. Brandmayer, working for the Argentine government, found a few fragments of Riochican mammals at a locality some distance south of Roth's in Patagonia. They also misunderstood the discovery at first, but it was followed up by Coleman Williams and me, working for the American Museum of Natural History. We found fossils of this age at several localities in the general vicinity of the Rio Chico in central Patagonia, and study of those enabled me to characterize the fauna and to name it Riochican.

Much the richest Riochican local fauna so far discovered comes from a remarkable deposit at São José de Itaborai in the state of Rio de Janeiro, Brazil, across the bay from the city of Rio de Janeiro. At that locality there is an isolated basin filled with limestone—or was, for the limestone has almost all been quarried out to make cement. There are (were) solution channels in the limestone, and these were early filled with marl and debris. In 1943 L. I. Price and others from the Brazilian equivalent of a national geological survey (Divisão de Geologia e Mineralogia) found some remains of mammals in the fissure fillings. For many years starting in 1945 large collections were made, and the mammals were studied by the Brazilian paleontologist Carlos de Paula Couto. He soon recognized that the fauna was at least approximately contemporaneous with the Riochican in Argentina, and he referred it to that age.

These earliest known South American Cenozoic mammalian faunas, those of Riochican age, are remarkable both for the extent and, in a different way, for the limitation of the diversification of the mammals in them. They already include five orders and fourteen families: Marsupialia (three families), Xenarthra (one family), Condylarthra (one family), Litopterna (two families), Notoungulata (five families), Trigonostylopoidea (one family), and Xenungulata (one family). Obviously a great deal of evolutionary divergence and expansion had already occurred among these mammals. It is probable that most of it and possible but less probable that all of it had occurred in South America itself.

It is, however, the limitation of the number of basic stocks and of ecological specialists that is most peculiar in the Riochican. All the mammals known from this age represent divergent lines of just three basic stocks, and the same is still true of the following Casamayoran and Mustersan faunas. There were marsupials, all of which could have been and probably were derived from primitive Cretaceous opossums, Didelphidae in a broad sense. There were Xenarthra (pronounced zee-nar'-thruh) represented in these three earliest known South American Cenozoic faunas mostly by armadillos, which constitute the family Dasypodidae. Their origin is quite uncertain and will be further discussed. And there were relatively abundant herbivores, ungulates in a broad sense, all of which could have been and probably were derived from primitive, relatively generalized ungulates classified as Condylarthra.

The collections from these faunas are now so extensive that it can be asserted with considerable confidence that in Riochican, Casamayoran, and Mustersan times all the South American land mammals belonged to those three basic groups and to no others. Such a mix is not only peculiar; it is absolutely unique. No other continent, present or past, is definitely known ever to have had a fauna consisting of just those three basic stocks, and it is quite unlikely that any ever did. It is clear that North America and Europe and highly probable but with less complete evidence that Asia and Africa in the early Cenozoic had mammals from considerably more than three such basic stocks. For Australia there is virtually no direct evidence, but by reasonable extrapolation backward from later faunas it is highly probable that the origins of the Cenozoic mammals of that continent were even more limited than those of South America, with only two basic stocks. One of those was originally the same as one in South America, deriving from opossumlike marsupials, but the other, represented by the still surviving egg-laying monotremes, the platypus and the several so-called spiny anteaters or echidnas, was quite unlike any of the South American basic stocks.

In North America, for example, at times approximately equivalent to the span of Riochican–Mustersan in South America, there were also marsupials and ungulates as basic stocks. But the marsupials there, all opossums, Didelphidae, were not nearly as abundant or as diversified as those of South America. The ungulates were about equally abundant and diversified on the two continents, but apart from survivors of the most primitive, originally ancestral group, the Condylarthra, the ungulates had already evolved in quite different ways on the two continents with just one peculiar exception that will require further discussion. The greatest contrast, however, is that in North America there were at least eight orders of land mammals not derived either from ancestral marsupials or from ancestral ungulates. As will appear on further analysis, one of the eight may or may not have had some relationship to the third South American basic stock, that of the Xenarthra, but the other seven early North American orders definitely had no South American relatives. Thus North America had a much more varied, more balanced, more ecologically complete early Cenozoic fauna than South America. That was probably true of all the rest of the world with the exception of Australia and probably of Antarctica, which has no native land mammals now but could well have had some in the early Cenozoic. No fossil land mammals have yet been discovered there.

South America was already surely an island continent in Riochican time and must have been so for an indefinite but geologically long time before that. This is clear from the fact that each of the three original stocks had become sharply diversified in ways unique to South America and demonstrating evolution in isolation. That is not so evident for the Xenarthra in Riochican time, when the positive evidence includes only armadillos, but in the Mustersan there are known specimens, still rare, of at least two and perhaps three other families of xenarthrans. Their absence in the present Riochican and Casamayoran collections is probably due not to their later origin but to chances of preservation and collection or to geographic and ecological factors.

The general characteristics of successive faunas and the histories of the separate orders and families of mammals will be discussed in later chapters. Just here concern is with the origin of such a peculiar mix and of each basic stock in the earliest known faunas. The next step is to consider possible connections of members of the basic stocks with mammals living elsewhere.

First consider the marsupials. It has already been noted that extremely primitive and closely similar marsupials are known from the Cretaceous in both South and North America. No Cretaceous or earliest Cenozoic mammals are yet known from Australia, but ancestral marsupials must have been early present on that continent, almost surely in the late Cretaceous. Those three continents have not been parts of a single land mass since mammals evolved, and therefore marsupials cannot have arisen on such a mass and then have become separated when the mass split into three (or more) separate continents. Early marsupials must somehow have spread among the three continents after their earliest forms evolved. Marsupials also spread to Europe in their primitive form as didelphids, but that is rather beside the point. The spread may have occurred at any time from late Cretaceous through early Eocene, when what are now North America and Europe were parts of the same continent. When they split apart, around the end of the early Eocene, the marsupials were in a dead end in Europe and became extinct there, as they did also for a time in North America.

Cretaceous marsupials certainly spread directly between South and North America. The available evidence does not indicate in which direction they spread, and although some authorities insist that it was from North to South America others are equally confident that it was in the opposite direction, and no one really knows. The problem of spread to or from Australia involves further difficulties.

It is reasonably certain that Australia has never been directly connected to either South or North America. It has long been known that, whenever they may have originated, marsupials were abundant in North America in the late Cretaceous. There has also long been some, now increased, evidence of some early faunal connection between North America and Asia. It used to be believed that Australia had formerly been directly connected to Asia, and even when that idea was given up by almost all students of the subject, it still was evident that for some undetermined time there had been stepping-stone islands between Asia and Australia and that some animals had spread from one continent to another along those stepping-stones. One that basis until fairly recently the favored hypothesis was that marsupials spread from North America to Australia by way of Asia. (It apparently did not occur to anyone that it could have been Australia to North America by way of Asia.)

More recent research has made that hypothesis so nearly impossible that it can hardly be supported at present. For one thing, the late Cretaceous and early Cenozoic mammalian faunas of some parts of Asia have become fairly well known, and there are no definitely identifiable marsupials in them. That is suggestive, but, as often is true of negative evidence, it is not conclusive. Asiatic marsupials might just have been missed in collecting so far, or they may have been living in regions where fossil mammals of appropriate age are not yet known. However, there is another recent development that makes the Asia–Australia hypothesis seem really impossible. Marsupials probably got to Australia in the Cretaceous and if not then certainly quite early in the Cenozoic. If they spread *from* rather than *to* Australia, that was certainly in the Cretaceous because of our positive knowledge that they were then in both Americas. But there is now rather extensive and widely accepted evidence that at those times Australia was nowhere near Asia and that stepping-stones between those two continents did not yet exist. Australia was then fairly close to East Antarctica, possibly even a part of that land mass. Then in the early Cenozoic Australia started to drift north, and it probably reached approximately its present position and relationship to Asia sometime in the Miocene, tens of millions of years too late for the initial intercontinental spread of marsupials.

The evidence is still not quite complete enough to call this a settled theory in the strict scientific sense of the word "theory," but at present the most probable hypothesis is that marsupials spread between South America and Australia in one direction or the other by way of Antarctica. It is, however, quite unlikely that a continuous and practicable land connection was involved. The dispersal of mammals over such a land connection is rarely or never in one direction only. Thus, if there had been such a route between these two continents some of the many different early South American mammals other than marsupials would probably have reached Australia. On present evidence it cannot be absolutely ruled out that some did so, but that seems highly improbable. As with other mysteries that will be met in this history, a complete solution still evades us, but progress toward one has been made and more can be expected.

It is reasonable to suppose that marsupials did not originate on a hypothetical and improbable land mass including two, three, or all of the continents now North America, South America, Antarctica, and Australia, but probably on only one of them at first. There is some evidence in favor of North America as the area of origin, and

Fig. 3. Possible continental configuration in approximately mid-Cretaceous time. This is a diagram, showing topological relationships of land masses, rather than a map, showing their shapes. Two main masses, Laurasia in the north and Gondwanaland in the south, are indicated. By the end of the Cretaceous, and probably well before that, Gondwanaland had begun to break up. Shallow seas on the continental masses (epicontinental seas) not shown in this diagram complicated the geography. The names in parentheses show in a summary way where the present continents came from, including the North American island of Greenland and the Asiatic subcontinent of India.

that is perhaps the consensus of those concerned with such matters. However, the possible evidence for the other continents is not merely negative: at present it is completely lacking either one way or the other. It would seem to be wisest and fairest just to say that marsupials probably did first evolve in a region now in one of these four continents but that we simply do not know which. The true directions of early spread of course depend on where the origin occurred.

To a certain point the mysteries about the Xenarthra have been partly cleared up. This group, evidently comprising mostly armadillos, glyptodonts, sloths (tree and ground), and anteaters, may have acquired its definitive characteristics in South America (but see added note, p. 47–49). Practically the whole of its complex later evolution did occur on that continent. Only toward the end of the Cenozoic did members of the order Xenarthra spread, clearly from South America, partly by island hopping or overseas dispersal and partly over an eventually continuous land connection from South to Central America. Thus, members of the order reached North America and also islands in the Greater Antilles. In those lately occupied areas the xenarthrans, especially the now extinct ground sloths, underwent some but limited further evolution. Outside of South America xenarthrans now survive only in Central America and as a single species of armadillo onward into the southern United States.

Although the Xenarthra certainly evolved mainly in South America they must have had ancestors there or somewhere else. Even after they became distinct from the ancestors of most other mammals, such prexenarthran ancestors might have given rise to xenarthran relatives on other land masses. That is the xenarthran mystery not yet solved to general satisfaction. There is a group of now fairly well-known mammals in the North American Paleocene, Eocene, and Oligocene that was named Palaeanodonta by the great North American paleontologist W. D. Matthew (1871–1930). Some of those creatures resembled armadillos, although they did not have bony plates in the skin as all armadillos do, and also resembled pangolins now living in Africa and southern Asia. The pangolins are often called scaly anteaters, although they are quite different from the South American xenarthran anteaters and are now usually called Pholidota to distinguish them from the Xenarthra. The groups now called Pholidota and Xenarthra had been put together as early as the eighteenth century in a larger unit of classification called Edentata, "toothless."

(Most "edentates" in that broad sense do have teeth, but the South American anteaters and the pangolins do not.)

Matthew believed that his Palaeanodonta were also Edentata in the old, broad sense and that they represented a third offshoot of the edentate ancestry, diverging from both the Xenarthra and the Pholidota. Thus both the marsupials and the xenarthrans would have some sort of early connection with early ancestral, probably Cretaceous, groups that also reached or arose in North America. That was generally accepted by students of mammals until 1970 when R. J. Emry maintained that one family of Palaeanodonta (the Metacheiromyidae of previous authors) not only resembled pangolins but were in fact members of the same family (Manidae) and had nothing to do with the Xenarthra. Emry did not go into the fact that another branch of the Palaeanodonta (the family Epoicotheriidae) does not resemble pangolins. Two leading students of fossil mammals, especially those of South America, R. Pascual and B. Patterson, have since (in 1972) maintained that the Palaeanodonta were derived from the same ancestry as the Xenarthra and that the resemblance of some of them to pangolins is convergent.

Quite recently, in late 1978, the discovery of an unquestionable pangolin (manid) in the middle Eocene of Germany has been announced. Although it has not yet been fully described, it is clearly more advanced, shares more specialized or derived characters with the Recent pangolins, than the middle Eocene palaeanodont *Metacheiromys* of North America. This makes it unlikely that Emry was right in considering *Metacheiromys* directly ancestral to the living *Manis* and weakens but does not in itself disprove his view that the palaeanodonts were Manidae and not just convergent toward the latter.

Since this chapter was written and sent to the publisher, the problem of the origin and affinities of the Xenarthra has been further complicated by notice of a discovery in the People's Republic of China. I am indebted to Minchen Chow and Su-yin Ding, both of the Institute of Vertebrate Palaeontology and Palaeoanthropology, Academia Sinica, Beijing (Peking), for a preliminary publication, notes, and photographs recently (May 1979) received. The specimen in question is a nearly complete skeleton from the late Paleocene Nonshan formation in Nanxiong, Guangdong, southern China. It has been named *Ernanodon antelios* by Ding, who classifies it as a "primitive form of xenarthran."

If this is indeed a xenarthran, it is the earliest known from outside of South America. That poses difficult questions as to where the Xenarthra originated and how they came to be distributed in South America and south China, areas extremely remote from each other and not directly connected, certainly since long before the Xenarthra originated and probably never. The possibility that *Ernanodon* is a xenarthran must be taken seriously on the authority of Ding and of Chow, who in personal communication supports Ding's views, but it may not yet be entirely established. *Ernanodon* has some primitive features, not clearly xenarthran and apparently casting little light on relationships. Definite and no longer similarly primitive xenarthrans were present in South America at the same time, and *Ernanodon* cannot be in the xenarthran ancestry. Among its derived or specialized characters only a few have been definitely stated to be Xenarthra-like. Notable among them are the "incipient development of a xenarthran type of articulation on the posterior thoracic vertebrae" and the presence of two spines on the scapula. In South America at this time xenarthran articulation was not incipient but fully developed. The two-spined scapula, while suggestive, is not conclusive. Some xenarthrans do not have two distinct spines and some nonxenarthrans, including some insectivores, do.

Ernanodon also has derived, specialized, or advanced characters, for example in the humerus, that seem to be adaptively convergent to those of edentates in the broad sense. The details are not so close to those of xenarthrans, or of other xenarthrans. Some of the derived characters of *Ernanodon* differ even more markedly from any South American Xenarthra and also from both families of North American Palaeanodonta: Metacheiromyidae and Epoicotheriidae. Thus, pending further study, two hypotheses in addition to possible reference to the Xenarthra may not yet be fully excluded: (1) that *Ernanodon* belongs to a distinct branch from a general edentate or preedentate stock, or (2) that it has only convergent resemblances to the Xenarthra, Palaeanodonta, and Pholidota and is of quite separate ancestry.

As to the biogeographic problem, Ding suggests several alternatives: that edentates in general (and presumably xenarthrans) originated on Gondwanaland, that they originated on the northern continents with *Ernanodon* in China as evidence in support of that, or "that it may not be entirely improbable that *Ernanodon* is a relic of earlier immigrants from (or to) the South via a route other than the one from the north, or by other means or route" (Ding 1979, pp. 63–64). There is some implication of the involvement of continental drift. Such points will need further discussion when the characters and affinities of *Ernanodon* have been more fully studied.

At present it seems necessary, or at least prudent, to say that we do not know where the Xenarthra originated or what their ancestry was. We do know that xenarthrans were present in South America in the late Paleocene or earlier and that almost all of their later evolution occurred on that continent.

As for the ungulates, it has been noted that all probably arose from members of the relatively primitive order called Condylarthra. Condylarths are known from late Cretaceous rocks in both South and North America and they also occur in the early Cenozoic of South and North America, Europe, and Asia. Some of those from South America are so like some from the northern continents that their placing in different families may exaggerate the moderate differences. Condylarths are not now definitely known from Africa, but the Paleocene and early Eocene mammals of that continent are practically unknown. The somewhat later complexity of indigenous African ungulates suggests that early condylarths had been there and had undergone a progressive radiation within that continent. It is, however, quite unlikely that condylarths, or any other placental ungulates, ever occurred in Australia.

From those facts and reasonable inferences it is easy to form a hypothesis. Perhaps condylarths originated on the likewise partly hypothetical continent called Laurasia, which in pre-Cenozoic times included all the lands now distinguished as North America, Europe, and Asia. Perhaps then the incipient ungulates spread, or island-hopped, from western Laurasia, now but not then distinct as North America, to South America and also to Africa from central Laurasia, now Europe and during part of the Cenozoic but not at some earlier times and not now separated by sea from what is now called Asia. Thereafter the many other families and orders of ungulates evolved at times separately on each of what are now North America, Europe, Asia, and Africa, but with some interaction by faunal interchange from time to time between North America and Eurasia and between Eurasia and Africa. In contrast, during most of the Cenozoic the ungulates evolved in complete isolation in South America.

That hypothesis becomes less purely hypothetical as it goes along, but the earlier part could almost as well be called imaginary history. It is a reasonable possibility, but it is not the only possibility. It is even possible that Ameghino was right, for the wrong reasons, on this point and that ungulates did first evolve in South America. On that point, and some others that have been suggested in connection with this history, we may well repeat a remark often quoted by W. B. Scott, who was introduced in chapter 2. Scott derived the quotation from Jack Robinson, an old frontiersman whom he met in 1877 at Fort Bridger, Wyoming. When anyone told "Uncle Jack" anything he would say, "Well, mebbe it is, but I don't believe it."

There is a most peculiar circumstance that becomes relevant here. Throughout most of the Cenozoic the great majority of South American ungulates belonged to the order Notoungulata. No other group seems more typical of South America or more surely to have evolved there. But a few specimens of apparent notoungulates have been found in the United States, Mongolia, and China. The rocks in which they occur are of approximately the same age in North America and in Asia and may be considered as latest Paleocene or earliest Eocene, depending on just where the artificial line is drawn between those two epochs. Calling these fossils "apparent notoungulates" may be excessive caution, for their dentitions do have distinctive characters otherwise known only in early and still relatively primitive or unspecialized South American notoungulates. A modicum of caution is in order because the dentitions are distinct enough to warrant classifying them in a family not known in South America, named Arctostylopidae by the W. D. Matthew previously mentioned, and because the structure of their ears is not yet known. The ear structure of South American notoungulates is well known, highly complex, and unlike that known in any non–South American mammals.

If, as is after all reasonably sure, the Arctostylopidae really are notoungulates, there seem to be only two possible explanations. Either the Notoungulata started their evolution outside South America, perhaps in southern North America for example, and the Arctostylopidae are late survivors of that basal stock, or some still primitive South American notoungulate lineage left the island continent of South America and reached North America by waif or sweepstakes dispersal across the sea barrier and before long, geologically speaking, also passed from North America to Asia. The authorities Pascual and Patterson, previously cited in other connections, lean toward the former alternative, but I find the latter alternative somewhat more probable. Discovery of early mammals, preferably Cretaceous or Paleocene at latest, in Central America may eventually settle the matter. In any event it is highly probable that most or all of the known families of South American ungulates originated on that continent.

All that has been discussed so far in this chapter does not solve the mystery of why the South American Cenozoic mammalian fauna started with just the three basic stocks of marsupials, xenarthrans, and ungulates, but some light has been cast on that mystery. In general terms, the paucity and imbalance of basic stocks seem most probably to result from South America's already having become an island continent not long after marsupials and placentals had become differentiated and when the placentals were just beginning to radiate into what later became numerous orders in terms of classification. Then South America had or received as waifs from across the sea barriers only a scanty representation of such mammalian diversity as was developing in the great land masses, periodically joined and separated, that are now North America, Eurasia, and Africa.

References

Simpson, G. G. 1978. Early mammals in South America: Fact, controversy, and mystery. *Proceedings of the American Philosophical Society,* 122: 318–328.

The following were received after the paper cited above was published:

Chow, Minchen. [English summary of a paper in press, 1979]. A new edentate from the Paleocene of Guangdong.

Ding, Su-yin. 1979. A new edentate from the Paleocene of Guangdong. *Vertebrata PalAsiatica,* 17: 57–64. (Text in Chinese, with a briefer English version.)

South China "Redbeds" Research Group [authors not named]. 1977. Paleocene vertebrate horizons and mammalian faunas of South China. *Scientia Sinica,* 20: 665–678.

Storch, G. 1978. Ein Schuppentier aus der Grube Messel—zur Paläobiologie eines mitteleozänen Maniden. *Natur und Museum,* 108: 301–307.

CHAPTER 6

First Phase:
The Old-Timers Alone

During almost certainly all of the Paleocene and much but probably not quite all of the Eocene, it has been shown, the known South American mammalian faunas consisted of just three major groups: marsupials, xenarthrans, and ungulates. Each group had already become diversified and somewhat specialized by evolution on a continent completely isolated. These are the real old-timers, the oldest faunal stratum of the Age of Mammals on this continent. Their communities, their environments, in general their ecology while they monopolized this spendid isolation, are now to be considered. Those are the topics for this chapter dealing with the three land mammal ages Riochican, Casamayoran, and Mustersan. What eventually happened to these old-timers will be told in later chapters.

It is necessary to bear in mind that our positive information, especially in the early phases, usually comes from small parts of a large continent. Inference yields generalities that are probably valid for the continent as a whole, but the details are likely to be local. In particular localities and areas many different situations occurred and events happened for which there may be no direct information. The force of that remark is at once revealed by the fact that although they have similarities that indicate approximate contemporaneity the Riochican faunas of Argentina (several localities in Patagonia) and Brazil (only Itaborai) are markedly different in some respects. Undoubtedly the environments and general ecology of the two were dissimilar in some ways.

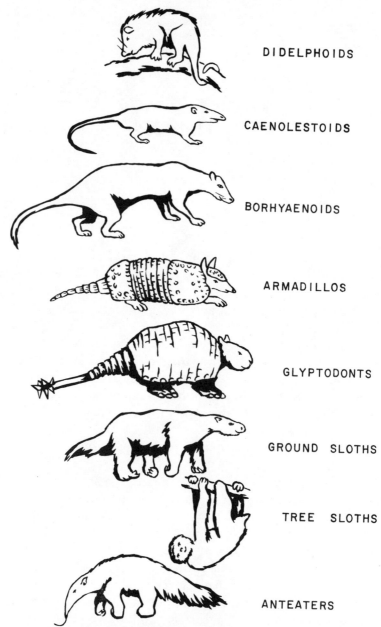

DIDELPHOIDS

CAENOLESTOIDS

BORHYAENOIDS

ARMADILLOS

GLYPTODONTS

GROUND SLOTHS

TREE SLOTHS

ANTEATERS

Fig. 4. Some marsupials (*three upper drawings*) and xenarthrans (*other drawings*) descended from old-timers of the first faunal stratum. The didelphoid (opossum), caenolestoid, armadillo, tree sloth, and anteater shown are still living. The others are restorations of mid-Cenozoic representatives of their groups.

CONDYLARTHS

LITOPTERNS

NOTOUNGULATES

ASTRAPOTHERES

PYROTHERES

Fig. 5. Some ungulates descended from old-timers of the first faunal stratum. The condylarth restoration is based on a North American specimen, because the skeleton is not known in any South American condylarth, but the more primitive forms must have looked very much alike on the two continents. The litoptern shown is the Pleistocene *Macrauchenia*. The highly varied notoungulates are represented by a hegetothere and a rather generalized early form (isotemnid). Astrapotheres and pyrotheres are represented by their type genera. The body of *Pyrotherium* is inadequately known and so is not included in the restoration.

In Patagonia the Riochican sediments are predominantly water-laid sands deposited on a low floodplain by streams flowing from hills somewhere to the west. There were trees, in clumps or forests, and doubtless also much low, shrubby vegetation. There were alligatorlike crocodilians in the streams and doubtless also fishes, although the latter are not known for this age. The climate was at least warm temperate and perhaps subtropical, in either case very different from the cold present climate of the now tree-less Patagonian plains and mesetas.

The Patagonian Riochican fauna is dominated by ungulates, all but one of those known being small, primitive, browsing animals. Four litoptern species of two families (Macraucheniidae and Proterotheriidae) have been found, the two families then being less clearly distinct and much less specialized than their later descendants. As usual in early South American faunas the notoungulates are most abundant and most varied: ten known species in four or five still not very different families (Henricosborniidae, ?Notostylopidae, Oldfieldthomasiidae, Interatheriidae, Isotemnidae). One large ungulate, the xenungulate *Carodnia,* already had specialized, sharply crested teeth also evidently adapted to browsing, probably on small trees or on higher bushes than those eaten by the much more numerous smaller browsers. Two perhaps omnivorous condylarths, the most primitive ungulates, are known. Armadillos were present but very rare, and there are no other known xenarthrans. The only marsupials definitely known are four species of the peculiar family Polydolopidae. Those animals had enlarged piercing or nipping lower incisors followed (in most genera) by a crested, shearing cheek tooth and then by crushing and chewing molars. As will be more fully considered when discussing the history of marsupials, the ecological position of the polydolopids is uncertain. They may have been eaters of seed and small fruit, but probably also ate some animal food.

As the Itaborai fossils occurred in fissures and caves, nothing very definite can be inferred about their environment from the rocks. The animals whose bones are found in them certainly did not live in the fissures and caves. The fossils themselves indicate a well-watered region with a warm climate, as in Patagonia, but the fauna was different in ways difficult to interpret ecologically.

Only two species of notoungulates have been described from Itaborai, but one of these is fairly abundant there. There is also an abundant trigonostylopid, member of a group of browsing ungulates not known from the Patagonian Riochican but common in the immediately following Casamayoran. *Carodnia,* first found in Patagonia, is common at Itaborai. There are some condylarths and litopterns not markedly different from those known from Patagonia. There is also a relatively primitive polydolopid. The most remarkable feature of the Brazilian Riochican fauna is the abundance and variety of opossums, Didelphidae in a broad sense; thirteen different genera have been described. This family is not known at all from the Patagonian Riochican or Mustersan and is rare in the intervening Casamayoran.

So many and such diverse genera of opossums are not known from any other one locality at any one time, including the present. As to the specific, presumably ecological, reason for their occurrence just here and just at this time, I have no suggestions. The occurrence warrants the general inference that a remarkable South American radiation occurred in the family Didelphidae in early Cenozoic times and that most of its lineages became extinct thereafter.

Three small predaceous marsupial carnivores, borhyaenids, are known from Itaborai, none from the Patagonian Riochican, although a primitive genus, *Patene,* occurs in both the Itaborai Riochican and the Patagonian Casamayoran. A characteristic of the known Riochican faunas is that there seems to be a poor balance between mammalian carnivores and herbivores. In what may be considered well-balanced faunas elsewhere or in South America at later times, mammalian carnivores are fewer than herbivores but nevertheless constitute an appreciable and varied part of a mammalian community.

The apparent imbalance of the low carnivore-herbivore ratio in the Riochican and also in the Casamayoran and Mustersan can be at least partly explained by the fact that not all carnivores are mammalian and that reptilian carnivores were present during those ages. There were crocodilians in variety, some of them crocodiles in a limited sense, some more alligatorlike, and some (the genus *Sebecus,* found in both Riochican and Casamayoran) with high, narrow snouts and large, daggerlike teeth—impressive predators. In the Casamayoran, at least, and possibly also in the other faunas here in question there were also large, predatory, boa- or pythonlike snakes. Thus the abundant crop of herbivorous mammals did not lack predators.

The rocks of Casamayoran age that immediately overlie those of the Riochican at some localities in Patagonia are extraordinarily different from the Riochican rocks. They are almost entirely of volcanic origin, mostly volcanic ash, some, at least, of which was transported by running water after it fell. Much was also altered by groundwater or by weathering that converted it into an odd kind of rock that swells greatly and becomes soggy when wet. That is bentonite, named after Fort Benton, Montana, and its principal component is a clay mineral called montmorillonite, named for a locality in France. Throughout Casamayoran time and, as will later be recounted, for millions of years thereafter there was a series of tremendous volcanic explosions that covered thousands of square kilometers under deep deposits of ash.

In spite of that sensational volcanic activity, the region now known as Patagonia was habitable and was inhabited by great numbers of mammals and other animals. There is some, but scant, evidence of trees, but there must have been abundant vegetation as evidenced by the presence of great herds of many species of herbivores. The ash containing their remains accumulated on a vast plain, not far above sea level and with some streams and small lakes in which there were fishes, frogs, and crocodilians, including the formidable *Sebecus* that has been mentioned as already present in Riochican time. The climate in this part of southern South America must have been humid and warm, perhaps even more so than during the Riochican.

The known Casamayoran fauna has the same mammalian orders as the Riochican except for the Xenungulata, known from the Riochican only, and the Casamayoran and later Astrapotheria and Pyrotheria, not yet found in the Riochican although they must have existed then. The families, too, are largely the same. Apart from families of the unshared orders, only two families of notoungulates first appear in the known record for Casamayoran

time: Archaeopithecidae and Archaeohyracidae. The Archaeopithecidae were still quite primitive as notoungulates went and
not markedly unlike some Riochican forms which nevertheless
seem nearer to the ancestry of what eventually evolved into a
quite distinctive family (Interatheriidae). The Archaeohyracidae,
however, were more advanced than anything known in the
Riochican. The crowns of their molar teeth were beginning to be
higher than in earlier or than in other contemporaneous notoungulates. That represents an incipient change of herbivorous diet
from browsing on relatively soft vegetation to grazing on grass or
other harsh vegetation.

The predaceous carnivores were still all marsupials, as they
would continue to be throughout most of the Cenozoic, and the
mammalian carnivore-herbivore ratio was still low, but less so than
in the known Riochican. There was also one big, already rather
specialized marsupial carnivore, a borhyaenid, convergent toward
doglike placental carnivores. This doubtless fierce creature, *Arminiheringia auceta* Ameghino, was at least as large as a robust
Recent timber wolf. Convergent evolution had already made up
for the imbalance of the absence of any placental carnivores in
ancient South America. Among other marsupials, opossums are
very rare in the Patagonian Casamayoran but must still have been
present in some numbers elsewhere in South America. The
strange polydolopids were at their height. They barely survived
into the Deseadan and became extinct thereafter.

The Condylarthra were also at their height as far as the known
record shows. They survived into the Friasian (middle Miocene),
when they were already extinct elsewhere in the world, and they
then became extinct as such also in South America—various of
their early offshoots survive to the Recent as other ungulates and
as the odd African aardvark. Litopterns were numerous but still
quite primitive. Notoungulates dominated the fauna, with 7
families and 23 genera described from the Casamayoran by 1967.
Others may occur in collections made since that date but not yet
described in print. In the Casamayoran they were all relatively
primitive and had not yet acquired characteristic divergent
specializations that became prominent in later faunas. As previ-

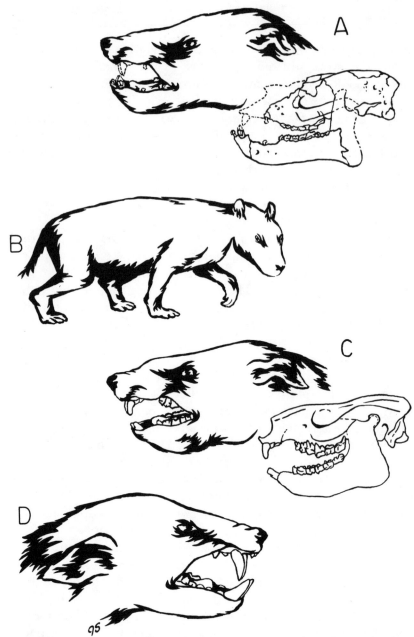

Fig. 6. Some early Eocene, Casamayoran, mammals from Patagonia: *A*, a trigonostylopid, *Trigonostylops*, skull and restoration of head; *B*, restoration of a primitive notoungulate, an isotemnid, *Thomashuxleya; C*, a slightly specialized notoungulate, a notostylopid, *Notostylops*, skull and restoration of head; *D*, a large, predaceous marsupial borhyaenid, *Arminiheringia*, restoration of head.

ously noted, the Casamayoran Archaeohyracidae do provide a partial exception to that generalization.

Among the Xenarthra, armadillos seem to be abundant in the Casamayoran. They are usually represented by isolated bony plates, which are so many on one individual that their abundance in collections doubtless gives an exaggerated impression of the abundance of the animals in the fauna. Nevertheless, a considerable part of the skeleton of one was found, and among other interesting things it revealed that this armadillo had enamel on its teeth. Enamel is totally absent on the teeth of all known later armadillos.

Volcanic activity similar to that of the Casamayoran continued through the Mustersan age, but there was some uplift of the Patagonian plains that led to post-Casamayoran erosion. The deposits with Mustersan fossils are consequently more patchy and local in Patagonia than those of the Casamayoran. The Mustersan fauna is somewhat less well known, but there are some recent collections not yet described. The lack of such warm-climate animals as crocodilians and boalike snakes and the relative scarcity of marsupials in the published collections have been taken to indicate that the climate had become somewhat cooler in central Patagonia latitudes, but that may be a chance effect of the smaller collections.

What we do know about the Mustersan shows us a mammalian fauna in transition. A now archaic polydolopid marsupial does occur here. The predaceous borhyaenids are present but rare, probably by luck of sampling. No condylarths are known in the Mustersan or thereafter in Argentina, but we know that they survived into the Miocene in tropical South America.

Among the still dominant notoungulates the primitive Henricosborniidae and Archaeopithecidae are not known after the Casamayoran and the also rather primitive Notostylopidae, Oldfieldthomasiidae, and Isotemnidae have become less common in the Mustersan. Among those, only the Isotemnidae, and they somewhat questionably, are reported in post-Mustersan faunas. The most striking change is that in two families of notoungulates, the Archaeohyracidae and the Notohippidae, the molar teeth have become high-crowned. There is a definite trend toward teeth more of grazing type, a trend that later appeared also independently in some other notoungulates. At around this time there was perhaps an expansion of grasses and of grasslands in South America, but that is hypothetical. Certainly some of the old native ungulates were adapting to a coarser diet, one that wore down their grinding teeth more rapidly.

Among the Xenarthra, sloths and glyptodonts are first known from the Mustersan. They then already had their peculiar special characteristics and must have been evolving for some time. The most probable explanation for their apparent absence in the Riochican and Casamayoran and rarity in the Mustersan is that they were restricted to or most common in more tropical parts of the continent from which we have as yet few or no fossils of these ages. They eventually became abundant in Patagonia as well.

Here for the time being we will leave the faunal succession. In the next few chapters the histories of the South American old-timers, those whose ancestors formed the first faunal stratum, will be followed. Then in chapter 11 the faunal succession will be resumed with the introduction of the members of a second faunal stratum.

Added note: After this chapter was written but before it was in type the discovery of a rich sequence of late Paleocene and early Eocene mammalian faunas in the northern Argentinian provinces of Jujuy and Salta was announced. Descriptions of these faunas had not been published when the present book went to press.

References

The comments on the mammal-bearing strata are based mostly on my unpublished field notes and observations. Most of what is known about the three faunas here under consideration is given in the following two-volume memoir, which also gives citations to the numerous short papers on the Itaborai Riochican by Paula Couto.

Simpson, G. G. 1948, 1967. The beginning of the Age of Mammals in South America. *Bulletin of the American Museum of Natural History*, 91: 1–232, and 137: 1–260.

CHAPTER 7

Marsupials

Australia has long been known as the Land of Marsupials, but South America has also been a land of marsupials. The reason why the marsupials became especially numerous and varied on just these two continents is the same for both of them. In Australia there were, in all probability, no placental mammals in the early Cenozoic. The marsupials underwent an adaptive radiation that took them into many of the ecological niches or ways of life that were occupied by placentals on most other continents. Well along in the Cenozoic, placental rodents of the rat family, Muridae, did reach there. That may have inhibited convergent rodentlike evolution among the Australian marsupials, where only the wombats, not really ratlike, did become adaptively similar to some larger rodents elsewhere. The only native land placental other than the murids in Australia is the dingo, and it is almost certainly a feral form of semidomesticated dogs introduced by the aborigines. It was no coincidence that the so-called Tasmanian wolf, more distinctively called the thylacine, which is the most doglike marsupial in appearance and habits, became extinct on the continent of Australia when dingos became common there. A few thylacines did survive on the island of Tasmania and may still do so although none has been seen lately.

In South America, as has been noted, the early marsupials were accompanied by placentals, but the latter were limited to the strange xenarthrans and to numerous ungulates. Notably there were no placental insectivores, rodents, or carnivores, which were abundant in North America, Eurasia, and Africa. Thus, the marsupials here, too, had an adaptive radiation that led into many ways

63

of life occupied by placentals on the northern continents and Africa. As will later appear, placental rodents did reach South America fairly early in the history. Incipient evolution of truly rodentlike marsupials was limited, probably for that reason.

The conservative classification used in this book and outlined in chapter 4 recognizes eight families of known South American marsupials, provisionally grouped in four superfamilies. One family, Necrolestidae, is not here placed as to superfamily. Its one known genus, *Necrolestes,* might well be put in a superfamily of its own, but this is now questionable. Some students of marsupials classify the South American forms in several more families than eight. A point of view on that different arrangement and the reasons for not adopting it here will appear in due course.

A history of South American marsupials naturally starts with the family Didelphidae, the opossums in a broad sense of the word. They are the oldest marsupials known from South America, or from anywhere, and the family's most primitive members are close to or may represent the ancestors of all other South American marsupials and possibly of the Australian marsupials as well. Didelphids are also incomparably the most abundant marsupials in South America today, where the only other surviving family, Caenolestidae, includes only three genera by the most split classification. A leading student of didelphids (Osvaldo Reig) recognizes 14 genera and 71 species in the modern fauna. To some other students that arrangement seems unduly inflated, but no one doubts that living didelphids are both abundant and highly diverse. They cover a vast area and one with many different environments: nearly all of South America and much of southern North America. The species and genera have limited ranges to which they are particularly adapted, and the numbers at any one place are of course much smaller than those given for the area as a whole.

Primitive didelphids and most of the living ones were and are essentially omnivorous. They may eat insects, worms, snails, crustaceans, eggs, amphibians, reptiles, birds, mammals, carrion, fruit, and other succulent vegetable matter to the extent of being menaces to farmers' crops in some areas. Within this broad regimen some species are more carnivorous and some more herbivorous, specializations carried to greater extremes in some extinct genera. The ecologically most peculiar living didelphid is the yapok, *Chironectes minimus,* which is aquatic and carnivorous, eating mostly crayfish and fish. Yapok is an Indian name from Guiana. *Chironectes* is from Greek roots for "hand swimmer," although it is the hind feet that are webbed and are used most in swimming. The species was mistaken for an otter when first discovered.

The extraordinary variety of didelphids in the Riochican fauna at Itaborai in Brazil was mentioned in the preceding chapter. It is as if these animals, isolated on a continent where there were no others like them, were experimenting with a great variety of incipient ecological specializations. The less anthropomorphic inference is that they represent disruptive natural selection acting initially on numerous small dispersal and marginal populations, among which those that prospered spread so that many of them came to occupy overlapping territories (became sympatric in technical language) as at Itaborai in Riochican time.

In the Casamayoran, in addition to at least one fairly average didelphid, there was another, more peculiar, named *Caroloameghinia* after his collector brother by Florentino Ameghino. Two incomplete lower jaws with some teeth and one incomplete upper jaw likewise with some teeth were the basis for this tribute of one brother to another. (I have since balanced the equation by naming a Patagonian fossil of the same age *Florentinoameghinia.*) With the usual dualism of his interpretations Don Florentino recognized the correct ancestry of the genus, in the Didelphidae, but completely misunderstood its resemblance to what he thought were its descendants, the placental ungulates. The lack of shearing crests and the presence of somewhat more than the main cusps primitive for marsupials are indeed resemblances to the most primitive ungulates, some condylarths, but the resemblance is only adaptive and convergent. *Caroloameghinia* was certainly a marsupial, one less carnivorous than most didelphids but so nearly allied to the latter that the consensus now places it not in a separate family, as Ameghino did and others long followed, but in a subfamily, Caroloameghiniinae, of the Didelphidae.

Didelphids also occur in intervening faunas, but they are next well known in the Santacrucian, early Miocene, where one named *Microbiotherium* by Ameghino is fairly common. The name means "short-lived mammal." There is no evidence that it was any shorter lived than other mammals of its size, but there is no rule that scientific names of animals must make sense, just that they be distinctive and their application clear. Ameghino recognized the relationship of *Microbiotherium* to didelphids but put it in a separate family. The most obvious distinction is that the small external (buccal) cusps of the upper molars are less developed than in didelphids. In 1906 Sinclair, the first to study this genus after Ameghino, considered it to belong to the Didelphidae and so have most later students, while usually retaining a subfamily Microbiotheriinae. The subfamily was long considered extinct, but as early as 1955 Reig pointed out that the living genus *Dromiciops* closely resembles *Microbiotherium* and may even be identical with that genus. Ever since he has considered the Microbiotheriidae as a family distinct from the Didelphidae and still living in the genus *Dromiciops* = *Microbiotherium* (?) and perhaps some others.

That may seem a minor point, perhaps a tempest in the taxonomic teapot. So it is in a way, and yet it bears on some matters of more general interest. It has not been too surprising to find that a genus of mammals first described and named from fossils and supposed to have been extinct for perhaps 10,000 or perhaps even up to a million years is in fact still living. An example famous among zoologists is a genus of small Australian marsupials supposedly extinct for at least ten thousand years and named *Burramys* by Robert Broom on the basis of fossil bones that he found in a cave in 1894. In 1966 one was found alive and, as reported, friendly in a ski hut in the so-called (with considerable exaggeration) Australian Alps. *Dromiciops* was known and named in 1894, only seven years after *Microbiotherium,* so the observation in 1955 that it might be a living microbiothere is not as dramatic as the history of *Burramys* but it may be in one respect even more remarkable: if *Dromiciops* is accepted as generically identical with

Microbiotherium the genus has survived as such for about 20 million years. That might be the world record for a mammalian genus.

A matter of broader importance is exemplified by the fact that *Microbiotherium,* with or without *Dromiciops,* is by some authorities included in the subfamily Didelphinae, by others (probably a majority at present) placed in a separate subfamily Microbiotheriinae in the family Didelphidae, and by still others put in a family of its own, Microbiotheriidae. Whether a group of organisms given a name in a classification, and then technically called a taxon (plural *taxa*), is a genus, a subfamily, a family, or a taxon of some other rank is not a "true or false" question. Although more definite criteria have been proposed for such ranking, none is really workable as a hard and fast rule. The ranking is usually affected by custom or tradition, but in any particular case it generally depends on personal opinion, taste, and judgment as to convenience, balance, and clarity.

In this example I have for some time placed *Microbiotherium* in the Didelphinae. This judgment is supported by Reig's listings and analyses of many characters of living and fossil opossums and their relatives, although Reig ranks the group in question as a separate family. There is not a single known character of *Microbiotherium* or of *Dromiciops* that does not also occur in genera referred by Reig himself to the Didelphinae. Combinations of characters do occur in these genera and not as identical combinations in other genera of Didelphidae. That is how the genera are defined and why they are given generic rank in classification: each genus does have its own combination of characters that occur separately in different combinations here and there throughout the family. In this situation my judgment is that subfamily or higher rank is not warranted, and similar considerations apply to other questions of ranks in classification.

A student of such matters once remarked in a cynical mood that some other taxonomists seem to think that if you can tell two animals apart they belong to different genera, and if you can't they belong to different species.

Besides continuation of the Didelphinae into their present flourishing populations, there is in the late Cenozoic another group of opossum relatives that unquestionably merits separation as a subfamily, at least, although it is not surprising that this group is sometimes placed in a family of its own. It is here considered a subfamily of Didelphidae called Sparassocyninae for its only now well-defined genus, *Sparassocynus*. In age that subfamily ranges from Huayquerian to Uquian or in other terms approximately early Pliocene to early Pleistocene, but it is best known from beautifully preserved skulls and jaws of Chapadmalalan age found in the sea cliffs near the city of Mar del Plata in Argentina. The molar teeth were more carnassialized than in other didelphids, which means that they had evolved strong shearing crests and reduced the more usual didelphid combination of crests with pounding and grinding parts. The ear region is even more distinctive as the middle ear has two large cavities, one below and one above (hypotympanic and epitympanic), both enclosed in bony walls. These animals were small, highly predatory carnivores, representing an ecological niche not at that time occupied by other South American mammals.

The other carnivores in South America from the Riochican (at least) to about the end of the Pliocene, when they became extinct, are now all referred to the family Borhyaenidae. They clearly arose from an early offshoot of the Didelphidae which tended to become less omnivorous and more carnivorous, presumably preying for the most part on the extremely numerous native ungulates. Typically they were cursorial predators, but they branched out to include many variations in size, bulk, and various anatomical details. Ameghino distributed them in seven different families, but there is now general agreement that they are best placed in a single family. However, they did become so varied that their most recent student, L. G. Marshall, divides them into four subfamilies, now well distinguished in a justified arrangement.

Members of the subfamily Hathlyacyninae remained small to medium sized and were apparently less fully carnivorous and predaceous than many of their larger relatives. Marshall thinks that some of them were semiarboreal. Although they differ in anatomical detail, the Proborhyaeninae and Borhyaeninae were all large terrestrial predatory carnivores. The Prothylacininae were also

Fig. 7. Restoration of *Prothylacinus,* an early Miocene (Santacrucian) marsupial carnivore of the family Borhyaenidae.

large, some also apparently strictly carnivorous but some probably nearly omnivorous, perhaps a secondary development from carnivorous ancestors such as occurred to greater degree in the bears among placental carnivores.

In general appearance and doubtless also in the activities of many of them, these animals were somewhat doglike. In appearance they were less catlike but must also have occupied some of the ecological roles played by cats on other continents. This has become a classic example of evolutionary convergence, which is classical too because in spite of the striking adaptive similarities no able anatomist could mistake any of these marsupial carnivores for a placental carnivore. Ameghino recognized their distinction and put them in a separate order (his Sparassodonta) which he believed, correctly as we now think, to be derived from primitive opossums, but again he erred as regards their descendants: he believed them to be ancestral to the placental carnivores.

Their resemblance to the Tasmanian wolf or thylacine of the Australian region is closer than to any placental carnivore. This resemblance is indeed so great that even a good anatomist could believe it to indicate a special relationship closer than the mere fact that all the animals involved belong to the very broad group Marsupialia. Sinclair, who was an able anatomist, referred all the Borhyaenidae of our present classification to the Australian family Thylacinidae. For some years this was accepted as evidence for a special and close connection between South America and Australia. There is still some dissent or marginal doubt, but it seems

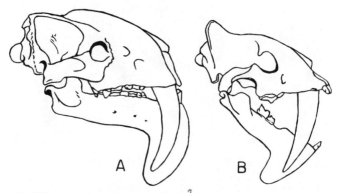

Fig. 8. *A, Thylacosmilus,* an early Oligocéne (Huayquerian) marsupial saber-tooth, family Thylacosmilidae; *B, Smilodon,* a Pleistocene placental sabertooth, family Felidae, subfamily Machairodontinae.

almost overwhelmingly probable that borhyaenids and thylacinids evolved separately in their respective continents. The fact that their resemblance is closer than in most undoubted examples of convergence is explained by their both having arisen from primitive didelphids or didelphidlike ancestors. Thus not only convergence but also an element of evolutionary parallelism is involved.

The South American marsupial family Thylacosmilidae provides another classical, obvious, but even more striking example of convergence. *Thylacosmilus,* from the Huayquerian of northern Argentina, had great saberlike canines, and the whole appearance of its skull, jaws, and dentition is amazingly like that of the famous placental "saber-toothed tigers," which were cats in the broadest sense but not tigers in any proper sense. It is a reasonable hypothesis that *Thylacosmilus* evolved from some early branch of the Borhyaenidae, but it appears suddenly in the known record and its ancestry is not yet known, or recognized.

The second still living family of South American marsupials is now almost always designated as the Caenolestidae. There is some doubt about the technically proper nomenclature of the family and its subfamilies, but that is not important here and the general usage will be followed. The first notice of a member of this family was published in England in 1860 and a few trapped specimens turned up at intervals thereafter, but they were considered great rarities and had hardly been seen in the wild except by unlettered natives until the late 1960s when more appropriate search by a student of Australian and American marsupials, J. A. W. Kirsch, found that some of them are rather common in the remote, mostly Andean, regions where they occur. Now the living forms are usually classified as comprising three genera, one with five species and the other two with one species each. They do not have any real popular names. In English the name "rat opossums" is usual, but this is an invented book-name and an inept one, as they are neither rats nor opossums and do not closely resemble either. In Spanish they are sometimes called *ratones runchos,* an equally inept name, "mice opossums." *Runcho* is a dialect name for opossum in Colombia, not generally understood in other Spanish-speaking countries.

The molars of these animals differ from the primitive marsupial pattern in being more squared off, but the most striking feature of the dentition is the presence of two very large lower incisors pointing almost straight forward. Many Australian marsupials have similar enlarged and forward-pointing lower incisors. On that account a large Australian group including kangaroos and their allies is often called Diprotodonta, "two first (or anterior) toothed." For some years students of these animals suggested that there is in fact a special, close relationship between caenolestids and the Australian diprotodonts, another supposed tie between their two continents. Now, however, it is agreed that this is another case of evolutionary convergence, here as in the case of the Borhyaenidae-Thylacinidae, between two groups both marsupials but distinct in origin. In habits and diet the caenolestids are even more ecologically convergent toward the placental insectivores. Like the latter, the caenolestids eat not only insects but also worms and other invertebrate animals and probably such small vertebrates as they can obtain. Kirsch found that the live animals relish meat and kill and eat newborn rodents presented to them. He suggests that the adaptive selection for the enlarged lower incisors was not only, or not primarily, to grasp food but also to pierce and kill it.

Ameghino pointed out correctly as early as 1897 that the living caenolestids are clearly related to a number of fossil forms that he had been describing under several other family names and placed in a distinct order Paucituberculata, a term also used by some modern authors who divide the Marsupialia into several orders. Sinclair referred them all to the Caenolestidae, divided into three subfamilies. The surviving subfamily, Caenolestinae, probably present throughout the Cenozoic, has the least specialized dentition. They now live in relatively cool parts of South America, well up in the Andes and on the cool island of Chiloë, and may owe their survival to this climatic tolerance. However, members of the same subfamily lived in evidently warm, even tropical climates earlier in the Cenozoic. The Palaeothentinae, known from the Deseadan to the Santacrucian, had an enlarged anterior lower molar with a low but well-developed shearing crest. In the third subfamily, Abderitinae, the anterior part of that molar had become a high, serrated blade. The family provides an interesting example of the extinction of lineages in some respects distinctly more advanced or specialized while the least specialized members of the family survived. The example is not unique and some evolutionists have even spoken of a law of survival of the less specialized, but the "law" has many exceptions.

In the family Polydolopidae there are also two or in the most primitive forms several enlarged, forward-pointing lower incisors. There is also a tooth with a large shearing blade, which used to be considered as a specialization of a first molar going beyond that seen in the Abderitinae. However, one of the earliest and most primitive members of the family, *Epidolops* from the Riochican of Itaborai, strongly suggests that the shearing teeth are not the same, not homologous, in the Caenolestidae and Polydolopidae. Some students have gone to the extreme of supposing that the two families arose separately from different didelphids. However, in other respects *Epidolops* is quite like the Caenolestidae, more so than are the later, Casamayoran polydolopids. That suggests that the two families did have a postdidelphid common ancestry and that their union in the same superfamily is valid on phylogenetic grounds. It is even conceivable that the shearing teeth in the two families are homologous after all, although that is an unorthodox suggestion. In any case, the Polydolopidae are clearly the more specialized family of the two, and they became extinct much earlier. They are fairly common in the Casamayoran, rare in the Mustersan and Deseadan, and unknown thereafter.

Most of the varied polydolopids were adaptively quite like the abderitine caenolestids. It is interesting that these two, potentially competing groups did occur together in the Deseadan, but polydolopids are not known thereafter. It is possible that they also occurred together in pre-Deseadan times, but perhaps in different regions, which may also explain why pre-Deseadan abderitines are not yet known. Both these groups have a somewhat limited resemblance to some of the smallest Australian kangaroos such as the bettongs, diprotodonts that also have one serrated, bladelike tooth in the lower jaw. The whole kangaroo family is basically herbivorous, but it is reported that bettongs are also partly carnivorous and avidly eat meat in captivity, at least. There is no way of knowing whether these somewhat similar extinct South American marsupials also had a taste for meat. They could hardly have competed with the larger borhyaenids but may have competed, ultimately without success, with the omnivorous to partly carnivorous opossums.

The next marsupial family to be discussed is one of the strangest, even in these faunas where almost everything is strange to modern eyes. It is also at present one of the rarest families of mammals in collections, known by only two specimens. The family is named Groeberiidae and both known specimens are of the genus *Groeberia,* named by Bryan Patterson for Pablo Groeber, an Argentinian of German origin who spent most of his life investigating the geology of Argentina although he had no special connection with discovery of the fossils named after him. The two specimens are from the same geological formation, the Divisadero Largo beds, in the outskirts of the city of Mendoza in Argentina. They are not known to have been quite contemporaneous, and the difference in adult size is so great that they are considered to represent different species. The specimens are poorly preserved, but they have determinable characters radically unlike any other known marsupials or indeed any other known mammals whatever.

In the lower jaws there is one pair (one tooth on each side) and in the upper jaw two pairs of enlarged, curved, constantly growing incisor teeth with enamel on the anterior (labial) faces. These are obviously powerful gnawing teeth, functionally like those of rodents, but there is no rodent with a set of gnawing teeth like these. Posterior to them there is a toothless gap and then a short series of molar teeth, short-crowned and with closed roots, with small cusps arranged differently from those in primitive marsupials. The face was very short and deep.

These highly specialized animals appear in the known record without any antecedents and then immediately—geologically speaking—disappear again forever. A possible hypothesis or a more or less educated guess is that they had been evolving for some time in a paleontologically unknown region or under special circumstances. Some plausibility is added by the fact that the whole fauna in which they occur is peculiar in detail, unlike any other known, and evidently representing some special ecological facies. The age is approximately Deseadan, perhaps early in that age or possibly even slightly before the Deseadan as currently understood. The time was apparently just before or possibly barely after placental rodents reached South America, and that suggests another guess, or two guesses. The origin of these marsupial gnawers may have been possible because there were previously no competing placental gnawers, and the extinction of these marsupials may have been from competition with more effective placental gnawers after those arrived.

When all that was known of *Groeberia* was a poorly preserved partial lower jaw it was suggested that it might have been derived from early caenolestoids. Further study with added knowledge from the better second specimen made that suggestion seem improbable. Both the caenolestids and the polydolopids were very different from *Groeberia* in almost all their nonprimitive characters, and their evolutionary trends were away from, not toward, any that might have led to *Groeberia*. It is more likely that groeberiids represented an early divergence and specialization from the early marsupial stock, but only the eventual discovery of older groeberiids, or pregroeberiids, can finally settle this question.

The family Argyrolagidae is equally strange in completely different ways and is much better known than the Groeberiidae. The Ameghinos discovered the first specimens of argyrolagids at Monte Hermoso, but those were such dissociated and puzzling scraps that in this case Florentino's talent for determining the ancestral, but not descendant, affinities of their fossils did not work. He was badly mistaken as to both ancestors and descendants. That is quite easy to say now but does not show that we are cleverer than the Ameghinos. It only shows that we now have a splendid series of fossils unknown to the Ameghinos, mostly from the sea cliffs near Mar del Plata, so prolific in fossils, and including even the associated parts of most of a skeleton.

The skeleton shows that these animals were bipedal, with large, powerful, two-toed, leaping hindlegs and a long, heavy counterbalance of a tail. To anyone accustomed to looking at the skulls of most other mammals, the argyrolagid skull is downright weird. It has enormous eye sockets, so far back that there is practically no place for jaw muscles back of the eye where other mammals, including ourselves, do have part of the jaw musculature. It adds

Fig. 9. Restoration of *Argyrolagus*, a late Pliocene–early Pleistocene bipedal, leaping marsupial of the family Argyrolagidae.

to the strangeness that the nose is prolonged in a bony tube formed well beyond the mouth opening. The teeth, too, are peculiar. There are two pairs of large upper incisors, the somewhat smaller medial pair curving downward and backward, and two pairs in the lower jaw, the decidedly larger medial pair curving forward and upward. Behind the incisors there is a toothless space and then in both upper and lower jaws there is a close-pressed series of five columnar teeth, the outlines of their cross sections differing somewhat in the various known genera and species. All the teeth grew continuously throughout life as they wore down, not forming closed roots.

The argyrolagids are known in Argentina from the Huayquerian to the Uquian, approximately early Pliocene to early Pleistocene. A single specimen clearly of this family has also been found in Bolivia in beds of Montehermosan or Chapadmalalan age. Argyrolagids are distinctly rodentlike, and there were many placental rodents in the same faunas. However, none of the latter closely resembled the argyrolagids, which evidently had adapted to a distinct and for South America new ecological niche. Although readily distinguishable in anatomical details and unquestionably marsupials, they were remarkably convergent to some placental rodents on other continents. This bipedal, leaping and jumping, saltatorial or ricochetal locomotive system, often accompanied by other special features such as inflated sounding chambers in the middle ear (also present in argyrolagids), evolved repeatedly and independently several different times. It is present especially in the "kangaroo rats and mice," not kangaroos or rats or mice but Heteromyidae, in North America; the Dipodidae, jerboas, of Africa and Asia; and interestingly enough in Australia not among marsupials but in a native member, *Notomys,* of the rat family, Muridae. All of those are placental rodents, but originating from different ancestors in several different families. Most of them are especially at home in steppes and more or less arid regions, and the argyrolagids were probably steppe or pampa animals. There are still large areas in South America and in just the regions where their fossils are found that would seem excellent environments for them. It is curious that they became extinct there while closely analogous rodents survived on other major land masses. South America now lacks that adaptive type. A few heteromyids do live in South America, but they are latecomers confined to the far north of the continent and probably never came in contact with and did not replace the argyrolagids.

These creatures, like *Groeberia* and some others, again appear in the known record suddenly, without known ancestors, and disappear after a geologically short span without apparent cause.

The last marsupial family to be discussed, as the marsupials are classified here, is again a highly specialized, most peculiar one that appears in our known record abruptly without antecedents and disappears mysteriously in a geologically extremely short time. This is the family Necrolestidae, known from a single genus and species confined to the Santacrucian, approximately early Miocene. The first specimens were found by Carlos Ameghino and described by Florentino in 1891 as *Necrolestes patagonensis*. Ameghino considered this species to be an insectivore but believed that it was derived from ancestors we call marsupials (he did not so name them) and that it gave rise to all other Insectivora. Hatcher found some skulls, jaws, and skeleton parts of these little animals (the skull was only about $3\frac{1}{2}$ centimeters long), and Scott published on them in 1905. He agreed with the wrong part of Ameghino's usual two-way interpretation, deciding *Necrolestes* had nothing to do with marsupials but was a placental insectivore related to the golden moles of South Africa, as Ameghino had once said. Scott also agreed with Ameghino that this indicated a direct connection between Africa and South America. Although other suggestions were made, Scott's authority rightly carried much weight. No further study of the specimens themselves was made until 1958 when Patterson carried out further preparation of the Princeton specimens and reexamined them with instruments not available to Scott more than half a century earlier. He produced evidence that *Necrolestes* was a marsupial, and that has been widely accepted. There the matter rests for the time being at least. Patterson placed the Necrolestidae in the superfamily Borhyaenoidea but recognized that this was very tentative and rested on few or no really special (derived) borhyaenid characters. This suggestion had previously been made by the eccentric Danish genius Herluf Winge, but as little more than a wild guess. Winge had never seen a specimen of this animal, and his supposed evidence was far from impressive.

What was this mystery animal like? It had an uptilted nose, numerous incisor teeth (five above and four below), sharp canines, and molars with triangular crowns. The bones of the forelimb indicate clearly that it was a burrowing, indeed subterranean and thoroughly molelike creature. Again able anatomists had been misled by an extraordinary example of evolutionary convergence toward the golden moles (Chrysocloridae) of South Africa and the so-called marsupial moles (Notoryctidae) of Australia. In the latter case, as in that of the Borhyaenidae and Thylacinidae, the resemblance was particularly close because convergence was reinforced by parallelism on the basis of remote common ancestry among the most primitive marsupials. In all three of these independently evolved, molelike groups the resemblance even went so far as to involve the odd development of secondarily triangular molar teeth.

References

Simpson, G. G. 1971. *The evolution of marsupials in South America. Anales Acad. Brasileira Ciências,* 43 (supplement): 103–118.

Stonehouse, B., and D. Gilmore. 1977. *The biology of marsupials.* Baltimore, London, Tokyo: University Park Press.

CHAPTER 8

Xenarthrans: The Strange-Joint Mammals

The name Xenarthra is derived from Greek words meaning "strange joints," although the English pronunciation, zee-nar'-thruh, is neither the classical nor the modern Greek pronunciation of the words compounded in this name. The name was invented and applied to this group of mammals because in them some of the vertebrae are connected with each other in the backbone with an extra articulation not found in other mammals: they are strangely jointed.

Among the living animals, armadillos, anteaters, and sloths look so unlike and act and live so differently that it might hardly occur to anyone to classify them together without more anatomical study. Such study reveals that they do share not only strange joints but also other peculiarities that undoubtedly indicate a common origin, although one in the remote past. They have few or no incisors, and some (anteaters) have no teeth at all. On the other hand some armadillos have more teeth than the primitive placental ancestry. Only the earliest had vestiges of enamel, and thereafter all teeth were composed of dentine alone, in some two kinds of dentine of different hardness. Even the earliest known had lost the cusped molar pattern primitive for all placental mammals, and the molars, if retained, became continuously growing columns. All have powerful legs and well-developed claws, the claw on the third toe on the front foot often being exceptionally large. They also have the peculiarity that, whereas in placental mammals in general only one, the ilium, of the three elements that unite to form the pelvis is jointed to the backbone at the sacrum, in xenarthrans a second part of the pelvis, the ischium, is also connected to the sacrum.

No one now seriously doubts that the Xenarthra, despite their remarkable diversity, do form a natural group with a single origin. As to just what that origin was and when and where it existed there are serious doubts, mysteries still unsolved, as was discussed in chapter 5. Those problems are here partly evaded by treating the Xenarthra as a unit on their own and not as a part of the disputable and variously defined group called Edentata.

The Xenarthra, then, are an order of mammals highly characteristic of all South American Cenozoic faunas and long confined to that continent. Only toward the end of the Cenozoic did they spread from South America to Central America and, in decreasing variety, farther in North America and to some of the West Indian islands. They very early separated into three different stocks that may be ranked as suborders with the Xenarthra considered as an order. Each suborder became richly diversified in its own adaptive radiation. The names here and commonly used for those suborders are Cingulata, Pilosa, and Vermilingua. Cingulata means "girdled" or "girt" in neo-Latin and refers to the fact that members of this group have a bony armor over most of the body. Pilosa means "hairy" in classical Latin and was somewhat negatively applied to the many and varied sloths just because they are not armored. In fact, the Vermilingua are equally hairy and all the Cingulata did and do have hair, even protruding from their armor. Vermilingua is a term coined by zoologists from Latin roots meaning "worm" and "tongue," hence "worm-tongued" in reference to the extraordinary, long, sticky tongues of the anteaters. All three suborders survive today in greater or lesser abundance.

Most of the Cingulata or cingulates belong to two readily separable families, the Dasypodidae, armadillos, and the Glyptodontidae, glyptodonts. It has already been mentioned that the armadillos, known from the Riochican onward, are the first of all xenarthrans to appear in the fossil record as we know it today. It is nevertheless probable that glyptodonts had already evolved by that time, probable that ancestral anteaters had, too, and virtually certain that ancestral sloths had. Apparently they were just rare or absent in the limited areas and restricted environments from which adequate collections of fossil mammals have so far been made. Among living xenarthrans it is evident that armadillos are the most adaptable, or in other words are less particular about where and how they live. They now range farther south, down through Patagonia, and north, up into the United States, than any other xenarthrans. In spite of what looks to us like inadequate dental equipment, among them they eat practically anything. Most of them love ants for food but will also go after other insects, eggs, carrion, and some even kill and eat small snakes, young birds, and small rodents. Such a mixed diet is much like that of some opossums. A few armadillos became more exclusively carnivorous or, rarely, somewhat herbivorous.

As everyone knows, armadillos have a bony shield on top of the head, body armor that is partly fixed and partly in the form of movable rings, and a flexible, bony tube on the tail. The bony scutes that join like tiles of various shapes to form the armor are overlain by thin, horny scales that cover the same parts as the bony armor but usually have a different pattern. Many people also think that armadillos curl up in a ball for defense, which is true of one living form but is not true of the vast majority of armadillos, past and present. Armadillos do not climb trees, but they go almost anywhere else and are extremely able diggers. It is hard to catch one before it can dig itself in, and the tiny fairy armadillos of northern Argentina are almost as subterranean as moles. They also have a rear armor plate with which they plug their holes.

Armadillos were already quite varied in Casamayoran times, but with a single exception they are known only by separated scutes from that age and cannot be well characterized. More satisfactory knowledge begins with the Santacrucian. There are five reasonably well-known genera from the type Santacrucian in Patagonia, so varied that they are commonly referred to three different subfamilies. One of those subfamilies (Euphractinae) survives today and includes the common Patagonian armadillo, *Zaedyus* in technical nomenclature, "pichy" in the vernacular of Patagonians. Pichy is the Araucanian Indian word for "small," and the pichy, although much larger than the fairy armadillos, is below the average size for

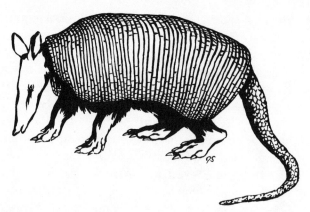

Fig. 10. Restoration of *Stegotherium,* an early Miocene (Santacrucian) ant-eating armadillo.

the family. It is thus somewhat odd that another branch of the subfamily in the late Cenozoic (Huayquerian and Montehermosan, Pliocene) produced giant armadillos with skulls about 27 centimeters (nearly 11 inches) in length.

Another subfamily, rather doubtfully identified from the Deseadan but definitely from the Colhuehuapian, is based mainly on the Santacrucian genus *Stegotherium,* which had a long, toothless snout and just five tiny, vestigial peglike teeth on each side in upper and lower jaws. It had evidently become adapted to a straight diet of ants and termites. As true anteaters, even better adapted to live on that abundant source of food, already existed, it is not surprising that the Stegotheriinae lost out in the competition and are not known after the Santacrucian.

The strangest Santacrucian armadillo is *Peltephilus,* which had a pair of horns on its nose, the only known horned xenarthran. It was also peculiar in having front teeth in the position of median incisors but probably not homologous with true incisors. It has been guessed that members of this subfamily, Peltephilinae (often given family rank), were carnivorous or carrion eaters. The subfamily is known from the Deseadan and somewhat doubtfully on into the Chasicoan, approximately early Oligocene to late Miocene.

Stegotherium and *Peltephilus* provide one of many instances in which the details of the history of South American mammals provide examples that bear on and illumine broader principles and processes of evolution. These two genera are rather closely related: they are usually classified in the same family and always in the same suborder. Nevertheless, they have become radically different in various adaptive features related especially to defense and to diet. Their common ancestor was almost certainly essentially omnivorous, and these descendants became specialized for quite different parts of that more generalized diet. On the other hand, *Stegotherium* and an anteater like the living *Myrmecophaga* are rather closely similar in skull shape and in tooth reduction, far along in *Stegotherium* and complete in *Myrmecophaga,* but they belong to different suborders and are not nearly so closely related to *Stegotherium* and *Peltephilus.*

Several general points about evolutionary patterns are involved here. First, adaptive patterns of similar kinds can arise entirely separately in different lines of descent. In attempting to assess genetic relationships one should not rely on such patterns, and one should take care about including them in overall assessment of similarities for classification of different animals, a procedure *phenetics* nevertheless insisted on by extreme supporters of one school of classification. On the other hand, this example shows that animals evidently more closely related genetically may develop markedly different characteristics and patterns, which again can be misleading if included in overall resemblance or difference as an assessment of affinity. Thus the careful student of evolutionary histories encounters and must evaluate restraints from two different, indeed opposite, directions.

Another point is that the difficult and often vague distinction between convergence and parallelism is somewhat clarified by the example of *Stegotherium* and *Myrmecophaga.* These genera are related, both are xenarthrans, and undoubtedly they had a common *parallelism and convergence* ancestry. That is the basis of parallelism when it does occur. But in this case their common ancestry was the same as that of all the other Xenarthra, and the other descendants include large numbers of animals that did not at all have the special characters that occur in both *Stegotherium* and *Myrmecophaga.* Thus the reasonable con-

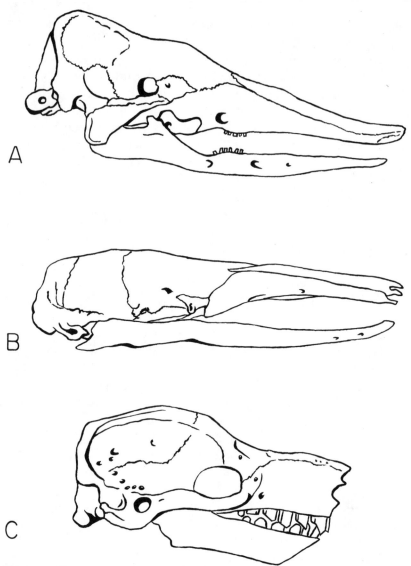

Fig. 11.   Skulls showing divergence in skull and dentition in two early Miocene armadillos and convergence of one toward a living anteater. *A, Stegotherium,* an early Miocene ant-eating armadillo; *B, Myrmecophaga,* a living anteater; *C, Peltephilus,* an early Miocene, probably carnivorous or scavenging armadillo. (The bony scutes on top of the skulls of the armadillos, which in *Peltephilus* included hornlike projections, have been omitted.)

clusion is that their resemblance, as far as it goes, is completely convergent and does not depend at all on their (fairly remote) common ancestry. On the other hand, among marsupials, and especially in the case of borhyaenids and thylacinids, which resemble each other much more closely than do stegotheres and anteaters, there is some reason to believe that the resemblance did depend to some extent on the genetic basis of a common ancestry. Thus parallelism was probably also involved along with convergence; some students consider parallelism the predominant or only factor in that example.

There are several subfamilies of much later appearance in the known record that also merit some notice. The Dasypodinae are known only from the Montehermosan on. Their special interest to North Americans is that they include the nine-banded armadillo, *Dasypus novemcinctus,* which is a South American species that has extended its range well up into the United States, where it is now the only native armadillo. A related but larger species, now extinct, was *Dasypus bellus* which ranged widely in what are now the southern states during the Pleistocene and even as far as where the city of Saint Louis now stands, the northernmost known record of natural occurrence for any armadillo. The extinct Pampatheriinae are known in South America from the Mustersan, approximate middle Eocene, into the Pleistocene. In the Pleistocene they reached what is now the United States, and the genus *Holmesina* spread through the south from Texas to Florida. It included some of the largest known armadillos, with skulls up to 30 centimeters (nearly 12 inches) in length. The teeth are lobed and the pampatheres are in that and some other respects the most nearly glyptodontlike of armadillos. It has been suggested that glyptodonts might have evolved from an early (Paleocene at latest) pampathere, but that is purely speculative and seems improbable.

The largest living armadillos belong to the genus *Priodontes,* confined to tropical South America. This genus is usually given a tribe or subfamily of its own, to which a few middle to late Cenozoic fossils have been doubtfully referred. The fairy armadillos, previously mentioned, form the subfamily Chlamyphorinae, not known by any fossils.

Some specimens from the Mustersan and Deseadan and one, better than most, of unknown age are generally referred to a family Palaeopeltidae. Members of this supposed family have been considered armadillos, glyptodonts, or neither one. They are so dubious and uselessly controversial that there would be no point in discussing them further here.

The fossil mammals collected in Argentina by Darwin in 1833 included part of a glyptodont, and in 1838 Richard Owen, then Darwin's friend but later his bitter opponent, named the genus *Glyptodon* that has given the name to the whole group, now classified as the family Glyptodontidae. The name is concocted from classical Greek roots meaning "carved teeth." The teeth are indeed unique and even one is unmistakable. All glyptodonts lacked front teeth, incisors or canines, but had a close-set battery of grinding teeth, generally eight in number, columnar, growing throughout life, and each with three lobes. In the earliest forms the sides of the lobes are rounded but in the later ones are more angular. They had no enamel but in all but the earliest had a central fore-and-aft line and across it a bar in each of the three lobes consisting of harder dentine and standing up above the rest of the dentine as slightly ridged under wear. They do look as if carved.

The most striking characteristic of the glyptodonts was not their teeth but the fact that they were the most heavily armored mammals that ever lived, veritable walking armored tanks. The head was topped with a bony helmet, and the top and sides of the body were completely covered with a bony mosaic, which in Santacrucian times had some moderately flexible areas but later became completely rigid. The tail was completely armored, in some species mostly with movable rings that gave it a limited flexibility and in others with only a few proximal or anterior rings followed by a completely fused, clublike end, sometimes probably with horny spikes although these are not preserved. In all of them the tail was evidently a formidable weapon of defense. It would seem that between this weapon and their armor they would be immune to attack, yet for unknown reasons they all became extinct.

In spite of the facts that glyptodonts have been known for al-

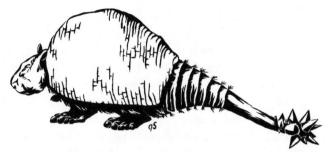

Fig. 12. Restoration of *Doedicurus,* a Pleistocene glyptodont, modified from a painting by Horsfall for Scott.

most a century and a half, are present and usually abundant in all South American faunas since the Mustersan and almost to the Recent, and have a truly voluminous literature both technical and popular, their classification is not entirely satisfactory. Ameghino placed them in four families, and although they are now almost always combined in a single family, Glyptodontidae, the same four groups are still often designated as subfamilies. Various authors have defined more than fifty genera in the family although the validity of some is dubious. The tail patterns seem almost infinitely varied, but other distinctions involve only minor details and the general anatomy is almost completely stereotyped in the later forms, at least. To the characteristics already mentioned may be added the uniformly deep and short skulls and jaws, the presence of a descending spikelike process from the cheekbone below the eye, the strong, heavily muscled legs, longer behind than in front, and the stout, blunt, almost hooflike claws. All were herbivorous and probably ate coarse, abrasive plants such as siliceous pampa grasses.

It has already been mentioned that glyptodonts are first known from the Mustersan and Deseadan and that the teeth then differed somewhat from those of later glyptodonts. Only fragments of the armor are known from those ages, and again the earliest really satisfactory specimens are from the Santacrucian. The Santacrucian glyptodonts are collectively known as Propalaeohoplophorinae. That twenty-two letter, nine-syllable word seems almost comically too much even to those who have to deal professionally with such things, but it resulted from an unwise but seemingly inevitable accretion. Someone—it happened to be Peter Wilhelm Lund in 1838—first named a late Pleistocene glyptodont *Hoplophorus,* "armor bearer," simple, euphonious, and appropriate. Someone else—not surprisingly Ameghino in 1887—named a possibly ancestral, older glyptodont from the Miocene *Palaeohoplophorus,* "old armor bearer." Then Ameghino, still in 1887, had a still older form from the Santacrucian which he considered ancestral to *Palaeohoplophorus* so he called it *Propalaeohoplophorus,* "before the old armor bearer." Substitute the two-syllable termination for a subfamily, -inae, for the final *-us,* and you inevitably have the monstrosity Propalaeohoplophorinae. This subfamily seems to combine animals by their being in about the same evolutionary stage rather than by any other criterion. This was the stage when parts of the body armor were still slightly flexible. The species were also considerably smaller than glyptodonts later became, but in general anatomy they were already like miniature, light models of the family as a whole. The largest of the Pleistocene glyptodonts reached a length of about 3 2/3 meters (about 12 feet).

In the Pleistocene, glyptodonts also spread into North America as far as what is now the United States, and they became fairly common in some parts of what are now the southern states from Arizona to Florida. One genus was closely related or possibly even the same as one known in Uruguay, but three other, somewhat more distinct genera were as far as known confined to what are now the United States and Mexico.

All the xenarthrans are curious and interesting, but in many ways the sloths are the most curious and interesting among them. They had a long history in South America and eventually occupied the entire continent from end to end and side to side. They were the first xenarthrans, and in fact the first native South American mammals, to reach North America, where they also proliferated and spread widely. They figure largely in the history of science and in the current study of such interesting points as the antiquity of man in the Americas and the causes of extinction.

A giant sloth was the first fossil mammal of which the entire skeleton was assembled as such and placed on exhibition. That skeleton was found near Luján in Argentina, which is significant because it is hardly a coincidence that the Ameghino boys who became great collectors and describers of fossil mammals grew up in Luján. Surely they were attracted to this subject by the local finds that had begun almost a century before they were born. That particular skeleton was sent in 1789 to Madrid, where it still is. It was described and figured in the large work by Georges Cuvier, an initial landmark in the history of vertebrate paleontology, entitled (in French) "Researches on the fossil bones of quadrupeds in which are restored the characteristics of several species of animals that the revolutions of the globe seem to have destroyed" in the chapter headed (also in French) "On the Megatherium, another animal of the sloth family but of the size of a rhinoceros, the almost complete fossil skeleton of which is preserved in the royal cabinet of natural history in Madrid," a publication dated 1812.

In North America Thomas Jefferson began the study of fossil sloths in a paper read to the American Philosophical Society in 1797 and published in 1799. The fragments available to him included a large claw, or rather the bone (terminal phalanx or ungual) that had been within a horny claw (not preserved), and he coined for it the vernacular name "megalonyx" or "great-claw." He believed it to represent a wild cat about three times as large as a lion. Jefferson had a brilliant mind and great erudition, but he was a poor naturalist and a worse anatomist. One of his vagaries as a naturalist was a firm belief that God would not permit any kind of animal to become extinct; therefore "great-claw" must still be living somewhere in the wilderness. Jefferson's friend and associate Caspar Wistar was incomparably more sophisticated in such matters, and in 1799 he published a memoir in which he demonstrated that *Megalonyx* (now established as a technical, not only vernacular, name) was a sloth. Cuvier took it from there.

After such early and illustrious beginnings and the constantly accelerating subsequent study, it would be pleasant to say that we now have in hand all we want to know about the history of sloths, but of course that is far from true. Study continues. There are still mysteries and gaps in knowledge. Classification is not yet in satisfactory form. The classification that is now usual and that must make do here has three families of the extinct ground sloths, formerly the most varied and widespread xenarthrans of all, called ground sloths because they were evidently terrestrial and not arboreal like the still surviving sloths, which are placed, perhaps erroneously as will appear, in a single, fourth family. There is also a poorly known and controversial fifth family here placed in the Pilosa as related to sloths, but perhaps so different that it could be misleading to call them sloths.

Most of the known history of sloths refers to the three families known as Mylodontidae, Megalonychidae, and Megatheriidae. Ameghino recorded the occurrence of two specimens of ground sloths in the Casamayoran. The specimens were mislaid and the reported occurrence was included in several later discussions, but in the 1960s Ameghino's specimens were found. Restudy showed that they could not possibly be xenarthrans of any sort. Probably from the Mustersan is an ankle bone (astragalus) of a ground sloth recorded by Ameghino, but it may just possibly have come from the overlying Deseadan. A claw (ungual) is also known from the Mustersan and is probably but not quite surely from a ground sloth.

The first known ground sloths of unquestionable identification and age are from the Deseadan. The known specimens are incomplete, but they suggest that a basic separation between Mylodontidae and Megalonychidae had already occurred. All three ground sloth families were present in Santacrucian times, but in the available collections the Megalonychidae are much the most common and completely preserved. At that time they were quite small and may have been semiarboreal although they are included in the vernacular expression "ground sloths." Their later descendants were larger but not truly gigantic. They had anterior teeth that look somewhat like canines but had not evolved from the canines of primitive placental mammals; that is indicated by the fact that the lower tooth bit behind the upper, whereas true lower canines bite in front of the upper, as can be verified by normal human occlusion. The few more posterior or cheek teeth in megalonychids had simple rounded or ovate cross sections.

Megalonyx itself is known mainly from the Pleistocene of North America, where it ranged as far north as Alaska, but it has also been found in the Amazon basin. Despite Jefferson's belief, it became completely extinct around the end of the Pleistocene more or less 10,000 years ago, as did almost all of the ground sloths. *Nothrotherium,* another megalonychid, was abundant in both North and South America during the Pleistocene. It was megalonychids that reached North America before the Panamanian land bridge existed and thus became the first native South Americans to do so. At an unknown date but perhaps around the same time some megalonychids also reached the Greater Antilles, then as now islands, by overwater waif dispersal and there evolved into several small to medium-sized species. These may possibly have survived into the geological Recent and thus have been the last living ground sloths, but they were all extinct before Europeans reached the islands.

The Megatheriidae were already larger than the Megalonychidae in the Santacrucian, and in the Pleistocene they became truly gigantic, quite as large as a rhinoceros, as Cuvier wrote, but with no other rhinoceroslike characters. The two largest species, common to the Pleistocene of both continents, are now often put in two genera, *Megatherium* ("big beast") and *Eremotherium* ("desert beast," although it was not confined to deserts and probably not typical of them). The two are so similar that this seems to be an instance of judging that if two animals can be told apart they belong to different genera. The megatheriids have cheek teeth roughly square in cross section and in the later forms wearing so as to form two transverse crests. Large as they are, they surely were not even semiarboreal, and with their very stout but relatively rather short hindlegs they probably could walk bipedally on occasion if not habitually.

The Mylodontidae have cheek teeth, generally three or four in number, oddly irregular in cross section, somewhat like what designers call free forms and unlike the teeth of the other families. They early differentiated into two groups, sometimes recognized as subfamilies, one confined to South America, with relatively long and slender snouts, and the other abundant in the Pleistocene

Fig. 13. Restoration of *Megatherium*, the largest ground sloth, Pleistocene. It could certainly stand and probably walk erect as well as on all fours. In the latter pose its fingers, or front toes, were curled inward and the feet rested on the knuckles.

in both South and North America, with short, wide snouts. One of the latter has become well known to many North Americans because of its occurrence in enormous numbers at Rancho La Brea in Hollywood, California. The nomenclature of these animals became quite confused because of uncertainty as to which of two related species belonged under the names *Glossotherium* and *Mylodon* proposed at the same time (in 1840) by Richard Owen, based in part on specimens collected by Darwin. The one at Rancho La Brea was long known as *Mylodon*, more recently usually as *Paramylodon* but sometimes as a species, or at most subgenus, of *Glossotherium*. The problem is annoying to specialists but of little importance to anyone else. Whatever they are called, these are all members of a group of closely related animals.

The ground sloths were all herbivorous browsers. Many of them on both continents in the Pleistocene frequented caves in some of which they left thick deposits of dung. From those the food habits of the animals can be determined in detail. For example *Nothrotherium* in what is now southwestern United States left dung that consists of the remains of desert shrubs such as Joshua trees (a species of yuccas), Mormon tea (*Ephedra*), and creosote bush (*Larrea,* a genus also present in dry climates in South America).

The living sloths include two genera, *Bradypus,* with several species known colloquially as ais or three-toed sloths, and *Choloepus,* with two species known colloquially as unaus or two-toed sloths. The toe number refers to the front feet; both genera have three toes on the hindfeet. All are strictly arboreal, hanging upside down under branches, hooked on by their enormous, curved claws. When undisturbed they move very slowly, and this has given them the name sloths, extended to all their extinct relatives, probably undeservedly as it is likely that the ground sloths were not so slothful. In fact, the tree sloths can move very rapidly in defense, and their slashing claws make them formidable. Clearly ancestral or very closely related fossils are not known; arboreal animals confined to tropical forests are poorly represented in the fossil record. The two living genera are placed in one family, Bradypodidae, but some esoteric details suggest that *Choloepus* might have evolved from a primitive member of the Megalonychidae and *Bradypus* from one of early nothrotherelike Megatheriidae. If that could be substantiated they should be placed in different families, but their quite close resemblance would require strong convergence between them if they really arose from such distinct sources.

The group here called the family Entelopsidae is obscured in a cloud of ignorance and disagreement. It is based primarily on two fragmentary lower jaws probably from the type Santacrucian. They seem to belong to something like a ground sloth but are peculiar in having a closed series of anterior (or mesial) teeth and in having bilobed posterior (or distal) teeth. So far, so good—this very inadequately known animal probably is distinctive enough to merit placing in a family of its own. But in the Deseadan there are some bilobed teeth named *Orophodon,* which are quite like the posterior teeth of *Entelops,* the only genus surely referable to the Entelopsidae. So why not just put *Orophodon* in the family Entelopsidae and go on our way? Because the two authorities best acquainted with the specimens themselves, Pascual and Robert Hoffstetter, agree that *Entelops* and *Orophodon* belong not only to different families but to different superfamilies. There is even more confusion: there is some, although entirely inconclusive, evidence that the peculiar bony scutes called *Palaeopeltis* might belong to *Orophodon* or a related genus known from teeth. That suggestion, first made by Tournouër and Gaudry, was followed by Hoffstetter in 1956, when he called *Orophodon* and its allies armored ground sloths ("gravigrades cuirassés" in his terms), but Hoffstetter later essentially abandoned that view and considered *Palaeopeltis* as a xenarthran of uncertain classification, not as a member of his Orophodontidae.

That mix-up has been treated here in greatly abbreviated form as an example of what can happen when knowledge is incomplete, in fact an example of confusion due to sheer ignorance. It is also a warning not to take the arrangement here used, with Palaeopeltidae in the Cingulata and Entelopsidae in the Pilosa, as final or even as well established. It does follow some authority, notably that of Patterson and Pascual.

The third suborder, Vermilingua, has only one known family, Myrmecophagidae, originally based on the living genus *Myrmecophaga,* the giant anteater. The name means literally "ant eater," which seems apt enough except that the principal food is termites, which although often called white ants are not ants. There are two other living anteaters, *Tamandua,* the collared anteater, and *Cyclopes,* the pygmy or silky anteater. The giant anteater is terrestrial and has a nonprehensile plumed tail. The collared anteater is partly and the pygmy anteater almost entirely arboreal, and both have prehensile tails.

The fossil record of anteaters is extremely incomplete. They are first known from the Santacrucian but must have existed long before that. The known fossils were already toothless, smaller than *Myrmecophaga* and with a shorter, but nevertheless elongated, snout. Origin from a very primitive armadillo, scuteless or losing its scutes, is conceivable but undemonstrable. A common ancestry with the sloths, independent of the armadillos, is hardly conceivable.

References

Hoffstetter, R. 1958. Xenarthra. In *Traité de paléontologie,* ed. J. Piveteau, tome 6, 2: 535–636. Paris: Masson. (This long article includes a large bibliography.)

Patterson, B. 1967. Xenarthra. In *The fossil record,* ed. L. B. H. Tarlo, pp. 771–772. London: Geological Society of London.

Scott, W. B. 1903. Mammalia of the Santa Cruz beds. P. I, Edentata. *Reports of the Princeton University Expeditions to Patagonia,* 5: 1–227.

See also the reference to Patterson and Pascual 1972, following chapter 1.

CHAPTER 9

Some Ungulate Old-Timers

The notoungulates are so numerous both in kinds and in individuals and so dominant in most of the fossil mammalian faunas of South America that they require a chapter devoted to them alone. This chapter deals with the even more diverse but much less numerous hoofed mammals that appear early in the South American fossil record and that are not, or not surely, notoungulates. They are here classified in six orders, although, as will appear, there is some question about that ranking for certain of them. They are the Condylarthra, Litopterna, Pyrotheria, Astrapotheria, Trigonostylopoidea, and Xenungulata. Except for the Condylarthra, which, as noted in chapter 5, probably did not originate in South America, these nominal orders are confined to South America as far as known and almost certainly did originate there.

In the earliest faunas condylarths are not abundant but are rather varied. Three genera currently considered valid occur in the Riochican. Two of those also are known from the Casamayoran, along with five other genera. Most of them are known by isolated teeth with a few imperfect jaws, but there is one notable exception: a crushed but nearly complete skull with its lower jaw was found in the Riochican of Itaborai. All of these early South American condylarths, although generically distinct, closely resemble North American Paleocene and early Eocene condylarths and there can be little doubt that those of the two continents had a common ancestry. Most of the South American genera especially resemble the North American family Phenacodontidae, and the placing of the South Americans in a separate family, Didolodontidae, may exaggerate their distinction. Paula Couto referred the best-known genus, *Asmithwoodwardia*, to the otherwise exclusively North American and Eurasian family Hyopsodontidae, thus clearly implying that a faunal exchange between South America and the northern continents involved two distinct stocks of condylarths. Although the teeth of *Asmithwoodwardia* do indeed closely resemble those of North American *Hyopsodus*, they also closely resemble those of another South American genus, *Ernestokokenia*, which Paula Couto himself places in the Didolodontidae. It is a reasonable hypothesis that the known South American condylarths represent a single original stock which in its proliferation produced a genus that came to resemble *Hyopsodus* by parallel evolution. That view was suggested by Malcolm McKenna in 1956 and has more recently been endorsed by Patterson and Pascual. It is also true that the Hyopsodontidae and Phenacodontidae are not so different that it is obviously necessary to separate them at the family level.

All the didolodontids have dentitions that are extremely primitive for ungulates. The molars are low-crowned, with more or less conical cusps and little or no development of crests (lophs and lophids, technically), and few additions of cusps to those primitive for placental mammals as a whole, all of the latter cusps being retained. Both upper and lower molars have become almost quadrate, a usual slight specialization common in ungulates and occurring also in some other groups. (See Figure 19B.)

In the Argentinian sequence condylarths became rare after the Casamayoran and are not known after the Deseadan, approximately early Oligocene. However, one occurs in the considerably later Friasian, approximately middle Miocene, of Colombia, an example of differentiation among widely separate local faunas within the general continental fauna.

In the Riochican through the Casamayoran and Mustersan the known Litopterna are represented mostly by isolated teeth although a few incomplete jaws with some teeth are known from each of the three faunas. In general, the litoptern teeth in those ages still resembled those of the condylarths, and in this respect early litoptern evolution was much more conservative than in the other noncondylarth orders. W. B. Scott placed the Didolodontidae in the order Litopterna, and in 1914 Frederic Loomis compounded the then existing confusion by publishing a supposed restoration of a Deseadan litoptern skeleton which was in fact a mixture of separate condylarth and litoptern parts. More recent students have come to make a consistent separation of the two orders, while recognizing that one, Litopterna, was derived from the other, Condylarthra. In spite of the resemblances, already in the Riochican the molars of condylarths and litopterns can usually be clearly distinguished, and within the Litopterna the two families that dominated later evolution of the order were already distinct: Proterotheriidae and Macraucheniidae. The most obvious distinction of the earliest known litopterns from contemporaneous condylarths was that the molar teeth were becoming more crested, more lophiodont, the lower molars tending to develop two crescentic crests.

As with a number of other groups of South American mammals, litopterns are first really well known in the Santacrucian fauna. The several genera of Santacrucian proterotheres here exhibit two somewhat different adaptive types. In both, the teeth are similarly low-crowned and strongly crested, the lower molars bicrescentic. In one, represented by *Diadiaphorus* and by *Proterotherium* itself, the feet have three toes, the middle toe slender but strong and the side toes of equal length, so small and short as to be doubtfully functional. In the genus *Thoatherium* there is only one toe, the ancestral side toes being reduced to mere nubbins.

Although quite distinct in many anatomical details, these litopterns were extraordinarily like horses in general appearance and adaptive characteristics. Once more Ameghino was misled by these convergent features, and he believed these litopterns to be especially related to horses, although not ancestral to them; as will be noted later, he picked a notoungulate family for that ancestral position. The feet of the three-toed proterotheres are superficially and mechanically like those of some extinct three-toed horses. The teeth are more obviously different but do have a functional resemblance to those of some browsing, not grazing, three-toed horses. *Thoatherium* is even more completely one-toed than one-toed horses, including all living members of the horse family. The

Fig. 14. Restoration of the horselike early Miocene (Santacrucian) litoptern *Thoatherium.*

remains of side toes in *Thoatherium* are even more vestigial than in *Equus,* and *Thoatherium* was probably the most completely one-toed (monodactyl) animal that ever lived. It is further remarkable that in this litoptern family the one-toed stage was reached by approximately early Miocene times, while in the horse family it was not reached until the late Pliocene, millions of years later. An obvious and important difference is that *Thoatherium* still had a relatively primitive browsing dentition, but all the one-toed horses had and have highly specialized grazing dentitions. Proterotheres survived into the Chapadmalalan, approximately latest Pliocene, but then became extinct.

The second litoptern family, Macraucheniidae, is represented in the Santacrucian by the genus *Theosodon.* The members of that genus were larger than the proterotheres and had three toes, with the side toes larger and more functional than in the three-toed proterotheres. The teeth were similar to those of the proterotheres but somewhat more complex. The neck was long, camellike, and the nasal part of the skull had retreated, indicating that the animals had a more or less tapirlike short proboscis. The terminal member of the family, *Macrauchenia* in the Pleistocene, had a neck still longer and evidence of a proboscis still more prominent but not elephantine. Its size, too, was exaggerated, as large as a modern camel. The Greek roots of *Macrauchenia* mean

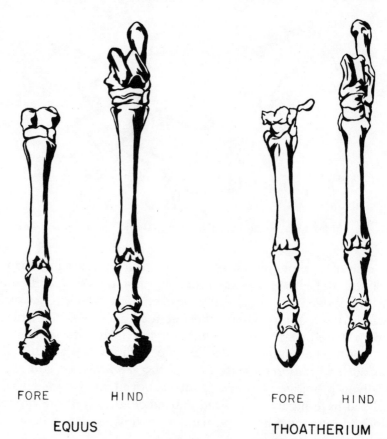

FORE   HIND   FORE   HIND

EQUUS   THOATHERIUM

Fig. 15. Comparison of forefeet (*left*) and hindfeet (*right*) of a modern horse, *Equus,* and an early Miocene litoptern, *Thoatherium,* the most completely one-toed mammal known. The close resemblance of these two kinds of feet is entirely convergent.

"long neck," but the name can also be interpreted as "big llama" because *Auchenia* was a name (invalid as now appears) previously given to the llama. Darwin, who collected the remains on which Owen based the name *Macrauchenia,* had the field impression that it was "a llama or *guanaco,* fully as large as the camel." Llamas and guanacos are small, humpless camels, and except for its proboscis *Macrauchenia* is overall convergent toward camels.

The other currently recognized family of litopterns is the

Adianthidae. These were small, delicate animals, Deseadan to Santacrucian in age, poorly known except for one nearly complete skull from probably early Deseadan beds near Mendoza in Argentina.

The Pyrotheria were first known (by Ameghino in 1888) and are still best known from the genus *Pyrotherium,* characteristic of what the Ameghinos called the *Pyrotherium* beds and fauna and, following Gaudry with slight modification, we now call Deseadan, approximately early Oligocene. Ameghino believed this animal to be a proboscidean, related to mastodonts and elephants, and considered earlier members of the family Pyrotheriidae to be ancestral to the latter. He believed that the pyrotheres were derived from condylarths, which is probably correct although transitional forms are not known, but the supposed relationship of descent to later proboscideans was based on convergence, again, and in this case not really close resulting similarity. Gaudry devoted a memoir to specimens of *Pyrotherium* collected for him by Tournouër and correctly denied their relationship to the Proboscidea. He wrote (in French), "In reality *Pyrotherium* is very different from all the large animals described up to the present day. It does not enter into any known order."

In 1911–1912, F. B. Loomis led an expedition to Patagonia financed by the class of 1896 of Amherst College as part of its fifteenth reunion celebration. The most important result of that expedition was a skull of *Pyrotherium,* which Loomis studied with the conclusion that the genus and its family do belong in the Proboscidea as Ameghino had thought. Recently Bryan Patterson has further cleaned Loomis' specimen, the only known skull of a member of this family, and found on restudy that Loomis's description and figure were largely incorrect and his conclusions completely wrong. Patterson's own conclusion, based on clear and undoubtedly accurate observation, nevertheless involves a serious difficulty to be discussed after a summary of other known or probable members of the Pyrotheria.

In the Casamayoran there is a very rare, very poorly known genus, *Carolozittelia,* which is probably but not quite surely a pyrothere. Likewise fragmentary but unquestionable pyrotheres

Fig. 16. The skull of the type pyrothere, genus *Pyrotherium,* from the early Oligocene (Deseadan) as reconstructed by Patterson, and a restoration of the head. Although some postcranial bones are known, they do not suffice for a restoration of the body.

have been found in the Mustersan of Patagonia. Specimens of *Pyrotherium* itself come from the Deseadan of Argentina and Bolivia, and no later pyrotheres are known. There is one specimen of inexactly determined early Cenozoic age from Peru that probably, but not surely, belongs in the Pyrotheriidae although it differs considerably from *Pyrotherium.*

Recently, Hoffstetter (in 1970) and Patterson (in 1977) have described two similar but distinct genera, *Colombitherium* Hoffstetter from Colombia and *Proticia* Patterson from Venezuela. They are related to each other, and *Proticia* may be ancestral to *Colombitherium.* They are also related to *Pyrotherium* but so different that they are placed in a separate family, Colombitheriidae. *Colombitherium* is probably Eocene in age; *Proticia* may be Eocene but is possibly older, Paleocene. *Pyrotherium* has upper and lower molars with two sharp transverse crests. *Colombitherium* has upper premolars and molars, the only teeth known, also with two transverse crests, but they are less sharp, have distinct cusps at outer and inner ends, and wear in a way suggesting an odd mechanism of chewing. *Proticia*'s lower premolars and first molar, the only teeth known, do not have fully formed transverse crests but have large, distinct, blunt cusps arranged in a way from which such crests could and quite probably did evolve.

Now for the problem arising from Patterson's restudy of the skull of *Pyrotherium.* The Notoungulata have numerous characters common to their more primitive members and modified but not wholly obliterated in more specialized notoungulates. The most evident of these characters involve the complex and, in detail, unique structure of the ear region and the equally striking, equally unique, and even more obvious structures of the dentition, especially but not only the molars. Now Patterson finds that *Pyrotherium* had a notoungulatelike ear structure and hence concludes, "That the Pyrotheria were notoungulates would seem evident." Of the dentition he says that "The cheek teeth of these early pyrotheres do not throw any certain light on the origin and affinities of the group." But they do throw some, not necessarily certain but surely suggestive, light on the origin of the group. As Ameghino already noted and Patterson iterates, the pyrothere cheek teeth could readily be derived from condylarths or more explicitly from didolodontids. That is especially clear in *Proticia,* which has the most primitive cheek-tooth structure known in a pyrothere.

Patterson suggests that there might be some resemblance to primitive notoungulate cheek teeth, but to me this seems illusory. As a detail Patterson writes that primitive notoungulates tend to form a cross crest on the posterior part of lower molars incorporating the cusps technically called entoconid and hypoconid and excluding the cusp called hypoconulid. This would then be similar to the posterior crest of the pyrothere lower molars. But the cross crest of the posterior part (the talonid) of primitive notoungulate molars is not formed by the entoconid and hypoconid but by the entoconid alone. In some variants it abuts against the base of the hypoconid but does not include that cusp. The most prominent feature of this part of notoungulate lower molars is a long, crescentic crest embodying the hypoconid and hypoconulid, an arrangement that would seem almost impossible in an ancestor of the pyrotheres. In other respects, too, such an ancestry for the pyrothere dentition seems out of the question.

So what do we now wind up with? Perhaps with a pyrothere ancestor that had ears like notoungulates but teeth like condylarths. The same ancestry could have given rise also to notoungulates if in a decidedly different line of descent its teeth evolved into the notoungulate, not the pyrothere, pattern. What then should we call such an ancestor, if it existed? A condylarth because its teeth were condylarthran? A notoungulate because its ears were notoungulatelike? A pyrothere because these became the largest and most strking of its early descendants? Or, as multiple choice has it, none of these? My own choice is "none of these" until and unless we actually find more remote ancestors of pyrotheres and of notoungulates than we now have. It should be noted also that there is another possible choice. It may be that both the pyrotheres and the notoungulates descended from condylarths as yet without either pyrotherelike or notoungulatelike teeth and without notoungulatelike ears. Then the pyrotheres and notoungulates may have evolved divergently as to dentition but in parallel as to the ear region. For the present I choose to let the pyrotheres stand on their own (incidentally very sturdy) feet as a provisionally distinct order. This is not a world-shaking problem, but it has been given in some technical detail as an example of the kind of tough, temporarily even insolvable, problems that a historian of life faces at times.

The same sort of problem does not arise in connection with the Astrapotheria. There are some resemblances to notoungulates in their cheek teeth, but those are limited and probably convergent as far as they go. There are no special resemblances in the ear or other structures and there is now virtual unanimity that they belong in a distinct order in classification. This order, as strictly defined, was never highly varied, but it is known from the Casamayoran to the Friasian, approximately early Eocene to middle Miocene, and geographically from southern Argentina to northern Venezuela and Colombia.

The earliest astrapothere, *Scaglia* from the Casamayoran, is known only from a single specimen, part of a skull and upper dentition of a young individual with milk teeth. The astrapothere *Astraponotus* gave its name to Ameghino's equivalent of what is now called Mustersan, but it is rare in collections of that age and not well known. In the Deseadan and Colhuehuapian the astrapotheres are reasonably well known, and there is a nearly complete skeleton of *Astrapotherium* itself from the Santacrucian. Patterson and Pascual say of these later members of the family that "they come in two sizes, large and very large."

The skull of the large Oligocene and Miocene astrapotheres had a bulging, domed forehead above the eyes, very short nasal bones suggesting that the animal had a small proboscis, and large tusks kept sharp by grinding against the somewhat shorter lower tusks. The lower tusks may have been used for rooting. There were no upper incisors, but there were six lower incisors with pretty, bilobed crowns. The usually five upper and four lower cheek teeth

Fig. 17. Restoration of the typical astrapothere, genus *Astrapotherium*, from the early Miocene (Santacrucian).

had rather high crowns but were simply crested browsing chewers. The body was long and the legs, especially the hindlegs, were surprisingly weak for such large animals. The feet were relatively small, and the hindfeet were apparently plantigrade, that is, flat on the ground when in walking position. Scott has speculated that the apparently clumsy disproportion of the animals might indicate that they were amphibious. The astrapotheres were somewhat convergent toward an extinct group of northern rhinoceroses called amynodonts, also possibly amphibious.

The Trigonostylopoidea are abundant in collections from the Riochican of Brazil and the Casamayoran of Argentina but only doubtfully present in the Mustersan and not known thereafter. They were long believed to be fairly close relatives of the astrapotheres, but restudy, including a well-preserved skull not previously known, showed that they are quite unlike astrapotheres in many anatomical features, including the ear region which also is not at all like that of a notoungulate. A resemblance to astrapotheres is that they do have upper and lower tusks, but these are small and not astrapotherelike in detail. The upper molars are low-crowned, crested, and more or less triangular in outline (less in the Riochican), unlike the characteristic astrapothere molars with four unequal sides. Why these animals flourished just where and when they did and then soon became extinct is among the many enigmas of history.

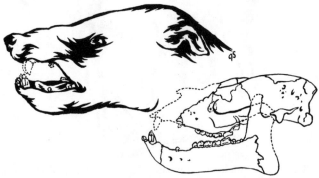

Fig. 18. Reconstruction of the skull and restoration of the head of the typical trigonostylopoid, genus *Trigonostylops,* from the early Eocene (Casamyoran).

Finally, for the present chapter, the Xenungulata, known only from the Riochican, were the largest and as their name ("strange ungulates") implies among the strangest of their time. The one known genus, *Carodnia,* was first discovered in Patagonia but is much more completely known from the Brazilian Riochican of Itaborai. It had chisellike incisors, small canines, and molars, upper and lower, with two sharp crests, curved but transverse. The forefoot is known and is heavy, elephantine, with five toes ending in relatively small, broad, flat hooves.

Paula Couto, who described the Itaborai specimens and on that basis proposed and defined the order Xenungulata, noted some resemblance to long-extinct early Cenozoic North American and Asiatic ungulates known as Dinocerata ("terrible horns"—the Xenungulata were not horned). He thought that this might indicate a phylogenetic relationship, but only through a common ancestry in the order Condylarthra. Some paleontologists, for example A. S. Romer, who had not made a personal study of the groups involved, have consequently made the Xenungulata and Dinocerata suborders of the same order, which almost necessarily implies a northern origin for the Xenungulata, but that has not been generally accepted. It remains probable that the Xenungulata originated in South America and that the really very limited resemblances to the Dinocerata were moderately convergent.

Patterson has restudied the Itaborai specimens of Trigonostylopoidea and Xenungulata. He has recently expressed in personal correspondence the opinion, contrary to his previous views, that those two groups of ungulates should both be included in the order Astrapotheria. Everyone including Patterson does agree that what are called Trigonostylopoidea, Xenungulata, and Astrapotheria are valid, distinct, groups (taxa in classification), so different that their rank should be higher than the family level. That is the most important point, and it is less important to decide whether that level is taken to be as three suborders in an order perhaps called Astrapotheria or as three separate orders. Pending publication of possible evidence that they are evolutionary units more closely related to each other than through a general condylarthran ancestry, the now customary status as three orders is here tentatively retained. If they were shown to have a common ancestry exclusive to them, the question would arise whether that ancestry should be considered astrapotherian, trigonostylopoidean, xenungulate, or, perhaps more likely, none of the three.

In that connection an item of evidence not previously published is that characteristic ankle bones (astragalus and calcaneum) almost certainly belonging to *Trigonostylops* are radically different from those of astrapotheres. These bones are not known in the xenungulates.

References

Patterson, B. 1977. A primitive pyrothere (Mammalia, Notoungulata) from the early Tertiary of northwestern Venezuela. *Fieldiana Geology,* 33: 397–422. (This also contains the redescription of the skull of *Pyrotherium* from Argentina.)

Paula Couto, C. de. 1952. Fossil mammals from the beginning of the Cenozoic in Brazil: Condylarthra, Litopterna, Xenungulata, and Astrapotheria. *Bulletin of the American Museum of Natural History,* 99: 355–394.

———. 1963. Um Trigonostylopidae do Paleoceno do Brasil. *Anales Academia Brasileira de Ciências,* 35: 339–351.

Gaudry, A. 1909. Fossiles de Patagonie: Le *Pyrotherium. Annales de Paleontologie.* Paris, 4: 28 pp.

Scott, W. B. 1910. Litopterna of the Santa Cruz beds. *Reports of the Princeton University Expeditions to Patagonia,* 7: 1–156.

———. 1937. The Astrapotheria. *Proceedings of the American Philosophical Society,* 77: 309–393.

Simpson, G. G. 1933. Structure and affinities of *Trigonostylops. American Museum Novitates,* no. 608, pp. 1–28.

See also the references to chapter 1 and the reference to Simpson 1948 and 1967 in chapter 6.

CHAPTER 10

Notoungulates

The ancient Greeks and Romans were given to personifying and anthropomorphizing many things in nature. Notos in Greek, Notus in Latin, was the personal name of the south wind. Technical nomenclature deals with names as neo-Latin even when the names are based on Greek or on barbaric languages (any language but Latin or Greek used to be considered barbaric). In the form *noto-* this word for a south wind, common to Greek and Latin in slightly different form, has often been used as a prefix meaning simply "southern." Thus the name Notoungulata means literally "southern hoofed [mammals]." When Santiago Roth coined this name in 1903 notoungulates were known only from South America. Now some are also known from North America and Asia, as was discussed in chapter 5, but the name is still appropriate for a group that was overwhelmingly South American throughout its known history.

In the rather conservative classification here followed there are fourteen notoungulate families in all, including the Arctostylopidae, not known from South America. Eight of those can be distinguished in the Riochican and Casamayoran, approximately late Paleocene and early Eocene. All were then still primitive, and the differences among the families are not striking. Another family (Notohippidae), more advanced and more distinctive, is first known in the Mustersan, approximately middle Eocene. In the Deseadan faunas so far discovered there are nine families, more than known in any one other land mammal age. Five of those are first known from the Deseadan. By Deseadan time, approximately early Oligocene, the families had become more distinctive and had more clearly adopted a variety of ecological roles. Thereafter there was marked differential extinction in a sort of weeding-out process. Only five families are known from the Santacrucian and only six from the approximate Miocene as a whole, Santacrucian to Chasicoan. Only three families are known from the Pliocene, taken as Huayquerian to Chapadmalalan, and all three survived into the Pleistocene but then became extinct.

The earliest South American faunas with known notoungulates, those of the Riochican, Casamayoran, and Mustersan, are especially interesting as to processes and episodes in evolutionary histories. Here this group is found in the midst of what can well be considered an evolutionary explosion. That is revealed in two different ways. For one thing, the notoungulates, which may not have been very far, geologically speaking, from their origin, were already quite diverse. In the eight notoungulate families of those three faunas more than thirty-five genera and about seventy species are listed in current classifications. These are from quite limited areas, and discoveries in other regions, some already made but not yet fully described, will add to those. This sampling from what were then, as now, marginal parts of South America shows clearly that the notoungulates were spreading profusely, opportunistically, over a large continent where there were relatively few other ungulates, and those, as summarized in the last chapter, were going off into increasing specialization, not occupying many of the ecological niches possible for ungulates.

A second point about this early flowering of the group is that some, at least, of its species were still extraordinarily variable. That probably was true of many of them, but it is best known by objective evidence for a comparatively primitive species with the rather formidable full technical name *Henricosbornia lophodonta* Ameghino, 1901. This genus was long so obscure that Henry Fairfield Osborn, its eponym, omitted it altogether in his prestigious classification of 1910 and other works. However, on my first expedition to South America in 1930–1931 my companions and I collected well over a hundred specimens of this one species. Although we did not find well-preserved skulls or any skeletons, its dentiton is now very well known, and as a result its extensive variation is well established. Study of this collection and of the Ameghinos' materials showed that Florentino Ameghino classified his fewer specimens of this one species in 16 species, 8 genera, 4 families, and 3 orders. This is given not as a criticism of Ameghino's work but as strong evidence of how extremely varied the teeth of individuals of this species were. Ameghino indicated that all his supposedly different "species" of this group were derived from condylarths, which is believed to be true of the single species to which they are now seen to belong, but he took their variants as indicating ancestral relationships to later groups as different as lemurs and rhinoceroses.

In the teeth of this species, and of some others equally old, there were variations then individual that were later to become fixed and then to characterize distinct genera and even families (but not quite orders). In an expanding group not yet settled into a narrow ecological niche such variation or, one might say, inexactness of genetic control of anatomical features may well occur. It contributes to the versatility of a population and to its possibility of moving into a variety of ecologies and adaptations. Once a derivative population does become more precisely adapted to a given ecology or niche, it is usual for centripetal or stabilizing natural selection to act to impede, slow down, or even to stop further change by weeding out the more marked genetic variants. Few of the notoungulates had yet reached that stage in these early faunas. More of them had in the subsequent Deseadan, as will later be seen.

The highly characteristic notoungulate dentition pattern is seen in its most primitive form in such early genera as *Henricosbornia* or *Oldfieldthomasia*, the anatomy of which is better known but the variation not so well known as in *Henricosbornia*. The notoungulates primitively had the dental formula that early became fixed in primitive placental mammals:

$$\frac{3 \cdot 1 \cdot 4 \cdot 3}{3 \cdot 1 \cdot 4 \cdot 3},$$

that is, three incisors, one canine, four premolars, and three molars on each side in upper and lower jaws. In the earliest forms all

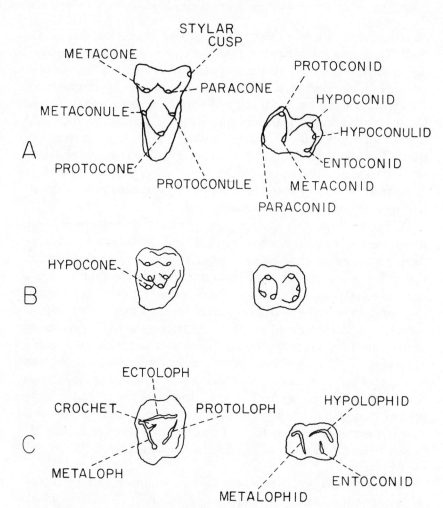

Fig. 19. Right upper (*left*) and lower (*right*) molars of three groups of mammals. *A*, a pattern primitive for placental mammals in general—not a portrait of a particular genus but showing the structure present with variations in almost all Cretaceous placentals, with the technical names of the principal cusps. *B*, a primitive didolodontid, somewhat stylized but like *Ernestokokenia* (Riochican and Casamayoran), for example. The hypocone was a new cusp not present in the most primitive placentals and still absent in some living ones. The other cusps are only slightly modified from the primitive placental pattern. *C*, a primitive notoungulate, essentially *Henricosbornia* (Riochican and Casamayoran). Most of the primitive placental cusps have been incorporated into crests (lophs above, lophids below) and a new crest, the crochet projecting from the metaloph, has appeared.

of these teeth were in a continuous and gradual series in each jaw, the canine simple and much like the adjacent incisor and premolar, the last premolar much like the more complex first molar.

The molars had a basic pattern that distinguishes them from those of any other mammals. That pattern is shown in figure 19C, which is diagrammatic but based essentially on *Henricosbornia*. The upper molars had three main crests or lophs, shown and named in the figure. There was also a smaller crest or spur, called the crochet (pronounced "crotchet," not "croshay"), extending from one of those. The crown pattern of the lower molars consists in the main of just two crests, here called lophids. (In the system of cusp nomenclature invented by H. F. Osborn and, with appropriate additions, now in general use, the suffix -id is used for most elements of a lower molar pattern.) In addition one of the cusps (entoconid; see figure 19A,C) has become a short transverse crest independent of the other two, a condition already noted in the last chapter as part of the evidence that pyrothere molars could not have evolved from those of a notoungulate.

Such apparently trivial or esoteric details of tooth structure are essential although not necessarily sufficient evidence for identifying and classifying many mammals, both living and fossil. The basic, primitive notoungulate pattern outlined in the preceding paragraph and in figure 19 occurs in all unquestionable notoungulates, although as mentioned in the last chapter some groups without it have from time to time quite questionably been considered notoungulates. These primitive notoungulate molar characters are still present in all later and more specialized notoungulates even though in other respects their molars may have changed greatly and added new structures while in other ways also the dentition as a whole may have become more specialized.

The peculiarity of the bones around the ear in notoungulates was also mentioned in the last chapter. Among the earliest notoungulates this is known in greatest detail in the Casamayoran genus *Oldfieldthomasia,* the ear region of which was studied and illustrated in serial sections. Its most prominent character in all notoungulates is the presence of two bubblelike, bone-enclosed cavities opening into the middle ear, one from above and one from below. Other special details include the fact that the tympanic bone, besides surrounding the lower (hypotympanic) cavity, forms a tube from the middle ear to the outer ear (nonbony and so unknown in fossils), with a crest along the lower or ventral side of the tube. On the lower surface of the skull behind the wall of the lower bubble (the bulla or hypotympanic cavity) there is a pit into which is inserted a projection from the throat bone or hyoid.

A double-bubble structure of the ear is by no means confined to notoungulates. It has arisen independently at least three times in marsupials, including the extinct forms *Argyrolagus* and *Sparassocynus* in South America, as mentioned in chapter 7. It has arisen also at least three times in rodents. However, it is not anatomically identical in origin among all those groups or between any of them and the notoungulates. It is evidently an example of repeated adaptive convergence, but what is it adapted to? Experiments on some rodents indicate that it increases the sensitivity of ears to sounds of certain pitches, perhaps to the calls emitted by other members of the same species or perhaps to sounds made by predators. By experimenting with models of notoungulate ears it might be possible to learn the pitches to which they were tuned, but that has not been done, nor are we likely to learn the sounds made by either their friends or their enemies.

One of the early and in general primitive families of notoungulates, the Notostylopidae, did become moderately specialized in some respects. The family is rare in the known Riochican, abundant in the Casamayoran, again rare in the Mustersan, and unknown thereafter. The type genus, *Notostylops,* is common in the Casamayoran, which the Ameghinos called "the Notostylops beds" or "Notostylopense." One species, *Notostylops murinus,* is particularly abundant. Here again subsequent larger collections with more precise field data than were possible for Carlos Ameghino have revealed extraordinary variability within that single species. Here, as with *Henricosbornia lophodonta,* that variability misled Florentino Ameghino, who placed specimens of this one species in 14 species of 6 genera, but in this case all in one family, Notostylopidae, a valid grouping and name in classification.

The most obvious specialization of this family is that the poste-

Fig. 20. Skull and restoration of head of *Notostylops,* an early Eocene (Casamayoran) notoungulate, primitive overall but with a slightly specialized dentition.

rior (third) incisors, the canines, and the anterior (first) premolars are always small and often absent altogether, leaving a toothless gap between the remaining incisors and the remaining premolars. The dental formula varies from the ancestral

$$\frac{3 \cdot 1 \cdot 4 \cdot 3}{3 \cdot 1 \cdot 4 \cdot 3}$$

to

$$\frac{2 \cdot 0 \cdot 3 \cdot 3}{2 \cdot 0 \cdot 3 \cdot 3},$$

even within one species. In mammals in general so much variation in the dental formula of a species is extremely rare. In *Notostylops* one upper incisor, the first, and one lower incisor, the second, are enlarged and bite against each other. That gives the animals a somewhat rodentlike appearance, but the large incisors are nipping, not gnawing, teeth. The molars are little modified from the most primitive notoungulate pattern. The most obvious distinction is that in the upper molars the crochet, a mere spur in the Henricosborniidae, has become long, almost crossing the gap between the protoloph and metaloph, and its crest, when little worn, bears a line of tiny cuspules.

In the dentition, at least, the Henricosborniidae seem to be the most primitive of known notoungulates, a survival into the approximately early Eocene Casamayoran of a stock that could have been ancestral to the other notoungulates. The Notostylopidae represent a moderately specialized offshoot that survived only into the next age, the Mustersan. Those two families do not sort easily into the major groups known also from later ages and so are here put into a seperate subdivision: the suborder Notioprogonia, a name derived from Greek words for "southern ancestor." (The known North American and Asiatic notoungulates, family Arctostylopidae, are also referred to this suborder.)

The other families known from these early faunas can be placed in the three major subdivisions originally based on later faunas and here treated as suborders of the order Notoungulata. The Typotheria were named from one of the latest surviviors of the order, long called *Typotherium,* "type beast," which doesn't seem to mean anything much. As a name for the genus, that is invalid— the proper name of the genus is *Mesotherium,* "middle beast," which doesn't seem to mean anything more—but the later animals of this suborder have almost always been called typotheres, and the name Typotheria for the suborder is technically valid. This suborder had already differentiated early in its history into three families.

The suborder Hegetotheria is also named from a genus, *Hegetotherium* ("chief beast," another nondescript name), and so are the Toxodonta, named for the genus *Toxodon* ("bow tooth," which does aptly describe its upper molars). Only one family in the three earliest faunas is referred to the Typotheria, but two, one of them not appearing in the known record until the Mustersan, had already become distinct in the Toxodonta. All three suborders have other, more advanced families in later faunas, and each has one family that survived into the Pleistocene, the Mesotheriidae in the Typotheria, the Hegetotheriidae in the Hegetotheria, and the Toxodontidae in the Toxodonta. The Hegetotheriidae survived only into the earliest Pleistocene (Uquian), but the others held on almost to the Recent.

The Typotheria and Hegetotheria were small to medium-sized animals, the Toxodonta medium-sized to huge. In all three, as in many but by no means all groups of mammals, the average size tended to increase as time went on. In all three the earliest members, Riochican and Casamayoran, had rather primitive dentitions, usually with the full dental formula

$$\frac{3 \cdot 1 \cdot 4 \cdot 3}{3 \cdot 1 \cdot 4 \cdot 3},$$

teeth all low-crowned (brachydont), and with molars not strkingly unlike those of the primitive Notioprogonia. Even at this level of evolution, however, there is a tendency for the upper molars to become more complex by further extension of the crochet and by the origin of other extensions from the main ridges or lophs, usually one called a crista but sometimes several cristas projecting inward from the outer ridge (ectoloph) and often uniting with the crochet, and sometimes one called an antecrochet projecting posteriorly from the anterior ridge (protoloph). The antecrochet may, but at this time level usually did not, meet and join with the crista, the crochet, or both.

The best-known early members of the Typotheria are the Casamayoran genera *Oldfieldthomasia,* placed in a family of its own, and *Notopithecus,* referred to the mainly later (Oligocene and

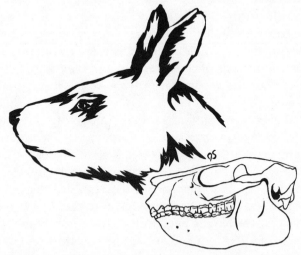

Fig. 21. Skull and restoration of the head of an early Eocene (Casamayoran) primitive interathere, *Notopithecus.*

Miocene) family Interatheriidae. The anatomy of the skull and dentition is well known and has been fully described for both. The dentitions have the general characters mentioned in the last paragraph. The skulls were still quite primitive and had the basic notoungulate characters, notably those of the ear region, in almost diagrammatic form.

In Deseadan and later times the interatheres related to and possibly descended from *Notopithecus* or one of its allies had become markedly specialized. In some of these the skulls and jaws did not differ markedly from those of their earlier relatives or ancestors. In others, notably *Interatherium* itself from the Santacrucian, skulls and jaws had become notably shorter, broader, and deeper. The dentitions had changed more radically, the teeth now high-crowned (hypsodont) and the median or anterior pair of upper incisors enlarged and grinding against two pairs of not particularly enlarged lower incisors. As usually found, the teeth have all been far worn down. In that condition the worn surfaces of the molars and posterior premolars have a fairly simple pattern that is bilobed, most clearly on the inner (lingual) side of the upper and the outer (buccal) side of the lower teeth. This has given some investigators the impression that the notoungulate pattern described earlier in this chapter had been lost in these typotheres and replaced by a simpler one. In fact, the primitive notoungulate molar pattern merely overlain by some later complications was present on the crowns of these teeth when they were first formed and unworn, but the crown pattern was soon virtually eradicated by heavy wear.

Nearly the whole skeleton is known in two of the Santacrucian typotheres (*Protypotherium* and *Interatherium*), and their feet are peculiar. In some, at least, and probably in all the early notoungulates the feet are five-toed, as is primitive for mammals, and the third or middle toe is somewhat the longest, also the usual primitive arrangement. These Santacrucian typotheres are four-toed, the original first toe having been lost. In the forefoot the first toe is absent, the fifth toe is reduced in size and function, and the second to fourth toes are fully functional but the third is slightly longer than the second, the fourth distinctly shorter than either. In the

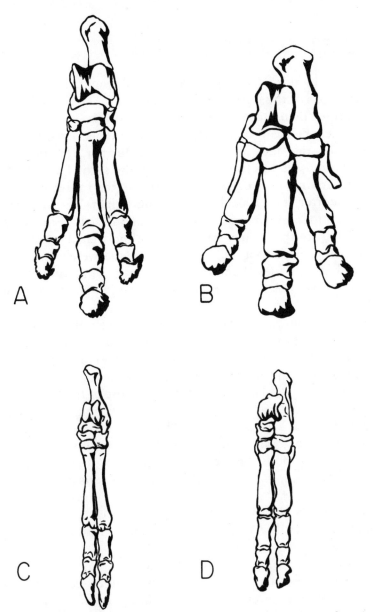

Fig. 22. Hindfoot bones of two South American living ungulates of northern origin and of two notoungulates of South American origin: *A*, living tapir, *Tapirus*, with three functional toes (digits II, III, IV) and weight-bearing axis on the middle toe (III); *B*, *Scarrittia*, an early Oligocene (Deseadan) leontiniid notoungulate, with the same functional toes as in the tapir and weight-bearing axis the same; *C*, living peccary, *Tayassu*, with two functional toes (digits III and IV) and weight-bearing axis between them; *D*, *Miocochilius*, a middle Miocene (Friasian) interathere. It had two functional toes (digits III and IV) with the weight-bearing axis between them, as in the peccary (on the front foot the weight-bearing toes were not homologous with those of peccaries).

hindfoot the third and fourth are of equal length, and the weight-bearing axis of the leg passes between them. The second and fifth are shorter than those and about equal to each other. In a somewhat later (Friasian) interathere from Colombia this odd specialization of the feet was carried still further. In this genus, *Miocochilius,* the forefoot is three-toed, the second and third toes (of the original five) equal and functional, the fourth present but much shorter and probably not bearing weight. The hindfoot has only two toes, equal in size, the third and fourth of the ancestral five. Thus, in this animal most or all of the weight was borne on two toes of each foot and in a forefoot the weight-bearing axis passes between toes II and III (a usual way of indicating which of the primitive toes I to V are involved) and in a hindfoot between III and IV.

No other notoungulates are known to have only two toes or to have the weight-bearing axis between two toes. In other groups of notoungulates in which the feet are known there may be five, four, or three toes, and in all the axis is in the middle toe, III. In the world outside of island South America most of the ungulates are distinctly divided into two great groups, definable in terms of the weight-bearing axis of the feet. In the Artiodactyla, including cows, sheep, pigs, and many others, the axis is between equal toes III and IV on both forefeet and hindfeet. In the Perissodactyla, including horses, rhinoceroses, and tapirs, the axis is in a dominant middle or finally (in horses) sole toe III. The strange diversity in this one South American order Notoungulata is a stunning example of the versatility, or perhaps the opportunism of evolutionary processes.

In the Deseadan, approximately early Oligocene, there mysteriously appeared another group of typotheres clearly related to the interatheres but even more specialized and of unknown more precise ancestry: the subfamily Trachytheriinae. These animals had carried high-crowned teeth to their extreme: the teeth kept growing throughout life and never formed roots, a condition called hypselodonty, as the end term of a trend through hypsodonty, high-crowned but eventually forming roots and ceasing to push out of their sockets. The molars had almost flat external (buccal) walls, and once the crown pattern was obliterated by wear they had three unequal internal (lingual) lobes. These animals are almost ideal ancestral types for the classical typotheres, *Mesotherium* and its close relatives, of the later Cenozoic and they are here placed in the family Mesotheriidae, but another mystery about them is that annectent forms are unknown from the Deseadan until after the Santacrucian—an interval of some millions of years. Probably they were living farther north than Patagonia, where most of this part of the fossil record is known.

In any event the Mesotheriidae, the classical typotheres, do appear well along in the Miocene and continue into the Pleistocene, where the genus that has been called both *Typotherium* and *Mesotherium* is fairly common in the fossil-rich surface beds of the broad Argentine pampas. This was the most specialized of all the typotheres, as might be expected of the last of them although this is contrary to the previously mentioned concept of "the survival of the less specialized." It had a broad, depressed, stout skull, which has been likened to that of a bulldog and more felicitously to a giant beaver, for the animal was much more rodentlike than doglike. Its dental formula had been reduced to

$$\frac{1 \cdot 0 \cdot 2 \cdot 3}{2 \cdot 0 \cdot 1 \cdot 3},$$

All the teeth are continuously growing (hypselodont). The incisors were large and rodentlike, and between them and the reduced premolars was a long toothless gap in each jaw.

For many years the Typotheria and Hegetotheria were confused and were usually lumped together under the former name, but they were already distinct in the Riochican. In some respects but not in all the hegetotheres did evolve in parallel with the typotheres. Their most primitive known representatives, the Archaeohyracidae, were on about the same evolutionary level as the typotheres in the earliest level, but as has already been mentioned (chapter 6) they more rapidly evolved high-crowned teeth.

The earliest hegetotheres are known from only a few teeth and incomplete jaws, but from the Deseadan, approximately early Oligocene, into the early Pleistocene they are reasonably well known. The virtually complete skeleton is known in one Deseadan genus, two from the Santacrucian, and one from the Chapadmalalan, a long span approximately from early Oligocene to late Pliocene. (Some others have been tentatively reconstructed from less complete data.)

As among the typotheres, the teeth of hegetotheres became continuously growing (hypselodont), their number was reduced —in this family to

$$\frac{1\cdot0\cdot3\cdot3}{2\cdot0\cdot3\cdot3},$$

—and the remaining incisors were enlarged and rodentlike. The hindlegs were much longer than the front legs, and the hindfeet were particularly long, flat on the ground when at rest and with a springing action when the animal was in rapid motion. These were clearly hopping and leaping creatures, much like rabbits both in habits and in appearance except that some of them had fairly long tails. It is interesting that when they evolved this rabbitlike habitus there were no rabbits in South America, although as will appear in the next chapter there were some true rodents. (Rabbits are not rodents in classification, not members of the Rodentia, although of course they do gnaw; so did the late typotheres and hegetotheres.)

Fig. 23. Restoration of *Propachyrucos,* an early Oligocene (Deseadan) hegetothere.

By the time true rabbits did reach South America, these pseudo-rabbits were already extinct.

The other suborder of Notoungulata, the Toxodonta, is not so nearly coherent as the Typotheria and Hegetotheria and is here divided into five markedly divergent families. These were highly numerous and were dominant notoungulates in much of the early Cenozoic, but finally in the Pleistocene, were reduced to a handful of species, all of which then also became extinct.

In the earliest faunas, Riochican and Casamayoran, the known members of this suborder all belonged to the most primitive family, the Isotemnidae. Up to now the only reconstruction of the whole skeleton of a pre-Deseadan notoungulate, or for that matter of any equally ancient South American mammal, is based on specimens of the genus *Thomashuxleya* collected by my first expedition to Patagonia in 1930–1931. Some other members of the family were equally or more common and are reasonably well known but not as yet by the whole skeleton. All the members of this family were still extremely primitive. In fact, the family can hardly be defined except by primitive characters, which as far as possible is preferably avoided in making a classification. The dentition differs from those perhaps even more primitive, for example that of *Henricosbornia,* by the presence of one or more accessory crests on the upper molars, the cristae. There is also a difference in that the isotemnids have fairly distinctive, more truly caninelike canine teeth, but it is possible that in this respect this family is more primitive than even the henricosborniids. The isotemnids are also larger than other notoungulates in the earliest faunas.

Fig. 24. Restoration of *Thomashuxleya,* an early Eocene (Casamayoran) isotemnid, primitive member of the suborder Toxodonta.

They differ from some contemporaneous and practically all later notoungulates just in being more primitive. That extends to the limbs, which have about the same proportions as in other primitive ungulates and have five functional toes on each foot, the middle one (III) somewhat the largest.

Here again, as was noted for some of the other primitive notoungulates, the species are markedly variable, and this is reflected in Ameghino's classification. For example, what is now seen to be one variable species, *Isotemnus primitivus* (a good choice of a specific name by Ameghino), although not particularly abundant in collections, was classified by Ameghino as seven species in five genera, all, however, recognized as members of the same family.

Another family, Notohippidae, appears suddenly in the Mustersan without surely identifiable precursors although it could have been derived from a rather precocious isotemnid. Its clearest distinction from then contemporaneous isotemnids is that the molars, although rooted, have much higher crowns. The crowns continued to become higher in later ages and in the poorly known Santacrucian genus, *Notohippus,* type of the family, were heavily coated with cementum. In that respect the molars came to resemble those of the advanced, grazing horses, including all the now living members of the horse family. *Notohippus,* the name given by Ameghino, derives from the Greek for "southern horse." Ameghino did decide, after some vacillation, that early notohippids were ancestral to the horses. The resemblance is only convergent in adaptation for grazing. The molar pattern apart from height of crowns and coat of cementum has all the diagnostic features of the notoungulates and none of the horses, and so has the ear region.

The Leontiniidae, prettily named by Florentino Ameghino after his wife and helpmate, née Léontine Poirier, are typically Deseadan, approximately early Oligocene, although they also are known from the later Colhuehuapian. In the Deseadan they are usually the most evident mammals although Ameghino named these beds after *Pyrotherium,* which is confined to them but is nowhere abundant and does not occur in some otherwise extensive Deseadan faunas. The leontiniid dentition retains the full primitive formula

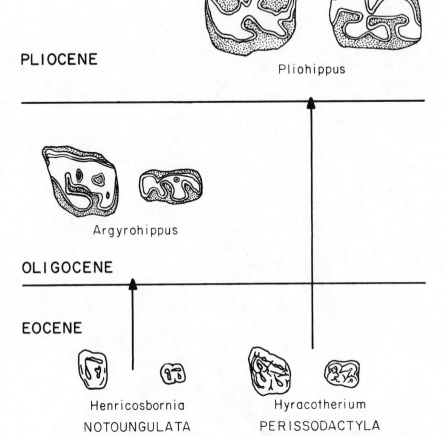

PLIOCENE

Pliohippus

OLIGOCENE

Argyrohippus

EOCENE

Henricosbornia

NOTOUNGULATA

Hyracotherium

PERISSODACTYLA

Fig. 25. Left upper (*to left in each pair*) and right lower (*to right in each pair*) molars of some notoungulates, native South American ungulates, and perissodactyls, originating in the Northern Hemisphere: *Henricosbornia,* lower Eocene (Casamayoran), with approximately the primitive molar structure for notoungulates as a whole, as *Hyracotherium,* early Eocene of North America and Europe, has for perissodactyls as a whole and the horse family (Equidae) in particular. *Argyrohippus,* early Oligocene (Deseadan), a notohippid, had already evolved high-crowned grinding teeth coated in cementum (stippled) and adapted to grazing on harsh vegetation. Some horses evolved grinding teeth with the same adaptations, shown here in the late Pliocene *Pliohippus* of North America, but they reached this stage much later than the South American Notohippidae and obviously entirely independently.

$$\frac{3 \cdot 1 \cdot 4 \cdot 3}{3 \cdot 1 \cdot 4 \cdot 3},$$

with low-crowned, rooted, and rather simple teeth in a closely continuous series. The canines are small, but the first upper and third lower incisors are enlarged like fangs or small tusks. The head is heavy, the body high at the shoulders. The forefoot in *Scarrittia,* much the best known genus of the family, has four toes, I lacking, V reduced and nonfunctional, II to IV functional, and the axis through III. The hindfoot has five toes, but I and V are reduced and apparently nonfunctional; II to IV have about the same arrangement as in the forefoot. (See figure 22B.)

The only reasonably well-known member of the family Homalodotheriidae is the genus *Homalodotherium* itself, also known incorrectly as *Homalodontotherium,* an eight-syllable

Fig. 26. Restorations of the early Miocene (Santacrucian) genus *Homalodotherium,* strange, clawed "ungulate" of the notoungulate suborder Toxodonta.

monstrosity of a name unusual even in a field of study burdened by a number of polysyllabic names. In either form the name is from Greek roots meaning "even-tooth beast," in reference to the full set of teeth in a closed and graded sequence. Although dissimilar in a number of details, the general aspect of the dentition is much as in the leontiniids, and the skull and skeleton except the feet are also much like them, as seen in *Scarrittia,* although more heavily built. The feet, however, are amazingly different. The forefoot has four nearly equal, heavy, functional toes, II–V, of nearly equal length, each bearing a large claw, not hoof. Digit I is a mere vestige and completely nonfunctional. The hindfoot also has four functional toes, II–V, all shorter and stouter than those of the forefoot, V being especially stout but stubby. It is not certain whether the hindfoot bore claws. If so, they must have been smaller than those of the forefoot. The forelegs of the animal were evidently digitigrade, that is, up on the bases of the toes when it walked, but the hindfoot was plantigrade, with the whole foot flat on the ground. The different pose of forelegs and hindlegs increased the elevation of the shoulders above that of the hips.

The homalodotheres appear in the known record at the same time as the leontiniids but survived longer, into the Chasicoan. *Homalodotherium* is from the Santacrucian. There is little doubt that the two families had a common ancestry, probably an unknown pre-Deseadan leontiniid, as that family is definitely the more primitive of the two.

It borders on fantasy that an animal certainly to be classified among the Ungulata, the hoofed mammals, should have claws, but this is not unique. In a time range overlapping that of the homalodotheres in South America there was a large group of clawed Ungulata called chalicotheres, belonging to the same order (Perissodactyla) as the horses. The chalicotheres ranged over all the continents other than South America, Australia, and Antarctica. They figured in a famous incident in the history of paleontology. Cuvier, generally hailed as the founder of scientific paleontology although he had less famous predecessors, believed that animals are so coordinated in structure that one could predict one part from another, and specifically that from a tooth the nature of the toes could be predicted. That, sometimes called Cuvier's law, is the source of the entirely untrue legend that a paleontologist can and does reconstruct a whole animal from one tooth or bone (see the appendix for a note on the restoration of extinct animals). In fact, the discovery of chalicotheres put an end to Cuvier's law as far as paleontologists themselves are concerned but unfortunately not as far as many nonpaleontologists still believe. According to the law, an animal with chalicothere teeth had to have hooves and could not have claws. It was soon discovered that in fact they did have claws.

It will not now come as a surprise to learn that Ameghino believed that primitive homalodotheres (he called them the equivalent of "homalotheres") were also ancestral to chalicotheres. On that W. B. Scott can be given the last word. He wrote that knowledge of some North American chalicotheres "conclusively shows that these animals are only aberrant perissodactyls and that they cannot be related to their South American analogues" (Scott 1930, p. 331). Adaptive convergence again—but again, adaptive for what? As there are no animals at all like these now living, imagination has roamed rather freely around this question as regards both the chalicotheres and the homalodotheres. E. S. Riggs, who collected the most nearly complete specimens of *Homalodotherium*, speculated in 1937 as reasonably as anyone that the powerful clawed forelimbs of that animal "indicate a prehensile member capable of digging in quest of food or of pulling down branches of trees in order to feed upon the fruit or foliage."

So, finally, in the account of the Notoungulata we come to the noble family Toxodontidae. The first known specimen of this family, and the first known of what much later came to be called the Notoungulata, was a skull purchased for eighteen pence from a farmer in Uruguay (then called the "Banda Oriental") by Darwin on 26 November 1833. On 19 April 1837, a few months after Darwin's return from the voyage of the *Beagle,* Richard Owen read a paper about that skull to the Geological Society of London. He gave the animal the name *Toxodon,* and after likening it to an astonishing array of other mammals he concluded "that it manifested an additional step in the gradation of mammiferous forms leading from the *Rodentia,* through the *Pachydermata* to the *Cetacea"* (quoted in Darwin 1839, p. 180; see reference following chapter 2). That remark must not be taken as referring to an evolutionary sequence. At that time Darwin was just becoming an evolutionist in a clandestine way, not made overt for more than forty years, and Owen never did become an overt evolutionist. His original classification of *Toxodon* seems merely nonsensical if one does not note that what he had in mind was the *scala naturae* or "great chain of being" as God's plan of creation and that he was placing *Toxodon* in the ladder or chain between rodents and pachyderms, the latter a term then referring to any large, four-footed, hooved, thick-skinned mammals. That was in fact a fair inference as to the adaptive characters of the genus, of course with no implications as to its phylogenetic position.

The name *Toxodon* is apt because it means "bow tooth," and in this genus the upper molars are extremely high-crowned and the crowns are strongly curved in vertical section, in that sense bow-like. Here there is another amusing touch of history. The skull Darwin bought for eighteen pence, a significant sum then but nevertheless one of the great bargains of history, had no teeth. The farmer's sons, as Darwin reported, had "knocked the teeth out with stones, and then set up the head as a mark to throw at." But 180 miles distant from there Darwin "found a perfect tooth, which exactly fits one of the sockets in this skull" and which led Owen to call the skull *Toxodon.* What made Owen think it belonged between rodents and pachyderms was that the two upper and three lower pairs of incisors (the uppers indicated by sockets in the type skull) were enlarged, continuously growing, and somewhat vaguely rodentlike, while the size, "that of a hippopotamus" as Darwin noted, and general aspect were pachydermlike in the terms then in use.

The whole dental formula of *Toxodon* is

$$\frac{2 \cdot 0 \cdot 4 \cdot 3}{3 \cdot 1 \cdot 3 \cdot 3},$$

and all the teeth are continuously growing, hypselodont. As in other such cases, the cusp pattern of the crowns is soon worn off,

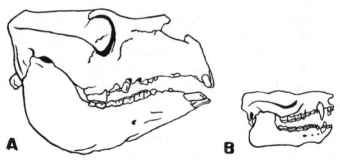

Fig. 27. Skulls of one of the last survivors and one of the earliest known members of the notoungulate suborder Toxodonta: A, *Toxodon*, late Pleistocene; B, *Thomashuxleya*, early Eocene. The skulls are drawn to the same scale. The difference in size and in specialization of skull form and dentition are evident.

and for the molars the resulting cross section of the teeth is interestingly characteristic of different genera and species. The lower molars are not bowed or arched and are nearly straight vertically. The pattern after wear can be amusing, as witness the name *Gyrinodon,* "tadpole tooth," given to one of the less common genera of the family. The skull of *Toxodon* was heavy, with short nasal bones suggesting the presence of a flexible fleshy nose, and the skeleton was heavy, powerful, stocky, with forelimbs shorter than hind, a bit of a hump at the shoulders, and both forefeet and hindfeet with three toes, II–IV, all functional, III longest and in the axis of weight bearing.

The first known toxodontids are from the Deseadan, and as with several other groups they are first really well known from the Santacrucian. From those beds complete skeletons of two genera have been described. The species of both are considerably smaller than those of *Toxodon,* and they had the primitive dental formula

$$\frac{3 \cdot 1 \cdot 4 \cdot 3}{3 \cdot 1 \cdot 4 \cdot 3}$$

The teeth were all very high-crowned but did eventually form roots and stop growing. The median pair of upper incisors and most posterior, third pair of lower incisors were already enlarged and somewhat rodentlike. The molars retained an only slightly modified notoungulate pattern in all but the latest stages of wear.

In the later Cenozoic, Friasian to Montehermosan, an interesting side branch of this family arose and evolved a single rhinoceroslike horn on its forehead. The horn itself, not having a bony core, is not preserved in the fossils, but as in living rhinoceroses its presence is clearly indicated by a rugose hump on the underlying bones.

Some, at least, of the later toxodontids may have been partly amphibious, and they seem to have converged adaptively to a limited extent toward both rhinoceroses and hippopotamuses. It is somewhat surprising to have to report that Ameghino did not consider them ancestral to either of those groups but placed them in an order of their own, Toxodontia, not ancestral to anything, which is still seen as valid for the Toxodonta as a suborder.

References

Chaffee, R. G. 1951. The Deseadan vertebrate fauna of the Scarritt pocket, Patagonia. *Bulletin of the American Museum of Natural History,* 98: 503–562 (includes most complete description of a leontiniid, *Scarrittia*).

Lavocat, R. 1958. Notongulés. In J. Piveteau, ed. *Traité de paléontologie,* tome 6, 2: 60–121. Paris: Masson.

Riggs, E. S. 1937. Mounted skeleton of *Homalodotherium. Geological Series of Field Museum of Natural History,* 6: 233–243.

Scott, W. B. 1912. Toxodonta of the Santa Cruz beds. Entelonychia of the Santa Cruz beds. *Reports of the Princeton University Expeditions to Patogonia,* 6: 111–300.

————. 1930. A partial skeleton of *Homalodontotherium.* From the Santa Cruz beds of Patagonia. Field Museum of Natural History, Geology, *Memoirs,* 1: 7–33.

Sinclair, W. J. 1909. Typotheria of the Santa Cruz beds. *Reports of the Princeton Expeditions to Patagonia,* 6: 1–110.

Stirton, R. A. 1953. A new genus of interatheres from the Miocene of Colombia. *University of California Publications in Geological Sciences,* 29: 265–348.

See also previous references, especially Patterson and Pascual 1972; Scott 1937; Simpson 1948, 1967.

CHAPTER 11

Second Phase: Aliens Appear

The word *deseado* means "desired" or "longed for" in Spanish. It is a strangely romantic name to be applied to a port and river in bleak, cold, gale-buffeted southern Patagonia. The origin of the name, known to few if any of the present local inhabitants, may seem romantic in the perspective of so many years but probably did not seem so to those directly involved in the year 1586. The Worshipfull Master Thomas Candish, whose name was sometimes written Cavendish, was then sailing from east to west around the whole earth with three ships, the *Desire,* 120 tons, flagship of the Master, or Admirall, and two even smaller vessels, the *Content* and the *Hugh.* The incident relevant here was recorded by the annalist of the "small Fleete," one Francis Pretty, a Gentleman lately of "Ey in Suffolke," as follows: "The 17. day of December in the afternoone we entred into an harborough, where our Admirall went in first: wherefore our Generall named the said harborough Port Desire."

The naming was of course in honor of the Admirall's flagship. It is not entirely apropos here but is of passing interest that at this port the party made early sightings of southern elephant seals and Magellanic penguins, not then noted under those later names but clearly described by Master Pretty.

When the Spaniards came, they transmuted "Desire" into "Deseado," and the town and river are still called Puerto Deseado and Río Deseado. What is stranger, or would surely have been least expected by either the Worshipfull Master Candish or the later pioneer Spanish settlers, is that the name Deseado was destined to become one of the most significant in the annals of South American geology and paleontology.

On his seventh expedition to Patagonia, in the summer of 1893–1894, Carlos Ameghino made an important collection of fossil mammals at a place called La Flecha ("the arrow," a recollection of the Indian frontier) in northern Santa Cruz ("Holy Cross"), which is the southernmost of the four political units of the large area colloquially called Patagonia. That site is near Puerto Deseado and the mouth of the Rio Deseado. In 1895 Florentino Ameghino described the fossil fauna from there, which he called the *Pyrotherium* fauna or Pyrothéréenne in his French version. Later, guided by Don Carlos, André Tournouër collected fossils of that fauna at La Flecha and elsewhere and sent them to Paris. There, as was remarked in chapter 2, Albert Gaudry, who never visited South America in person, studied the Tournouër collection. The point especially relevant here is that he applied the name Deseado to the fauna and to the geological strata in which it occurs. In more precise modern usage the name Deseadan in English or Deseadense in Spanish designates a land mammal age, the South American mammalian fauna that defines it, and the stage comprising the rocks of that age.

This is a good place to bring in an extraordinarily clear and instructive example of how the sequence of faunas, the progression of evolution, and the passage of geological time can be objectively determined in the field. South of the central Patagonian topographic basin in which lie the two lakes Musters and Colhué-Huapí (locally usually pronounced more nearly "Coluapi") there is a cliff or steep slope, a great barranca, often now called *the* Great Barranca by paleontologists. As a geological site it was discovered—one might say, "of course"—by Carlos Ameghino. The geological beds exposed in it are nearly horizontal, and as one climbs up any such rock exposure one is also climbing through time, from earlier to later.

Here and as far as I know nowhere else in the world the climber going up a single, continuous, steep slope climbs through four quite distinct geological ages, each with a fully characteristic mammalian fauna. In the post-Ameghinian terms now in use these are, from bottom to top and hence earlier to later, Casamayoran, Mustersan, Deseadan, and Colhuehuapian. Teaching himself as he went along, Don Carlos came to understand this sequence, and from that Don Florentino had the inescapable basis for a good part of the South American mammalian faunal sequence. Although Gaudry innocently named the oldest of these four faunas "Casamayor" after a locality not really basic or typical for it, the Ameghinos' concept of their "Notostylopense" and our concept of our Casamayoran really have as their typical representation the lowest fauna in the Great Barranca. This is the type locality and, with a little leeway, also the source of the names of our Mustersan and Colhuehuapian, each named for one of the two lakes in that general area. (Musters was a nineteenth-century English explorer of Patagonia; Colhué-Huapí is a corruption of Araucanian Indian words meaning "red island.") The Deseadan fauna is also present in its sequential place in the Great Barranca, but as already noted in this chapter its type and the source of its present name are satisfactorily located elsewhere.

The Deseadan is in more than one respect a key time and fauna in the geological and zoological history of South America. For one thing this is at present the oldest South American land mammal age for which there is a good radiometric check on age in years. It is fairly well established that beds with Deseadan mammals were being deposited about 35 million years ago but that such known deposition ceased about 34 million years ago. That permits reasonable correlation with the standard European epochs and the North American land mammal ages. It indicates that the Deseadan is early Oligocene in European terms and approximately eqivalent to the North American Chadronian, which is typically the oldest part of the famous Big Badlands of South Dakota. That is reassuring because for some time on admittedly inadequate previous evidence most of us concerned with this point have been calling the Deseadan "approximately" or "conventionally" early Oligocene in age. This has turned out to be correct.

Another interesting geological point is that it was at about this time that the uplift of the Andes although still moderate began to be significant. There had been and would continue right down to the Recent to be local or regional changes of elevation and incursions and withdrawals of the sea over parts of what is now land. In the early Oligocene the intermittent or episodic but continual uplift started to rear hills that would become the Andes mountains, a process that is still going on, as is evident from the earthquakes along the west coast and the active volcanos in the Andes. In the Deseadan age for the first time volcanos and lava flows began to appear among the relatively flat beds east of the hills that eventually would become high plateaus and mountains.

In Patagonia the Deseadan rocks continue to be composed almost entirely of volcanic debris as are those of the Casamayoran and Mustersan before and of the Colhuehuapian after the Deseadan. Now, however, not all is fine ash blown from distant volcanos and then reworked by streams and altered by weather. There is that, too, in the Patagonian Deseadan but also coarser materials, cinders and scoria, usually also reworked by water. In one particularly interesting locality a rich deposit of Deseadan mammals, found by my second Patagonian expedition in what we named the Scarritt Pocket, was mostly concentrated in what had been the crater of a small volcano. After the volcano stopped erupting it was deeply buried and much later was reexposed in essential cross section by erosion. In what had been a shallow crater lake large numbers of leontiniids (see chapter 10) had died, probably gassed by the volcano, and had been buried by successive ash falls from other volcanic vents in the region.

The Deseadan rocks are widely scattered in southern Argentina and generally lie on an eroded surface, indicative of a change in regional elevation of the land. For example, at a famous locality called Cabeza Blanca, "white head," because it is a hill with light-colored rocks at the top, the Deseadan beds lie directly on the Casamayoran, with no Mustersan or rocks of other intermediate age between them. For a time such occurrences led some paleontologists, mostly non-Argentinian, less skillful and less knowledgeable than Carlos Ameghino, to question whether a distinct Mustersan age and fauna existed. One North American who spent a whole successful summer at Cabeza Blanca—the one known skull of *Pyrotherium* came from there—even denied that the Casamayoran is present there; it is, but the Mustersan is not. The Mustersan does exist elsewhere, but there still is a break in continuity, a hiatus in the sequence of dated rocks and faunas, between the Mustersan and the Deseadan.

That brings up the question of the so-called Divisaderan, mentioned before only in passing. In the outskirts of the city of Mendoza, an Argentinian city at the foot of the Andes far north of Patagonia, there is a geological formation named Divisadero Largo ("long viewpoint") after a hill formed by it. The rocks are not composed of volcanic debris, as in the Deseadan of Patagonia, but are varicolored, water-laid clays and sands. They contain a small, extremely peculiar known mammalian fauna, classified in 7 families, two of them dubious as to identification, 9 genera, one doubtfully identified, and 10 species. All of the species, eight of the genera surely and the other doubtfully, and two of the families, one surely (Groeberiidae) and one doubtfully (unnamed at present), are completely unknown in any other fauna of any age. Three of the notoungulate genera, with one species each, are primitive, comparable in apparent evolutionary stage with some of the Casamayoran and Mustersan notoungulates. However, four other ungulates, two of them litopterns and two notoungulates, are definitely more advanced and on the evolutionary level of genera known elsewhere in definitely Deseadan faunas. The primitive and advanced ungulates certainly occur here together, not in successive faunas.

The fauna of the Divisadero Largo formation almost surely is approximately Deseadan in age, for survival of relatively primitive animals is much more likely than the early appearance of specialized ones decidedly more advanced than any in earlier well-known faunas. The possibility that this markedly distinct fauna is slightly earlier, geologically speaking, or slightly later than the known Deseadan faunas of Patagonia cannot be entirely ruled out. Pascual, the leading Argentinian student of fossil mammals, thinks it somewhat more probable that this fauna is slightly earlier than the typical Deseadan, and on that basis he has proposed a Divisaderan land mammal age partly occupying the hiatus recognized between Mustersan and Deseadan. I do not believe that the data now available justify that tentative conclusion.

That difference of opinion is of little real importance, but the situation is of special interest and merits this much discussion here for a different reason. As everyone concerned with this fauna agrees, it is not intermediate between the known Mustersan and typical Deseadan. It is aberrant, right out of the orderly progression of almost all other South American faunas. Whether it is of just the same age as some Deseadan fauna elsewhere or a bit earlier or a bit later is beside this point: it is different, neither ancestral to any other known fauna nor descended, as a whole, from any. As Pascual (in Pascual and Odreman Rivas 1971, p. 386) has written (in Spanish), this fauna "belonged to a distinct or geographic domain where archaic browsing types that had disappeared almost completely in Patagonia lived together with certain grazing types like the Hegetotheriidae of the Deseadan age." In addition to some degree of geographic separation or isolation, such a fauna must represent a distinct ecological difference, even though the ecological factors cannot be specified in detail.

A geological age is not a point in time. It is a geologically fairly short, definable span marked off in the continuous flow of time. A land mammal age is not definable by a fixed ecological community but by all such local communities as can be reasonably considered to have existed within the span of the same geological age. In the known Riochican of Argentina and Brazil we have seen that there is a somewhat limited example of land mammal faunas geographically separated and ecologically different, for example, notoungulates and few (no known) didelphids in Argentina, few notoungulates and many didelphids in Brazil.

In the Deseadan we have for the first time in this history numerous local faunas scattered over a very wide geographic area. Some have only slight ecological differences, but the Divisadero Largo local fauna, at least approximately Deseadan in age, has a strongly marked ecological distinction. The most important geographic addition to knowledge of Deseadan faunas, with some but less evident ecological distinction, is the fairly recent discovery of a rich fauna of that age in the Salla (pronounced sah'-yah) forma-

tion of Bolivia. That fauna occurs at a number of different exposures of nonvolcanic red beds in the Salla-Luribay basin. These
exposures are now at elevations of about 3,500 to 4,000 meters
(about 11,400 to 13,125 feet). Such elevations now entail a considerable difference from lowland faunas, but most of the Andean
uplift was post-Deseadan. The region was already above sea level
when this Deseadan fauna lived there, but was much lower than it
is now. Unlike the Divisadero Largo fauna, the Salla fauna may be
considered normal or in the overall mainstream of South American faunal evolution. The fauna has not yet been fully described,
but most of the genera so far listed in publications are identical
with or closely related to those previously known from Patagonian
Deseadan faunas. There are, however, some differences probably
due mainly to ecological (environmental) causes. For example toxodonts, leontiniids, and astrapotheres, common in most Patagonian Deseadan local faunas, are rare in the Salla fauna, and some of
the ground sloths and most of the rodents, about which more
later, are generically distinct.

Another and indeed the main reason for special interest in the
Deseado is inherent in what has previously been said, especially in
the last two chapters, and may here be summarized in a broader
context. By Deseadan times the old-timers, the first settlers, had
been fairly well sorted out, and each group was well along toward
adequate specialization in a particular way of life. Later history
involved mainly two processes as regards these particular groups.
Some rather slowly developed still further along the lines already
laid out in the Deseadan. Others one by one, and eventually a
majority, dropped out, became terminally extinct. Some scions of
the old-timers that suddenly appeared as totally new departures
late in the history are few in number and probably only apparently
exceptional. The most striking example is the argyrolagids (see
chapter 7), which suddenly appear in the known record in the
Pliocene and apart from being marsupials do not even remotely
resemble any known older forms. The most reasonable explanation is that their ancestors must have been evolving, perhaps from
the Deseadan or earlier, in parts of the vast regions from which we
do not yet have much or any fossil evidence. In the Deseadan itself

the occurrence of *Groeberia* (also chapter 7) without known ancestors or descendants is a similar phenomenon of the record, and there we know that the one fauna in which this genus and family are known was clearly exceptional both geographically and ecologically.

There are two sudden appearances in the Deseadan that represent historical events quite different from those noted in the last paragraph. These are further reasons for the special interest of this age and its fauna. These incursions into the Deseadan record, and

MONKEYS

OLD   NATIVE
RODENTS

Fig. 28.   A ceboid monkey and some caviomorph rodents, living descendants of the waifs that reached South America in the late Eocene or earliest Oligocene. These few examples are shown here just to emphasize the event of the arrival of their ancestors. The two major groups, South American primates and caviomorph rodents, are discussed in the next few chapters.

quite surely also into the continent not long, geologically, before the Deseadan, are by the orders Rodentia and Primates. They quite surely had no ancestors in South America when the old-timers became established there, and they and their descendants constitute a second faunal stratum in the eventual complex of the South American fauna. When they reached that continent, it was already an island. The original South American immigrants of these two orders must have reached there by island hopping or by unbroken overseas dispersal, waif or sweepstakes dispersal as such events are designated when the odds against successfully reaching another continent or island are high but with the passage of enough time are not prohibitive. These have been called the old island hoppers (later island hoppers will be discussed in chapter 14). These two orders have been unusually successful at island hopping, as is further indicated by the fact that eventually members of both hopped to various Caribbean islands.

It is now generally accepted that most and probably all of the large number of old native, second-stratum South American rodents came from a single ancestry on that continent. The possible but improbable exception is the American porcupine family, Erethizontidae, which is basically more distinct than the other families and could have had a separate immigrant ancestor. Thus one chance immigrant stock or at most two must be postulated. On the one-stock theory the whole South American complex is united in a group of its own called Caviomorpha. Where that, or those, ancestors came from is in dispute; in fact it is one of the most bitterly argued problems in mammalian history and geography. It is fairly well agreed that the only likely sources are North America and Africa. The question is, "Which?" There are rodents on both continents that could conceivably, hypothetically or theoretically, have given rise to the Caviomorpha. However, Eocene forms clearly close to the caviomorphs are not now known from either continent. The ultimate ancestor as it landed in South America is also unknown. There are students on both sides of the argument so well informed, so authoritative, and so evenly balanced in disagreement that anyone else can hardly argue against or for either view. A. E. Wood and B. Patterson have the ancestor of the caviomorphs hopping along islands from southern North America. R. Hoffstetter and R. Lavocat have them making the long (but then not quite so long as now) transatlantic hop from Africa. It is irrelevant that Wood and Patterson are North Americans, Hoffstetter and Lavocat French. Years ago I was on the North American side; now I am neutral and await some really convincing evidence on either side.

Wherever it came from, the ancestry of the caviomorphs did get there. By Deseado time this group had already diversified into the primitive but distinguishable members of all four main stocks (superfamilies) and at least seven families. They must already have been in South America for some time, but not necessarily a very long time geologically speaking. The most plausible view is that the ancestry arrived during the hiatus between Mustersan and Deseadan for which there is almost no known fossil record at present. There were no previous rodents in this vast and varied territory. In such circumstances adaptive radiation of an immigrant group can occur rapidly. The ancestral caviomorphs doubtless proliferated as rodents do and in a reasonable time, up to a million years or two or three, were well under way in the Deseadan. Incidentally, one of the arguments for considering the Divisadero Largo fauna immediately pre-Deseadan is that no rodents are known in it although rodents occur in all equally known Deseadan faunas. But the Deseadan record clearly requires the presence of rodents in immediately pre-Deseadan times. Thus the absence of rodents in the Divisadero Largo fauna must still be imputed to its peculiar ecology, not to the arrival of rodents in South America after that fauna lived.

For many years the earliest South American primates were from the Colhuehuapian, approximately latest Oligocene in age, but in 1969 Hoffstetter published a description of one, *Branisella,* from the Deseadan of Bolivia. The New World monkeys are now and probably always have been confined to tropical or at farthest subtropical forests, and their absence in the Deseadan of Argentina, if not due simply to lack of discovery, may well indicate that Bolivia then had a more appropriate climate and flora for this group. The Bolivian Deseadan is and was some 20° of latitude nearer the equator than the Argentinian, and the altitude was then still low in Bolivia.

Here the same biogeographic problem appears as for the rodents, and again it has led to the same dispute, which at present seems to be a deadlock. Again there are possible relatives on both sides of the Atlantic. Again there are, however, no known Eocene forms from either North America or Africa that can clearly be taken as ancestral to the South American ones. It is tempting, but not really necessary, to suppose that rodents and primates, which apparently got to South America at about the same time, came from the same place. Thus it is not surprising to find again that American students of this question almost all support the view that the primates went from North America to South America, while French students think they went from Africa. One American student, F. S. Szalay, has made the diverting suggestion that perhaps the South American monkeys evolved from North American ancestors and the African monkeys from South American ones. Again I am neutral while awaiting convincing evidence on either side.

The first South American primates were probably arboreal, as all their descendants are today. When they arrived in that continent there may already have been some arboreal xenarthrans, but the primates probably had no serious competition. The first South American rodents were mainly if not wholly terrestrial, were all small, and all had low-crowned molar teeth functionally but not structurally comparable with those of rats and mice. There might have been some competition with a few small marsupials, but if so it was not close and on the whole the primitive caviomorphs had access to a wealth of different ecological niches empty before they arrived.

One evolutionary development among the old native ungulates partly discussed in the preceding two chapters here requires further notice in a different context. Primitive ungulates in general and the primitive South American ones in particular were small to medium in size and had low-crowned (brachydont) cheek teeth (premolars and molars) indicative of more or less omnivorous or browsing diets. In the Deseadan some, relatively few, of the primi-

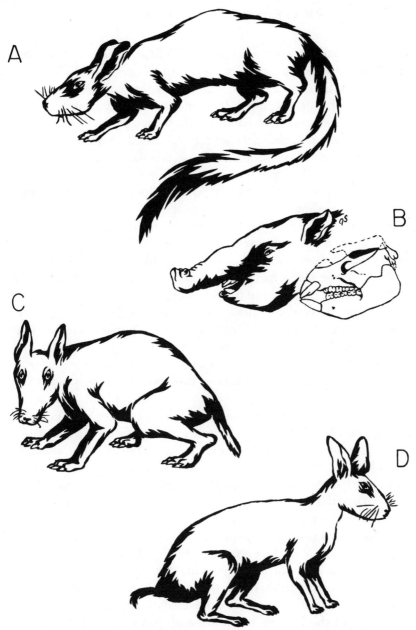

Fig. 29. Some characteristic early Oligocene (Deseadan) mammals: *A*, restoration of *Platypittamys*, one of the earliest known caviomorph rodents; *B*, *Pyrotherium*, reconstruction of skull (after Patterson) and restoration of head; *C*, *Propachyrucos*, a rodentlike, grazing hegetothere notoungulate; *D*, *Prosotherium*, another hegetothere.

tive, unspecialized sorts still survived. More evident, however, were larger ungulates variously specialized and definitely browsers on fairly succulent vegetation. The pyrotheres and leontiniids are among the striking examples. It seems ecologically significant that although pyrotheres and some other browsers do occur in the Bolivian Deseadan, the data so far published indicate that they were there much less abundant than in the Patagonian Deseadan.

Another overall adaptive trend in ungulates includes the evolution of high-crowned (hypsodont to hypselodont) cheek teeth indicative of feeding on abrasive vegetation, especially siliceous grasses. In the North American Miocene there were many different lineages in the horse family. Some of them continued to be browsers as the ancestors of all of them had been, but by the end of the Miocene some had become grazers. In North America all eventually died out and the browsers everywhere became extinct, but grazers survived in Eurasia and Africa as the horses strictly speaking, asses, and zebras. It has been shown that some notoungulates already showed a trend toward grazing in the Eocene (Mustersan). In the early Oligocene (Deseadan) there were a number of different notoungulates fully adapted to grazing. (See figure 25.)

Some paleontologists familiar with horses but not with notoungulates postulated that coarse grasses evolved and became widespread prairies in or shortly before the late Miocene. The notoungulate history would then suggest that such grasses evolved and prairielike pampas spread in South America some 20 or 25 million years earlier than in North America. That is unlikely, to say the least. The assumption of a new adaptive type by an evolving group of animals depends not only on the existence of an environmental possibility but also on the existence in a population of animals with the genetic background and possibility for adaptation to that environmental factor. In this case the most likely hypothesis is that grasses had existed widely, not necessarily in the form of prairies or pampas, in the Eocene or earlier and that some notoungulates simply had the genetic background and possibility to become grazers earlier than some horses did.

So much then for the Deseadan, which has been given perhaps

disproportionate attention here for reasons that have been stated. Unfortunately the Deseadan is followed by an almost complete gap in our knowledge of South American mammals, a hiatus longer than any other in the whole sequence from Riochican to the present. The time gap from Deseadan to Colhuehuapian has been radiometrically dated as about 9 million years. The faunas, too, indicate evolutionary changes consistent with the passage of a long time. Deseadan mammalian local faunas are much more numerous and geographically widespread than Colhuehuapian so that the terms of comparison are unequal. It is, however, probable that no species are common to the two and only a few genera. The most noteworthy change is that there are several families in the Deseadan that are unknown in any later age and that were probably extinct before the Colhuehuapian. Among them are the marsupial Polydolopidae (last known member in the Bolivian, not Patagonian, Deseadan), the Xenarthran Palaeopeltidae, the Pyrotheriidae, and the Isotemnidae.

The Colhuehuapian raises a question for historians that is not very serious but is instructive enough to be mentioned. In Patagonia there is a widespread group of sedimentary rocks that were deposited in a fluctuating sea that expanded from the Atlantic over what is now land. That fluctuation went on for a long time, even speaking geologically, and the marine beds are not everywhere of the same age although they have commonly been lumped under the name of Patagonian formation or group, with other more local geographic names for various subdivisions. The type Colhuehuapian near the Great Barranca is overlain by part of that marine group and so is an approximate equivalent of the Colhuehuapian in the valley of the Chubut River. To the south in Santa Cruz Province the type Santacrucian is underlain by part of the marine group. Thus one can say and several have said that the Colhuehuapian is pre-Patagonian and the Santacrucian post-Patagonian, and the two land mammal ages have been distinguished and separately named on that basis. But that statement can be misleading. There is no known geological section where Colhuehuapian and Santacrucian beds both occur with part of the Patagonian marine beds between them. Since the Patagonian beds are not of the same age everywhere, it is possible, for example, that the part of them known to overlie the Colhuehuapian is later in age than the part known to underlie the Santacrucian. In that case it would be possible from the known stratigraphic relationships for the Colhuehuapian to be of the same age as or even to be later than the Santacrucian. The historian must distinguish between what is objectively known, like the sequence of faunas and ages in the Great Barranca, and what is deduced, like the stratigraphic relationships just outlined.

The principles involved are important, but in this case, as I said above, the problem is not very serious. The known Colhuehuapian and Santacrucian faunas are not quite identical, and close study of evolving lineages running through both makes it practically certain that the Colhuehuapian is in fact older than the Santacrucian, as was already established in other terms by the Ameghinos. Thus the sequence is all right, but the faunas of the two ages are nevertheless very much alike, more so than is usual for formal recognition of separate faunal ages. The designation of a Colhuehuapian age as such rather than as early Santacrucian is a matter of taste and usage, not of fact. Usage does favor recognition of the two as separate ages, and it is to my taste to follow usage in this respect.

The Santacrucian faunas are known only from a limited region in southern Patagonia, but in conjunction they are especially important in this history because they are particularly rich, represented in museums by large collections including a remarkable number of nearly complete skeletons of individual mammals as indicated in previous chapters. They represent the continuation of phase 2 in the history of South American mammals. In this phase, ushered in by the Deseadan, the mammalian communities are a complex of descendants of original settlers, belonging to the orders Marsupialia, Xenarthra, Condylarthra, Litopterna, Notoungulata, and Astrapotheria, to which have been added the latecomers, but early island hoppers, Rodentia and Primates. (The Condylarthra are not known from the Santacrucian but are known to have been present in South America then because they are known there in both older and younger faunas.)

There are a number of Santacrucian local faunas, but all in the same general region and similar in composition aside from details. The beds in which they occur were deposited by streams and floods and consist mostly of volcanic debris, more or less like the earlier Casamayoran to Colhuehuapian beds in other parts of Patagonia, but also with some pebbly sediments from erosion of the rising Andes to westward. The whole mass of sediments was laid down across a low sloping plain left by the retreat of the Patagonian sea. The area must have had ample rainfall and large amounts of grasses, bushes, and trees to have fed the great herds x of both browsing and grazing mammals. The climate must also have been much more equable and warmer than it is in that region now, and perhaps more so than it had been early in the Cenozoic or ever was again. Perhaps one indication of such a climate is that fossil monkeys are known from Patagonia only in the Colhuehuapian and Santacrucian, indicating the presence of tropical or subtropical forests then and possibly not either earlier or later in that region. The last inference is doubtful, however, because fossil primates are rare in most South American fossil faunas and may simply have been missed in collecting.

Marsupials were present in enormous variety, especially caenolestids and the carnivorous borhyaenids, and so were armadillos, glyptodonts, and especially ground sloths. Rodents had continued their expansion and within their still somewhat limited size range are near dominance in these communities. The notohippids, grazing notoungulates, were not varied but were abundant in the earlier local faunas. They seem to have become extinct before the end of the Santacrucian. Other grazing notoungulates continued to be common.

It is worthy of note that a good many fossil birds have also been discovered in the Santacrucian beds. Among them is the earliest *birds* known member of the rhea family, the so-called South American ostriches. There were also many flightless running birds, phororhacids, some of them enormous, with great, hooked beaks. It has sometimes been said that these and other flightless South American birds such as the rheas survived because there were long no placental carnivores on that continent. That speculation is far

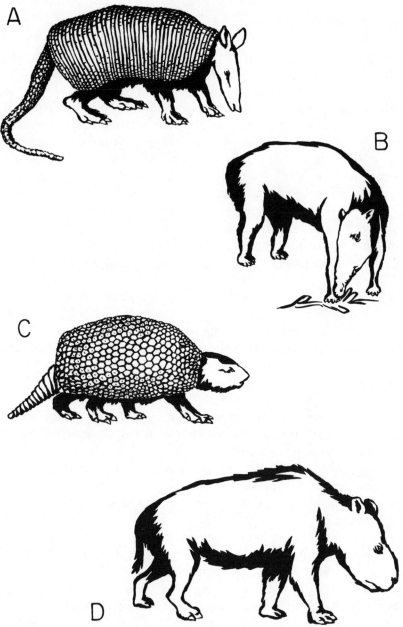

Fig. 30. Some early Miocene (Santacrucian) mammals: *A*, restoration of *Stegotherium*, an ant-eating armadillo; *B*, *Astrapotherium*, a tusked browsing ungulate, type of the order Astrapotheria; *C*, *Propalaeohoplophorus*, a glyptodont xenarthran; *D*, *Nesodon*, a toxodont notoungulate.

Fig. 31. Restoration of some early Miocene (Santacrucian) mammals, continued from figure 30: E, *Prothylacinus*, a carnivorous marsupial borhyaenid; F, *Hapalops*, a megalonychid ground sloth xenarthran; G, *Thoatherium*, a one-toed litoptern; H, *Neoreomys*, a caviomorph rodent.

from convincing. Rheas still survive although there have been placental carnivores in their communities for at least 2 million years. Most of the phororhacids became extinct before, only a straggler or two after, placental carnivores reached South America. Many of the borhyaenids that lived among these birds for many millions of years were highly predaceous, and there is little reason to think them incapable of killing a phororhacid. Moreover the phororhacids themselves were evidently predaceous, and they were more likely to kill than to be killed by mammals. Their staple food was probably small notoungulates and some rodents after those arrived.

Although the nominal type locality of the Friasian, like those of all the land mammal ages for South America, is in Argentina, this age there is inadequately defined and its fauna, or faunas, poorly known. A few mammals now considered to be of this age were collected by Carlos Ameghino and described by Florentino, who gave one of the local faunas the name "Friaséenne" in his French texts, for the Rio Frias, with more particular reference to fossils collected there by Santiago Roth. Roth made similar collections at various localities along the eastern front of the Andes in Patagonia, and considerably later (1930) Lucas Kraglievich re-studied specimens from Rio Frias, Rio Fenix, Laguna Blanca, and elsewhere and laid what basis there is for what is called the Friasian age and fauna, although it can hardly be said to have a single type locality or local fauna. What little is known of Friasian faunas in Argentina indicates a continuation of what I have here called phase 2 of the history, with mammals intermediate in evolutionary advance between those better known from the earlier Santacrucian and the later Chasicoan. Geologically, the Patagonian Friasian beds indicate that another, more emphatic uplift of the growing Andes was in progress and that the uplift was probably beginning to cast the rain shadow that made Patagonia a desert.

Much the best known fauna referred to the Friasian is the La Venta fauna of Colombia, collected by R. A. Stirton of the University of California and others in the 1940s but still not fully described. Although a few isolated finds older than this have been made in Colombia and Venezuela, this is the oldest fairly well-known mammalian fauna from northern South America. It represents for the most part an orderly advance of much the same groups as in the Patagonian Santacrucian, demonstrating that at this time there was a thoroughly distinctive South American mammalian fauna and that it occurred with only local geographic differences both in the far south and in the far north of that continent. The last surviving known condylarth, *Megadolodus,* is in the La Venta fauna, and so is the strange interathere *Miocochilius* briefly discussed in chapter 10.

Perhaps the most interesting element in the La Venta fauna is that it includes at least three and probably four species of monkeys referred by Stirton to three genera, one, *Homunculus,* first known from the Santacrucian of Patagonia. Colombia was tropical then, as it is now, and this region must have been partly forested although some of the other mammals indicate the presence also of savannahs. The La Venta formation was deposited by streams of the Magdalena River drainage already established as the major drainage system of what is now Colombia. Besides mammals the La Venta fauna includes many fishes, some aquatic snakes, and highly varied crocodilians.

After the Santacrucian the main sedimentation forming deposits east of the Andes in which the remains of mammals were buried moved northward. Along the foot of the Andes, such deposits extended into northern Patagonia in Friasian time. In the next age, the Chasicoan named for a site in southern Buenos Aires Province, the sedimentation began to extend over the vast plain that is now the pampas region of Argentina. Mammals of this age have been found at several localities, the others even farther north than Chasicó. The type fauna represents another advance in phase 2 faunas, without any striking novelties. Knowledge of this age and its faunas seems to require both restudy and further collecting.

The next land mammal age, the Huayquerian, begins to usher in the first forerunners of phase 3, or the Great American Interchange, and discussion of it is deferred for a couple of chapters.

References

Hirschfeld, S. E., and L. G. Marshall. 1976. Revised faunal list of the La Venta fauna (Friasian—Miocene) of Colombia, South America. *Journal of Paleontology,* 50: 433–436.

Hoffstetter, R. 1974. El origen de los Caviomorpha y el problema de los Hystricognathi (Rodentia). *I. Congreso Argentino de Paleontología y Bioestratigrafía*, preprint, 27 pages.

———. 1976. Introduction au Deseadien de Bolivie. *Paleovertebrata*, 7-III: 1–14.

———. 1977. Phylogénie des Primates. *Bulletin et Mémoires, Societé d'Anthropologie de Paris*, 4: 327–346.

Lavocat, R. 1974. What is an hystricomorph? *Symposia of the Zoological Society of London*, no. 34, pp. 7–20.

Pascual, R., and O. E. Odreman Rivas. 1971. Evolución de las comunidades de los vertebrados del Terciario Argentino: Los aspectos paleozoogeográficos y paleoclimáticos relacionados. *Ameghiniana*, 7: 373–412.

Simpson, G. G. 1974. Chairman's introduction: Taxonomy. *Symposia of the Zoological Society of London*, no. 34, pp. 1–5 (introduction to discussion of the origin and classification of "hystricomorph" rodents by Lavocat and Wood).

Szalay, F. S. 1976. Systematics of the Omomyidae (Tarsiiformes, Primates) taxonomy, phylogeny, and adaptations. *Bulletin of the American Museum of Natural History*, 156: 159–449 (includes discussion of origin of South American primates).

Wood, A. E. 1974. The evolution of the Old World and New World hystricomorphs. *Symposia of the Zoological Society of London* no. 34, pp. 21–60.

See also reference to Scott 1932, given after chapter 2. Unfortunately there is no reliable post-Ameghinian review or revision of the Argentinian Deseadan.

CHAPTER 12

Old Native Rodents

By old native rodents I mean the group here called Caviomorpha, the descendants of some early rodent stock that reached South America overseas from either Africa or North America before the early Oligocene. As noted in the preceding chapter they first appear in the known record in the Deseadan, just after the Mustersan-Deseadan hiatus in that record. The ancestral stock probably reached South America during the time represented by that gap in present knowledge.

The classification of these rodents here adopted follows Wood and Patterson (cited at the end of this chapter) and Patterson and Pascual (previously cited) as summarized in chapter 4. Four superfamilies are recognized, and six families spread among all four superfamilies were already present among the earliest known South American rodents. That arrangement may give an exaggerated impression of the divergence that had already occurred. In fact most of the Deseadan rodents were similar, and their dispersion into separate families and superfamilies is in considerable part due to the more pronounced differences among their descendants. With the exceptions noted, the following features characterize these Deseadan rodents:

Dental formula reduced to $\dfrac{1 \cdot 0 \cdot 1 \cdot 3}{1 \cdot 0 \cdot 1 \cdot 3}$

Cheek teeth (premolars and molars) low-crowned (brachydont) or high-crowned but rooted (hypsodont) and in only one genus (*Scotamus*) continuously growing (hypselodont)

Molars, when unworn, with four transverse crests or a relatively simple derivative of such a pattern (but this has been questioned)

153

Size generally small to minute

Skull hystricomorphous except possibly in the most primitive known genus, *Platypittamys*

Lower jaw hystricognathous

The terms "hystricomorphous" and "hystricognathous" are formidable, but they can be explained quite simply and they designate functional and anatomical characteristics that are both interesting and important in a number of different ways. For example, one question on which these characteristics have a bearing is the geographical one of whether the caviomorph ancestry came from North America or from Africa. That was briefly summarized in the preceding chapter and will here be mentioned again in this different context.

Let us first understand hystricomorphy. In all mammals there is a powerful muscle called the masseter, a term derived from the Greek word for "chewer." It is involved in chewing, biting, and in rodents also in gnawing. In primitive mammals it is attached to the skull along the cheekbone (zygoma), an arrangement that happens still to be present in ourselves. (You can feel the masseter if you put your fingers on your cheek and clench your jaws.) That arrangement was also present in the most primitive rodents, especially in the Eocene epoch. It is preserved in only one living rodent, the sewellel or mountain beaver (not related to the true beaver beyond the fact that both are rodents). In all other living rodents and most of the fossil rodents after the Eocene the arrangement has become more specialized by the masseter's attachment farther forward on the skull. However it occurred, this change had a functional result related to fore-and-aft motion of the lower jaw in gnawing and chewing. The change was brought about by quite different anatomical arrangements in different groups of rodents.

In the caviomorph rodents and some others this functional specialization occurred in what is an extremely peculiar way compared with most mammals. The masseter muscle is compound, and a powerful part of it is attached to the side of the facial part of the skull in front of the eye socket and cheekbone. Another part of the masseter complex remains attached in a more posterior posi-

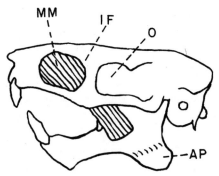

Fig. 32. Somewhat generalized diagram of the skull, jaw, and one of the jaw muscles of a caviomorph rodent. *AP,* the angular process of the lower jaw (the mandible or dentary) here deflected outward (toward the reader). IF, rim of the large infraorbital foramen, an opening in the anterior wall of the orbit. *MM,* the massiter medialis muscle at its origin on the side of the face; from here it passes through the infraorbital foramen and is inserted on the lateral side of the lower jaw (other muscles of the masseter complex are not shown in this diagram). *O,* orbit or eye socket; the posterior opening of the infraorbital foramen is in the anterior part of the orbit.

tion on the cheekbone. Instead of going directly to the lower jaw, the division of the masseter attached to the facial part of the skull goes first through a large opening in the anterior wall of the eye socket and then down to the lower jaw. All mammals have an opening, the infraorbital foramen, in that position, but except for the caviomorphs and some other rodents it is very small. A branch of the facial nerve goes through it (as is true of us), but with those exceptions no muscle does.

That peculiarity was noticed by early anatomists especially in the Old World (African, Mediterranean, and southern Asiatic) porcupines of the genus *Hystrix,* which was their name in Latin. This arrangement of the masseter muscle came to be known anatomically as hystricomorph, "shaped as in *Hystrix.*" Classifiers long supposed that so unusual an arrangement probably evolved only once and therefore that all rodents possessing it had one origin and constituted a natural group which was called Hystricomorpha. However there is now a clear consensus among specialists studying rodents that a number of the rodents anatomically hystricomorph developed that condition independently of the ancestors of *Hystrix* and its closer allies. Therefore those anatomically hystricomorph rodents do not correctly belong to the group called Hystricomorpha in a classification. The debate about the geographic origin of the Caviomorpha mentioned in the last chapter can therefore be partially restated. Those authorities who believe that the caviomorph ancestry came from North America suggest that the caviomorphs are another group of rodents that independently acquired anatomical hystricomorphy. Those who believe in an African origin suggest that the Caviomorpha did inherit anatomical hystricomorphy from ancestral Old World Hystricomorpha.

Although I have simplified this rather complicated matter as far as possible, I must go on to another crucial complication. The attachment of the masseter muscle to the lower jaw normally occurs, as it does in us, on the outer side of the posterior part of the jaw. Sometimes, as in us, the area of attachment is simply a flattish area on the jaw, not otherwise particularly distinctive. In most mammals, however, including the rodents, it also involves a sort of backward projection of the lower part of the jaw, an angular process so called in comparative anatomy. Usually this angular process lies in the same vertical plane as other parts of the jaw and its row of teeth. That is the primitive condition for placental mammals in general and for rodents in particular. However, in *Hystrix* and a number of other rodents the angular process projects strongly outward (laterally) and that makes a functional difference in the action of the masseter muscle. This is called hystricognathy, "*Hystrix*-like jawedness." Most hystricognathous rodents are also hystricomorphous, and so with one possible exception are all Caviomorpha. As mentioned above, *Platypittamys* may not be fully hystricomorphous. That is because it seems to have a relatively small infraorbital foramen and part of the masseter may not have passed through that opening. However, that may be merely apparent, because the only known specimens are crushed flat and one cannot be sure that a small part, at least, of the masseter did not go through the foramen as it does in all other known Caviomorpha. (A. E. Wood, who has a somewhat playful attitude toward names, gave the name *Platypittamys,* more or less meaning "pancake rodent," because the specimens were flattened by pressure from the entombing rocks; incidentally, those specimens were found in the same ancient crater as *Scarrittia,* mentioned in chapter 10.)

Now some students, especially Lavocat, an eminent French specialist on fossil rodents, have argued that although hystricomorphy has evolved independently several times, hystricognathy combined with hystricomorphy has not and that when these two occur together the rodents in question had a common ancestry. There is one still extant group, the so-called mole rats (which are neither moles nor rats), that is hystricognathous but not hystricomorphous. Lavocat explains that by postulating that the mole rats had a not exactly known hystricomorphous ancestry and later lost that characteristic. This concept of the unity of groups both hystricomorphous and hystricognathous has of course become part of the argument for African origin of the Caviomorpha. However, as Wood, also an eminent authority on fossil rodents, and others have pointed out, there are hystricomorphous and hystricognathous rodents in which the two conditions do not both occur. Both conditions are believed by these students to have evolved independently more than once; therefore, they see no reason why the combination could not have arisen independently in the relevant South American and African rodents. Moreover, there are North American Eocene rodents that could well have given rise to the Caviomorpha which then may have evolved in parallel with, not by descent from, African rodents that arose from similar and related more primitive Eocene forms in the Old World.

When viewed more broadly, even such details as have just been summarized here take on general significance as they bear on and exemplify matters of procedure and logic in problems of classification, functional anatomy, evolutionary descent, past geography, present distributions of animals, and several other subjects that need not be further discussed at this point.

The same six families of Caviomorpha that enter the record in the Deseadan early Oligocene were still present in the Santacrucian early Miocene. They had become more distinct from each other and more clearly related to later and still living caviomorph families. Five of the six Deseadan-Santacrucian families are in fact still extant, and their diverse characteristics and ecological roles can be most clearly put in terms of these numerous and for the most part still thriving present representatives.

One family, that of the New World porcupines (Erethizontidae) is familiar to all North Americans because in the Pleistocene it spread to North America and is still widely present here. In South America there are three surviving genera, one with many species, mostly less spiny than the North American porcupine. All porcupines are at least partly arboreal, and they variously eat fruit, nuts, leaves, and bark.

Surviving members of the Chinchillidae, still confined to South America, include not only the chinchillas but also the closely similar but somewhat larger vizcachas. They are all terrestrial, fairly large-eared, running and leaping animals that look and act rather like long-tailed rabbits. All are becoming rare, and after so many millions of years the family may be near extinction, at least as wild animals. The chinchillas have been killed off for their fur but are also raised in captivity for that purpose. The vizcachas are pursued for food and because they are considered pests if at all numerous.

The living pacas and agoutis are three genera of the similar and sometimes united families Dasyproctidae and Cuniculidae, widespread in South America and in tropical North America. They are fair-sized animals, up to about 10 kilograms (22 pounds) in weight.

Fig. 33. Restoration of *Neoreomys*, an early Miocene (Santacrucian) member of the caviomorph family Dasyproctidae.

They have extraordinarily long hindfeet and have a rapid, bounding run. They resemble the late notoungulate hegetotheres in general adaptive type, a fact with a possible bearing on the extinction of the hegetotheres. The meat of pacas and agoutis is delicious, which makes them eagerly hunted.

The family Octodontidae takes its name from the living genus *Octodon,* "eight-tooth," so called not from the number of its teeth but because a cross section of its continuously growing molars is like the numeral 8. The most primitive known caviomorph, *Platypittamys,* is now referred to this family, but its low-crowned teeth had not yet taken on the 8-form. In the Santacrucian the genus *Acaremys* did have high-crowned molars like a figure 8 when worn. The family is now confined to southern South America. There are five somewhat diverse living genera with numerous local popular names little known outside South America. The species of *Octodon* itself are known as degus. This and all but one other of the living genera look like heavyset rats with disproportionately large heads. All are skillful diggers, and one genus, *Ctenomys,* with numerous species, spends most of its time underground. These animals look and act very much like North American pocket gophers and are of about the same size but lack the

Fig. 34. Restoration of *Platypittamys,* an early Oligocene (Deseadan) member of the caviomorph family Octodontidae.

cheek pouches of the gophers. They are called tucu-tucus because they make a sound like tucu-tucu; it is an eerie sensation to hear this sound coming from underground below one's feet.

Finally among all these families that have survived as such for about 35 million years there are the Echimyidae, the most varied and individually abundant of all the living Caviomorpha. They occur widely in South America and tropical North America and have many native names. All of them look more or less like rats, and many, but not all, have short, flexible spines in their pelts so that they are often known as spiny rats. Although some of them have molars with slightly high crowns, these teeth have roots even in the Recent species, when many caviomorphs have evolved continuously growing teeth. At some time in the complex history of the family they reached the West Indies by sweepstakes dispersal and evolved into distinct genera on Puerto Rico, Hispaniola, and Cuba. On Hispaniola, at least, they were apparently still living when Europeans reached that island (Haiti and Dominica), but all the island genera are now extinct.

The only known South American Deseadan and later family of caviomorph rodents unknown after the Friasian and thus nominally extinct may be extinct in name only. Two still extant families first known in the Friasian may have been descendants of unknown or unrecognized earlier members of the Deseadan-to-Friasian Eocardiidae. The two surviving families here concerned are both well knwn: the Caviidae and the Hydrochoeridae. The typical genus of the Caviidae is *Cavia,* the common "guinea pig," and there are three other genera of this family usually called guinea pigs or cavies although they have other local vernacular names. It is an old joke that guinea pigs are so called because they do not come from Guinea and are not pigs. It has been conjectured that they were called guinea pigs because they looked like the young of true wild pigs known from Guinea in Africa, or because they were brought to England by ships returning from South America after a voyage in the Guinea, that is, the slave, trade, or because the name Guinea was simply a sort of Shangri-La name for any place distant and unknown—none of which is very convincing. It is better to call these animals cavies, but the origin of that name also is uncertain.

Everyone knows that guinea pigs or cavies are dumpy little things with relatively big heads and no visible tails. They used to be used extensively as laboratory animals, and "guinea pig" has come to be a figure of speech for any animal or person used in experiments, but the cavies themselves are rarely so used now. They are pleasant pets and they are among the few animals that were first domesticated by American Indians, in their case raised as food.

A superficially quite different member of the cavy family is the mara or Patagonian hare, which is Patagonian but is not a hare. It has also been called the Patagonian cavy, but it does not look or act like the guinea pig cavies. It is large, has a more pointed nose, longer ears, and longer limbs, and runs more rapidly and indeed with a more harelike gait. Like the cavies and in fact practically all the Caviomorpha, it is good to eat.

Both the cavies and the mara have very high-crowned (hyp- see p. 153 selodont) cheek teeth, with simple bilobed or trilobed patterns when worn.

The other family first known in the Friasian and possibly derived from earlier Eocardiidae is the Hydrochoeridae, the one species of living capybaras and their more numerous extinct relatives. The Recent species, which ranges from eastern Panama through tropical South America, is the largest living rodent, with a length of about 1.3 meters (about 4¼ feet), a height of about 50 centimeters (about 20 inches), and a weight of about 50 kilograms (about 110 pounds). They have heavy, large heads, blunt noses, small ears, stubby tails, and partially webbed feet. They are semiaquatic and live only in the vicinity of permanent water. Some of their extinct relatives evidently had different habits. For example, the Pliocene *Protohydrochoerus* had longer legs and seems to have been a running animal adapted for life on the open pampa.

Like cavies, capybaras have constantly growing (hypselodont) teeth, and in the earliest members of the Hydrochoeridae the cheek teeth—one premolar and three molars in each jaw—

Fig. 35. Restoration of *Protohydrochoerus,* a probably cursorial member of the caviomorph family Hydrochoeridae.

resembled those of some Caviidae, but in later, more specialized members the lower premolar and the last upper molar became greatly complicated, the last upper molar especially becoming enormously large and with as many as nineteen transverse plates of enamel that are separated by cementum and wear into grinding ridges.

During the Great American Interchange, later to be discussed more explicitly, capybaras spread far into North America and are found as fossils in the southern United States, notably in Florida, Texas, and Arizona. Some of the fossil species, in both North and South America, were even larger than the living species.

The largest known rodent of all may not have been a capybara but was probably a member of a distinct family, Dinomyidae, that also is known first from the Miocene Friasian and includes just one still living species. The living animal is called a false paca or pacarana. It does considerably resemble a paca, even to the presence of rows of white spots on its sides, but it even more resembles a tremendously overgrown cavy, almost as large as a small bear but not as large as the living capybara. Its largest known relative and possibly the largest rodent that ever lived was a late Pleistocene species from Argentina called *Telicomys gigantissimus.* Although he didn't say so, L. Kraglievich, the Argentine paleontologist who coined the name *Telicomys,* evidently used the Greek roots in a sense that can be colloquially put as more or less "the

Fig. 36. *Dinomys,* the only living member of the family Dimomyidae.

rodent to end all rodents." This species, "most gigantic," was
nearly as large as a rhinoceros. Its smaller but still large living
relative typifies the genus *Dinomys,* which means "terrible rodent." As to their being terrible, those who know them call them
"good-natured and peaceful," so we can take it that they are terrible only in the sense of being terribly big compared to a mouse.
(Some dinosaurs, "terrible reptiles," were probably also good-
natured as far as we can judge.)

The pacaranas and also the true pacas, the fossil history of which
is not known, probably evolved from a common ancestry with, or
were an early offshoot of, the agouti family, Dasyproctidae.

In order to round out this summary of the Caviomorpha some
mention may be made of the families Heptaxodontidae and Capromyidae, omitted from the classification in chapter 4 and from
the previous part of this chapter because according to the present
usage they are not known ever to have occurred as such in South
America. The Heptaxodontidae comprise six or seven genera
known from Jamaica, Hispaniola, Puerto Rico, Saint Martin, and
Anguilla in the Antilles. The teeth and bones of these animals
resemble those of the Dinomyidae, and it is probable that they
represent the outcome of evolution on the various islands from a
waif stock originally dinomyid in South America. They have often
been referred to or confused with the Dinomyidae but do seem to
represent a limited radiation on the various islands from a single
origin. These animals are now all extinct, but their known remains

are geologically Recent and in some instances are found in what seem to be kitchen middens. Some species surely were still extant when Indians reached the islands and possibly when Europeans did so.

The Capromyidae of present usage are also confined to the Antilles and include three known extinct genera and four still living. The living genera are on Cuba, Jamaica, Hispaniola, and the Bahamas; the extinct ones lived on Hispaniola, Puerto Rico, and the Virgin Islands. The living animals are known collectively as hutias; the *h* in this originally Indian name is not silent and the name can be written *jutía* in Spanish. Hutias look like overgrown rats, despite which they are largely hunted for food and have poor chances of survival among the dense and hungry human populations of the islands.

The hutias resemble and seem to be related in some degree to the nutria or coypu, originally and still of South America but now escaped from fur farms and become pests in parts of North America and Europe. Coypus are known as fossils in Argentina from the late Pliocene Chapadmalalan. The living animals are aquatic and feed mainly on water plants, while the hutias are terrestrial and semiarboreal. There are other anatomical distinctions, one of the most interesting being that the female coypus have six pairs of mammae situated so far up on the sides that the young can suckle while mama is swimming. Hutias have two pairs in the usual position.

The hutias and coypus are often placed in the same family, usually as Capromyidae and sometimes as subfamilies of the Echimyidae. It seems probable that they evolved separately from early echimyids, and they are here put in separate families, the coypus as Myocastoridae, confined to South America, and the hutias as Capromyidae, confined to the Antilles.

Looking back over the whole history of the caviomorphs, we see that in the early Oligocene, when they first appeared in the now known fossil record, they had advanced markedly beyond the primitive placental mammal stage. They had acquired not only the basic specializations of rodents in general but also further specializations of their own, partly shared with some Eocene rodents known from North America and with some known from the Oligocene and later in Eurasia and Africa. They had also diversified in South America into six adaptive groups symbolized in classification as families. Definitely five and probably all of those families have descendants still living in the present fauna of South America. In the course of their history these groups became more highly specialized and also more diversified, giving rise to new adaptive groups as high as the family level in classification. From six at the beginning of the known record, the number of families rose to nine in the early Pliocene, ten in the late Pliocene and early Pleistocene, and eleven in the Recent. Two additional families evolved in the Antilles, and both lived into the geological epoch Recent or Holocene, although one has become extinct, probably in the sixteenth century as centuries are counted in human history.

Throughout their history in South America the caviomorph rodents, basically herbivorous although a few vary the diet with a bit of animal food, lived in the same communities with herbivorous ungulates, especially notoungulates before the Pleistocene. Some adaptive evolutionary trends occurred similarly in both groups, although not in all members of either one. In some lineages of caviomorphs and of notoungulates there was a trend toward larger individual size. There were also trends in both for the grinding teeth to become higher-crowned and eventually to grow continuously throughout life. In the course of that change both groups evolved molars with grinding ridges of enamel, although the patterns were very different in the two groups. In both, the grinding teeth also tended to develop cementum, so that the wearing surfaces involved three tissues of different hardness: enamel hardest, dentine, and cementum softest.

The notoungulates reached their acme in the early Oligocene. Thereafter, they did become more specialized, with surviving families increasingly divergent, but fewer families survived. From ten families of notoungulates in the Oligocene the number was reduced to six in the Miocene and three in the Pliocene and Pleistocene. All are now extinct. That decline closely follows the opposite trend among the caviomorph rodents. The latter reached an acme in the Pliocene with individuals ranging from minute to gigantic and including specialized groups able to occupy a great number of ecological niches, from waters to treetops and with diverse special food habits. It is true that some of the most extreme types of specialization among the Pliocene caviomorphs did die out, but all the Pliocene families survive, several in large numbers of species and of individuals. It is speculation, but reasonable speculation, that the decline of the notoungulates, and of other old native ungulates, and the rise of the old native rodents were related phenomena, that the rodents increasingly adapted to some aspects of ecological niches previously utilized by ungulates.

References

Fields, R. W. 1957. Hystricomorph rodents from the late Miocene of Colombia, South America. *University of California Publications in Geological Sciences,* 32: 273–404.

Scott, W. B. 1905. Glires [of the Santa Cruz beds]. *Reports of the Princeton University Expeditions to Patagonia,* 5: 384–489.

Walker, E. P.; F. Warnick; S. E. Hamlet; K. I. Lange; M. A. Davis; H. E. Uible; and P. F. Wright. 1975. *Mammals of the world.* 3d ed., rev. J. R. Paradiso. Baltimore and London: Johns Hopkins University Press. (Living Caviomorpha are described, not under that name, and each genus is illustrated in 2: 1009–1067.)

Wood, A. E., and B. Patterson. 1959. The rodents of the Deseadan Oligocene of Patagonia and the beginnings of South American rodent evolution. *Bulletin of the Museum of Comparative Zoology,* 120: 281–428.

CHAPTER 13

Primates

The fossil record of the order Primates in South America is exceedingly poor. Few specimens have been found, and there is some disagreement about what they mean in relation to the history and classification of the many Recent monkeys in South America.

As mentioned in chapter 11, the oldest primate now known from South America is *Branisella* from the early Oligocene, Deseadan, of Bolivia. It is known from a single specimen, a fragment of an upper jaw with the broken bases or roots of two premolars and the crowns of the last premolar and first two molars. One might expect, or even assume, that this early genus would be close to the ancestry of the large South American monkey family or superfamily, Cebidae or Ceboidea. Hoffstetter, who described and named the specimen in 1969, did not exclude that possibility but at first considered *Branisella* as so primitive that he was not sure whether it was yet a "real monkey" ("un singe vrai" in his words). Philip Hershkovitz, whose views are sometimes quite idiosyncratic, insisted in 1970 that *Branisella* "was neither platyrrhine nor ancestral to platyrrhines." Platyrrhines, meaning "flat noses," is used in some classifications as a name to include all the living South American monkeys and their fossil allies. Hershkovitz's remark means that in his opinion *Branisella* had an entirely different origin from the, or the other, South American monkeys as a group. Hoffstetter in 1977 riposted by putting *Branisella* in the Ceboidea, adding (in French) that "*Branisella* may represent . . . the ancestral morphotype of the Ceboidea."

In any case *Branisella* is certainly a primate, and I have tentatively put it in the Cebidae.

The next younger fossil primates are from the approximately late Oligocene Colhuehuapian of Argentina. One was described by J. L. Kraglievich (the son of L. Kraglievich), who named it *Dolichocebus* and tentatively placed it in the marmoset family (or subfamily) Callithricidae to which no other fossils have been referred. Hershkovitz puts it in a supposedly quite distinct family Homunculidae, in his opinion not ancestral or closely allied to either Cebidae or Callithricidae. Carlos Rusconi identified another Colhuehuapian primate as in the genus *Homunculus* ("little man"), a genus otherwise known only from the somewhat later Santacrucian. Again Hershkovitz disagrees. He has renamed this primate as *Tremacebus,* meaning a *"Cebus*-like monkey with a hole [in the wall of its eye socket]." He puts this genus in the Cebidae, where most other researchers still put *Homunculus* and also *Dolichocebus.*

Homunculus was originally described from the Santacrucian by Ameghino, who named a distinct primate family, Homunculidae, for it. W. K. Gregory once strangely classified it as a lemuroid, but as far as I know everyone else after Ameghino has put it in the

Fig. 37. Reconstruction of skull and jaw (essentially after Rusconi) and restoration of head of a late Oligocene or early Miocene ceboid monkey, one of the earliest for which the skull is known, put in the early Miocene (Santacrucian) genus *Homunculus* by Rusconi but moved to a distinct genus *Tremacebus* by Hershkovitz.

Cebidae except for Hershkovitz, who resurrected Ameghino's Homunculidae as a family quite independent of the Cebidae and included *Dolichocebus* in it, as noted above.

Except for some Brazilian late Pleistocene or quite likely geologically Recent specimens belonging to living species, the only other known fossil primates from South America are from the middle Miocene Friasian La Venta fauna of Colombia. Everyone, even Hershkovitz, refers these to the family Cebidae, along with most of the living South American primates, but they differ as to relationships within that family. Stirton first described these specimens in three genera: *Homunculus,* again, which Stirton believed related to the howler monkeys (subfamily Alouattinae), *Cebupithecia,* new with Stirton and by him believed related to the saki monkeys (subfamily Pitheciinae), and *Neosaimiri,* also new and believed related to the squirrel monkeys (subfamily Saimiriinae). Hershkovitz believed that Stirton's Friasian *Homunculus* is not related to true, Santacrucian *Homunculus* or to the howlers, courteously renamed it *Stirtonia,* and gave it its own subfamily, Stirtoniinae, in the family Cebidae. Oddly enough, Hershkovitz agrees with Stirton that *Neosaimiri* is related to *Saimiri,* the living squirrel monkey.

Cebupithecia is known from a nearly complete skull and lower jaw, much of the fore and hind limbs, and a number of vertebrae, including part of the tail, which apparently was not prehensile. It would be possible to make a reasonable reconstruction of the skeleton of this genus, but as far as I know that has not been done. Whatever one may think about its close relationships, the animal may have looked much like a saki monkey. However, as with some other South American monkeys, the appearance of sakis in life depends largely on the length and arrangement of their hair and the color of their faces, things that cannot be restored or even imagined from the bones of an extinct genus.

Neosaimiri Stirton and *Homunculus* of Stirton but *Stirtonia* of Hershkovitz are known each from a nearly complete lower jaw, sufficient to identify genera and species but otherwise meaningful only by interpretation of minor details.

So much for the fossil record, remarkably incomplete for a

group of animals undoubtedly abundant and varied throughout most of the history of South American mammals. The reasons for this paucity can be conjectured. These monkeys are now and probably have been from their start highly arboreal animals, and arboreal species are least likely to have their remains buried and preserved as fossils. They are now, and again probably have always been, most abundant in tropical or subtropical forests. Such regions are still largely forested, are most difficult to work in, and have been least throughly explored for fossils. Moreover, enormous areas of these forested regions are without exposures of rocks of suitable ages and likely to contain fossil mammals.

Let us then approach the subject from two other directions: first, what can be conjectured about the origins of South American primates from what is known about primitive and ancient primates elsewhere; second, what can be learned from the results of their history, that is, the primates of South American origin still alive.

In view of the scanty remains of South American primates and those from some other parts of the world, it is surprising that remains of very ancient, Paleocene and Eocene, primates are abundant in North America and Europe. These were already highly varied, but they can be fairly well sorted out into three groups. One is a group of families, four in recent classifications, that arose practically at the base of the whole primate family tree and each of which early evolved somewhat superficial but clearly divergent specializations. All were extinct by the end of the Eocene. They need not concern us further here because it is unlikely that any, beyond perhaps the very earliest and least specialized, were in or near any mainstream or branch of later primate history or ancestral to such a branch.

The two other early and primitive groups of primates, each now usually classified as a single family, appear in the record around the beginning of the Eocene, when they were common in both America and Europe, then essentially parts of the same continent. Some of them lingered on into the Oligocene and one even into the Miocene, but they are rare after the Eocene. North America and Europe began to drift apart around the end of the early

Eocene, and thereafter the early primates evolved independently on the two continents but within the two early Eocene families.

One of those families is the Adapidae, based on the middle Eocene genus *Adapis,* first described and named by Cuvier in 1821 on the basis of specimens found in gypsum quarries on the Butte de Montmartre in Paris. Cuvier thought that those incomplete remains belonged to some ungulate, and it wasn't until around the last quarter of the nineteenth century that it was generally realized that *Adapis* was a primate. It is interesting that Ameghino made the opposite error: he classified a number of early ungulates as "Prosimiae," that is, primitive primates. The best known adapid is *Notharctus* from the North American middle Eocene. As the continents drifted apart, so did the evolution of their mammals diverge, and *Adapis* and *Notharctus* differed enough so that some classifications put them in separate but obviously closely related families. In time it came to be suspected that the Adapidae were related to the living lemurs of Madagascar, and this was established beyond serious question by W. K. Gregory in a large monograph on *Notharctus* published in 1920.

The other early family here under consideration is now usually called Omomyidae, for the genus *Omomys* named by the pioneer North American paleontologist, Joseph Leidy in 1869. It was the first American fossil primate to be discovered. (*Notharctus,* named by Leidy in 1870, was the second.) Leidy had only part of a lower jaw and did not recognize *Omomys* as a primate. The Greek roots of its name mean "shoulder mouse," which is not at all clear. Neither is the fact that the word roots of *Adapis* may mean more or less "similar to a bull" or may mean "rabbit" and that those of *Notharctus* do mean "fake bear"—Leidy thought at first it was a raccoon. It is well to remember that these truly brilliant early scientists were dealing with bits and pieces of creatures hitherto completely unknown, and also that the scientific names of animals do not have to mean anything but are just the given names of animals known from particular specimens.

A skull of an omomyid was found in 1881 and was soon recognized to be related to the tarsiers living in the Philippines and

Indonesia. It was found by J. L. Wortman in the Bighorn Basin of Wyoming, and it was Edward Drinker Cope, the great nineteenth-century North American paleontologist, who spotted its relationship to the tarsiers. Many other fossils of this family are now known, and the anatomy and classification of members of the family have now been well worked out, for the North American forms most recently and completely by Szalay in 1976. Knowledge is not even now quite as good for the Omomyidae as for the Adapidae.

Thus we have two large families in the early Cenozoic, one related to the living lemurs and one to the living tarsiers. The two living groups are still relatively primitive; that is, each family, genus, and species has its own special characters, but these animals retain overall characters present in the Eocene primates and lost in the living monkeys, apes, and men. They are often referred to as prosimians, "premonkeys."

The living prosimians can be divided into two distinct groups. One, markedly diverse but all rather certainly descendants from a single ancestry, includes the lemurs and their kin, broadly speaking, and the lorises and theirs, also broadly speaking. The whole complex is usually divided into eight or more families, but the details need not concern us here. The lemurs are now confined to Madagascar, and although a number of extinct forms have been found there those are all of late Pleistocene or Recent Age. Older fossil lemurs are unknown except in the form of the Adapidae. The lorises and their kin such as the galagos or bush babies live in Africa and southern Asia. (That the dwarf lemur of Madagascar is sometimes considered closer to the lorises than to the other lemurs is one of the complications that need not delay us here.) Early Miocene forerunners of these animals have been found in Africa and somewhat later ones in southern Asia.

By the 1920s there was a strong consensus that both the Old World and the New World monkeys evolved from prosimians either lemuroid or tarsioid, belonging either to early Adapidae or early Omomyidae in the terms used here. There was no general agreement as to which group was the ancestral one. For example, two eminent authorities of that time carried on a lively controversy, the North American W. K. Gregory arguing for lemuroid ancestry and the British Frederic Wood Jones for tarsioid ancestry. Now, a half-century later, it is depressing to have to say that although Gregory and Wood Jones are gone the controversy is not. Among able present-day paleontologists Philip Gingerich, for instance, argues strongly for lemuroid ancestry. Hoffstetter and Szalay, by no means in agreement on other points, hold with some others just as strongly to the view that the ancestry was tarsioid.

No poll has been taken, but the consensus now probably favors the tarsioid hypothesis. However, scientific controversies cannot be settled by polls, only by evidence that can either confirm or falsify a hypothesis. In this case evidence that could be really conclusive in either direction simply does not exist at present. No fossils that can be considered intermediate between either lemuroids or tarsioids and either the New World or the Old World monkeys or definitely ancestral to one or both of the latter groups have yet been found. On both sides of the present Atlantic the oldest known monkeys, simians as successors to prosimians, occur in the Oligocene. The Eocene ancestors of the New World monkeys almost certainly occurred either in North America or in Africa but are not definitely known in either. If they were in North America, that was most likely in what is now Central America, and the Eocene mammals of that region are almost unknown as yet. In Africa no primates at all are known before the Oligocene, but there are few known Paleocene or Eocene African mammals of any sort. What we need seems to be less debate and more discovery.

The New World and Old World monkeys are distinct, natural groups each with anatomical characters unlike the other. From the Oligocene, at least, onward they evolved separately, the New World monkeys radiating primarily in South America, the Old World monkeys perhaps primarily in Africa but probably in a broader region involving also much of southern Eurasia. It is probable that the New and Old World monkeys had a common ancestry somewhere before those geographically separate radiations began. Szalay has suggested that the common ancestry may in fact have been the South American monkeys, which had North American tarsioid (omomyid) ancestors, but there is little support for this view at present. As mentioned in chapter 11, Hoffstetter and some others maintain that the common ancestry was in the earliest African monkeys, which had a probably European but possibly African tarsioid (here, too, omomyid) ancestry. There is a third possibility that seems to me at least as probable but that also lacks critical evidence at present. This is that the common ancestry was a particular subgroup of omomyids, probably, or adapids, possibly, not yet known or in any case identified, the same subgroup present in both what is now North America and what is now Europe before those regions were separated. Then that one ancestral subgroup, which would not itself belong among either of the two separate groups of monkeys, could have given rise to each of the latter separately in areas then or soon geographically distinct. This hypothesis, too, cannot be adequately tested on evidence now available.

Still other hypotheses can be imagined, but only one more will be briefly mentioned. It has been suggested, although not very strongly espoused, that monkeys, primates of simian grade, arose over a considerable area of what is now South America and Africa when those two were united. The original population was then divided when the continents drifted apart, and its descendants evolved independently on the two. Although this hypothesis might conform with one school of biogeography, it is too improbable to be seriously supported. There is good evidence that the separation of South America and Africa occurred before prosimian primates, and even longer before simian primates, existed.

There is one further complication due to Hoffstetter. He maintains that two of the Oligocene genera known from North Africa (*Apidium* and *Parapithecus*) evolved in Africa from the same ancestry as the South American monkeys and not directly from that of the (other) Old World monkeys. That of course fits in with Hoffstetter's view that the New World monkeys were derived from early African monkeys. However, Elwyn Simons, who has made much the most extensive and detailed study of the two genera here in question, flatly disagrees and classifies those genera as a subfamily in the large Old World monkey family Cercopithecidae.

So much for what is known or conjectured about possible origins of the South American monkeys. Hershkovitz, now the leading authority on the living, but, I venture to say, not the fossil, South American mammals, classifies the living South American monkeys in 3 families, 16 genera, and 42 species. Other students recognize only 2 families, or occasionally 1, but as many as 64 species, which is probably an exaggeration.

The most widely known New World monkeys outside of South America, at least, are the capuchins, several species of the genus *Cebus* for which the superfamily Ceboidea and family Cebidae are named. They used to be the organ-grinders' monkeys when there were organ-grinders. They are still zoo favorites and occasional pets, but they can be nuisances as pets—they are mischievous and they cannot be housebroken. They are among the least distinctive of South American monkeys in many ways, although the ends of their long tails tend to curl up and are somewhat prehensile and one species has a hornlike tuft of hair on each side of the forehead. The closely related squirrel monkeys of the genus *Saimiri* are smaller and have relatively large, hairy ears and white faces with black eyes, nose, and mouth. The occurrence of an ancestor or close relative in the Miocene has been mentioned.

The squirrel monkeys are sometimes called titis, but that name more distinctively applies to a different genus, *Callicebus,* more nearly related to the night monkeys or douroucoulis. Most monkeys are diurnal, as would seem prudent for active tree dwellers and branch swingers, but the douroucoulis, genus *Aotus,* are nocturnal. Their most obvious features are their relatively enormous, highly sensitive eyes, which give them adequate night vision.

Another group of South American monkeys including the ouakaris and sakis, typified by the saki genus *Pithecia,* is characterized by usually long, shaggy hair and in another genus of sakis by a rather chic topknot and spreading beard.

The largest South American monkeys, much larger than any known as fossils, and the ones most likely to impress travelers in the tropical forests are the howlers, genus *Alouatta.* The curious resemblance of the generic name to the French word for "lark," well known in a French children's song, is pure coincidence. *Alouatta* is a more or less phonetic spelling of a Carib Indian name of these monkeys in Cayenne (not Central America as sometimes stated). These big monkeys have heads and bodies up to a bit over 0.9 meter (about 3 feet) in length and tails about equally long. They may weigh as much as 9 kilograms (almost 20 pounds). They have noble beards and coarse but glossy hair which in different species or varieties may be a brownish yellow, a rich red, or a pitch black in color. They are best known for their communal howling, especially at dawn and near dusk, which may be heard for several kilometers and must be heard to be believed. Howlers were the first monkeys whose behavior was studied (by C. Ray Carpenter) in the wild at length and in a thoroughly scientific way.

That monkeys hang by their tails is one of the things that everyone knows and that are not true as generalizations. No Old World and few New World monkeys can or do hang by their tails, but howlers can and do when they think it advisable. So do spider monkeys, *Ateles,* also fairly large—up to about 6 kilograms (over 13 pounds). They are scrawny animals, not very attractive, but highly prized by many human South Americans as food. The woolly monkeys, *Lagothrix,* are about as large as the spider monkeys and are related to them. They also have prehensile tails and are evenly covered with short wool all over except on the bare, dark face. They are arboreal but come down to the ground more readily than most New World monkeys. Then they may walk upright on their hindlegs.

The smallest of all living monkeys are the marmosets and tamarins, generally classified in four genera with a rather uncertain number of species (Hershkovitz says fifteen, but there are many more supposed species in the literature). An adult pygmy marmoset, genus *Cebuella,* may weigh only about 70 grams (about 2½ ounces). Even the largest marmosets do not exceed weights of about 900 grams (about 2 pounds). All have very long, nonprehensile tails covered with short hair or plumed with long hair. Some are otherwise unremarkable, but some have grotesque topknots, mustaches, ear tufts, or beards.

These little monkeys have a distinct resemblance to each other and do not so nearly resemble most of the other South American monkeys. They also have a reduced dental formula:

$$\frac{2 \cdot 1 \cdot 3 \cdot 2}{2 \cdot 1 \cdot 3 \cdot 2}.$$

The other South American monkeys have a formula of

$$\frac{2 \cdot 1 \cdot 3 \cdot 3}{2 \cdot 1 \cdot 3 \cdot 3}.$$

In the Old World monkeys (as well as in apes and humans) it is

$$\frac{2 \cdot 1 \cdot 2 \cdot 3}{2 \cdot 1 \cdot 2 \cdot 3}.$$

Largely, although not entirely, because of this different dental formula the marmosets and tamarins are almost always put in a separate family Callithricidae, although one may question whether overall differences from the more diverse Cebidae warrant more than subfamily rank. No known fossil South American primates are certainly related to the marmosets and tamarins although the Colhuehuapian *Dolichocebus* may belong here.

There is one other South American genus, *Callimico,* sometimes given the book-name Goeldi's marmoset, that has been something of a nuisance to classifiers who insist on separating the Cebidae and the Callithricidae. *Callimico* closely resembles marmosets in most respects but has the dental formula of the Cebidae,

$$\frac{2 \cdot 1 \cdot 3 \cdot 3}{2 \cdot 1 \cdot 3 \cdot 3}.$$

It could equally well be placed as a subfamily either of the Cebidae or of the Callithricidae, but some classifiers cut this Gordian knot (or complicate it) by giving this one little species a family all to itself.

Although several groups of South American monkeys moved into Central America in the Pleistocene and are still there, none expanded beyond the tropical part of the northern continent. A single specimen found in Jamaica suggests that monkey waifs from the mainland reached that island at some time in the past and that offspring there evolved into something unlike any mainland monkeys, but it is still too poorly known for proper evaluation.

The Recent South American monkeys are the end terms of a long adaptive radiation on that continent into many niches which are nevertheless ecologically limited to primarily arboreal habitats and to mostly succulent vegetable foods. (Some of these monkeys do eat small animals when they can catch them.) The fossil record is poor, but it gives an approximate date, late Eocene, for the beginning of that radiation and also suggests that it included some side branches outside the ancestries of the living primates.

References

Gingerich, P. D. 1977. The fossil record and primate phylogeny. *Journal of Human Evolution*, 6: 483–505.

Hershkovitz, P. 1970. Notes on Tertiary platyrrhine monkeys and a description of a new genus from the late Miocene of Colombia. *Folia primatologica*, 12: 1–37.

———. 1974. A new genus of late Oligocene monkey (Cebidae, Platyrrhini) with notes on postorbital closure and platyrrhine evolution. *Folia primatologica*, 21: 1–35.

Hoffstetter, R. 1969. Un primate de l'Oligocène Inférieur Sud-Américain: *Branisella boliviana* gen. et sp. nov. *Comptes rendus, Académie des Sciences*, 269: 434–437.

———. 1977. Primates: Filogenia e historia biogeográfica. *Studia geologica, Salamanca*, 13: 211–353.

Napier, J. R., and P. H. Napier. 1967. *A handbook of living primates.* London and New York: Academic Press.

Simons, E. L. 1972. *Primate evolution.* New York: Macmillan.

Stirton, R. A. 1951. Ceboid monkeys from the Miocene of Columbia. *University of California Publications, Bulletin of the Department of Geological Sciences*, 28: 315–356.

Walker, E. P. et al. 1975. *Mammals of the world.* (Primates, 1: 393–481.)

See also references to publications on primates following chapter 11.

CHAPTER 14

Third Phase:
The Great American Interchange

We are now coming to one of the most extraordinary events in the whole history of life: the mingling of advanced North and South American mammals, their interactions, their integration into faunas of different compositions, and finally the establishment of the present faunas of the two continents, faunas which taken as a whole are still characteristically different, but to a less degree and in other ways than most of the earlier faunas. The existence of this phenomenon was recognized as early as 1893 by Karl Alfred von Zittel (1839–1904), author of the most compendious nineteenth-century treatise on paleontology, in which he called attention to this interchange, saying of it (in German) that it was "one of the most remarkable faunal migrations in the geological record."

Much more is now known about this complex but fascinating subject, although parts are still debatable and some are still merely conjectural or quite unknown. Yet there is an unusually good record of these events. In Argentina there is known a virtually complete sequence of rocks and mammalian faunas for the relevant part of geological history, the Pliocene, Pleistocene, and Recent, a span of more or less eight million years as those epochs are defined in the present work. Outside of Argentina the record is less complete or less well known, but there already are mammals for some part of the sequence from most South American countries. In North America the relevant record is quite well known with one serious exception important for this subject: the late

Cenozoic sequence for what is now tropical North America, or in that sense Central America, is not a blank and is useful as far as it goes, but as yet it does not go very far.

This chapter will present a general running narrative, and some of the special problems and analytical details will be given in the following chapter.

The interchange started in a small way about 7 or 8 million years ago at a time here placed in the early Pliocene (although Marshall and some others put it in the late Miocene), represented by the Huayquerian land mammal age in South America (see chapter 3). Mammal-bearing deposits of that age occur widely along the eastern slopes of the Andes and out into the plains beyond them. The Andes had been considerably uplifted by that time but had not yet reached their present height. The sediments forming part of the plains and underlying most of the pampas in both northern and southern (Patagonia) Argentina represent vast amounts of detritus from the rising cordillera. At present the region east of the southern Andes in the belt of prevailing westerly winds is relatively arid. In Huayquerian times aridity was already affecting the far south, but there are large fossil trees in rocks of this age in northern Argentina and also faunal evidence that this region was well watered and wooded. For example, porcupines occur there in the Huayquerian, forest dwellers not later or now known to occur anywhere in Argentina.

The total mammalian biomass, that is, the amount of matter incorporated in all the mammals living at any one time during this age, probably was about the same as during most of the earlier parts of the Cenozoic in South America. Nevertheless, the makeup of the mammalian fauna had changed considerably even before the radical changes of the Great American Interchange, soon to be considered in more detail.

It might be expected that faunas living in nearly or quite complete isolation would reach an approximately stable equilibrium within, say, two or three million years at most and thereafter change little until isolation ended or some other environmental upheaval occurred. Here in South America isolation apparently was complete through the Paleocene and all but perhaps the very end of the Eocene, a span of about 25 million years. The record so far known is deficient for the earliest and the latest parts of that span, but the evidence we do have shows that there was continual and even fairly rapid turnover at the level of mammalian genera, some turnover of families, even some, mostly by extinction, above the family level.

The arrival of caviomorphs and primates around the end of the Eocene was a break in complete isolation, but thereafter isolation was again complete until the middle or late Pliocene, a lapse of at least 30, perhaps 35 million years. (That has been questioned, but it is a strong consensus view and is supported by the available facts.) As shown in the preceding chapter there was expansion but little turnover among caviomorph families from the late Oligocene onward, but within those families there was great, continuous turnover of genera. In the Huayquerian those old native rodents, the caviomorphs, were near the height of their diversity. For reasons that have been previously suggested, the known record of South American primates is as yet a blank in the Pliocene. It is probable that the group either was still expanding or had reached approximately its present extent by Huayquerian time.

Among marsupials two new families, Thylacosmilidae and Argyrolagidae, are first known from the Huayquerian of Argentina although both must have been evolving elsewhere in South America well before that age. Both became extinct in the late Pliocene or early Pleistocene. The marsupial predators, Borhyaenidae, were still present but apparently fewer, and they also became extinct by about the end of the Pliocene. The Didelphidae, oppossums in a broad sense, were expanding toward the dominance they still maintain within their ecological domains.

The most striking change in the overall composition of the Huayquerian mammalian fauna is the marked reduction in the diversity and probably also the individual abundance of ungulate herbivores. As has been noted, as early as the early Eocene there are six orders and twelve families (as here classified) in the known record. Turnover of both genera and families was rapid in the later Eocene and the Oligocene. From the early Miocene into the Pliocene generic turnover continued, but change in families was by extinction. Here in the Huayquerian only two orders, Litopterna and Notoungulata, and five families are still present. As suggested in the preceding chapter, this reduction can reasonably be ascribed to the great increase in numbers of caviomorph rodents, evidently more successful herbivores than most of the old native ungulates, especially the smaller ones. The final blow, bringing extinction to these last remnants of old native ungulate evolution, was yet to come during the Great American Interchange.

We thus can ascribe part of the unsteadiness of faunal equilibrium during continental isolation to the long, slow effects of the one previous limited breach in that isolation. The rise of the Andes also represents an important topographic change that had environmental effects for the faunas. For the South American mammals as a whole, that would be more likely to increase faunal diversity, as it surely increased environmental diversity, and hence more likely to increase proliferation of new species than to induce marked turnover overall. Such environmental effects doubtless did affect the turnover, but it does seem that there was also turnover during isolation because on a continental scale, at least, evolution in isolation does not soon (geologically speaking), if ever, lead to an approximately static equilibrium. Increasing evidence from pre-Pleistocene fossil discoveries in Australia, the other continent especially characterized by evolution in isolation, bears out this rather general but still probable and definite conclusion.

The Huayquerian fauna also includes an extraordinary novelty, an invader from another world. This is the genus name *Cyonasua* by Ameghino, *cyon-* from Greek *kyon,* "dog," because the animal was somewhat doglike, and *-nasua* from *Nasua,* the generic name of the coatimundi (Latin *nasus,* "nose"—coatis are nosy), because *Nasua* is a collateral relative of *Cyonasua. Cyonasua* belongs to the raccoon family, Procyonidae (so does *Nasua*), and it is the first placental (nonmarsupial) carnivore known in the history of South American mammals. It certainly came from what is now Central America, and its ancestry was more broadly North American. At about the same time that this North American immigrant reached

South America, the first South American immigrants (later than the early Cenozoic) reached North America. Three genera of relatively small ground sloths are known from what is called the Hemphillian land mammal age in North America, nearly equivalent in age to Huayquerian in South America although not with precisely the same span.

Thus there was at this time a small interchange of mammals between the continents, a sort of presage of the Great American Interchange that was still to come. It is reasonably certain that there still was no continuous land connection between the two continents and that the few members of this beginning interchange moved from one to the other by waif dispersal, most likely involving island hopping. That is supported by geological evidence and also by the fact that evidence of this interchange is limited to so few kinds of mammals and that what is known about the mammals of Central America at about this time, although that knowledge is still limited, suggests that Central American mammals were still almost if not quite all of North American ancestry.

We move on, then, to the latter part of the Pliocene epoch, represented by the Montehermosan and Chapadmalalan land mammal ages which include very approximately the time from about 2 to about 5 million years ago. The known faunas of these two nominal ages are similar, and some students do not separate them. Although I continue to do so formally (see chapter 3), it is not necessary to treat them separately in the general narrative. A more precise revision of the type Montehermosan, especially, will be necessary before the relationship between the two can be well evaluated. Both are based primarily on strata and their contained fossils in areas in southern Buenos Aires Province, almost all along the shores where wave erosion has exposed these relatively old parts of the sediments underlying the pampa. The Chapadmalalan fauna is now much the better known of the two, and this summary will be based mainly on it.

In chapter 2 I noted the significant visits first of Charles Darwin and later of Florentino Ameghino to the locality Monte Hermoso for which the Montehermosan land mammal age and stage is named. The arroyo Chapadmalal, type locality for the Chapadmalalan, was also near the source of fossil mammals collected and described by the Ameghino bothers. That the Chapadmalalan fauna is now so well known is due even more to the work of two remarkable fossil collectors resident in the resort city Mar del Plata, near Chapadmalal. The late Lorenzo Scaglia started collecting as an amateur and made an imposing collection that became the nucleus of a municipal natural history museum. His son Galileo Scaglia continued collecting as a highly successful professional and is the director of the museum now named for Don Lorenzo. This has become a mecca for vertebrate paleontologists, many of whom, Argentinian and North American, have studied its fossil mammals.

The sediments and faunas of the typical Montehermosan and Chapadmalalan indicate a plains or pampas region with rich meadows, some trees, considerable rainfall and streams, probably at least as warm as the present climate of the region and probably not yet affected by the coming Ice Age. Deposits of similar age along the pre-Andine front farther north in Argentina, in Bolivia, and elsewhere have as yet scanty and not completely studied known faunas. They may be expected to represent different environmental conditions and corresponding local differences in the faunas.

Regarding the Chapadmalalan fauna, Osvaldo Reig, one of the Argentinian students of the Scaglia collections, has written (in Spanish):

Its place in time . . . makes knowledge of it particularly important as a basis for problems of correlation and for the significance of faunal elements for the question of establishment of the Pliocene–Pleistocene boundary. For the history of our neotropical faunas the Chapadmalalan faunal complex constitutes for the pampas environment the time of greatest evolutionary maturity of a special living community [biocenosis] developed under the conditions of continental isolation of South America, immediately before the establishment of conditions favorable for the massive interchange of animals with the North American continent. [Reig 1958, p. 242]

Most of the families descended from the earliest faunal stratum appear here as relicts fated for extinction. Exceptions are the Didelphidae, the opossums well along in their expansion as evident in the now living fauna, and the Dasypodidae, armadillos, including some lineages also destined for extinction but others ancestral to the quite diverse living forms. The few old native ungulate families noted for the Huayquerian still survive in the Chapadmalalan. From the second stratum the caviomorph rodents still flourished in the Chapadmalalan as they do today, and most of them differed only generically, at most, from their living allies and descendants. We do not know how well the primates were doing, as they evidently did not live in the type regions of the Montehermosan and Chapadmalalan, but we can assume that they, too, were flourishing elsewhere in South America.

There are also new forerunners of the Great American Interchange in the Montehermosan-Chapadmalalan. *Cyonasua,* the oldest of the known forerunners, survives from the Huayquerian, and here is also a strange relative of the raccoons (Procyonidae), *Chapadmalania,* so much larger than other known procyonids that it was at first mistaken for a bear. Another placental carnivore family appears in the Chapadmalalan for the first time in the known record: the Mustelidae (weasel family) represented by a skunk of a genus, *Conepatus,* still living all over South America and as far north as southern Utah. There is also the first hoofed mammal of late North American origin, a peccary akin to the genus *Platygonus.* This genus became abundant and widespread in North America in the Pleistocene but then became extinct there. Its South American close relative or possible synonym *Catagonus* was also long supposed to be extinct, but it has lately been found living in remote, poorly explored parts of the Paraguayan Chaco. The earliest noncaviomorph rodents *known* from South America, field mice of the family Cricetidae, also appear in these faunas. The reason for here stressing the word *known* is among the topics discussed in the next chapter.

Although the known new immigrants are still few, they suggest that spread from North to South America now involved either a greater probability of waif dispersal or the opening of a land route not yet very effective. It is of course possible that more North

Fig. 38. Some terminal members of South American lineages: *A*, restoration of *Toxodon*, a terminal Pleistocene notoungulate; *B*, *Dinomys branickii*, still living but on the verge of extinction and clearly a terminal species among the caviomorph rodents; *C*, restorations of *Macrauchenia*, a terminal Pleistocene litoptern.

American mammals had reached South America than are known from the southern part of that continent, but it seems probable that once a northern group effectively colonized South America its spread to the southern part of that continent would have been rapid in geological terms.

In the region around Mar del Plata the beds of the Chapadmalalan stage are immediately overlain by the type sediments with the type fauna of the Uquian land mammal stage and age. A number of other but less well-known mammalian faunules of about this age are known from scattered localities in South America. Evidence from the typical fauna clearly shows that there was now an open land connection between North and South America and that the Great American Interchange was at its height.

In the Uquian besides the Cricetidae, Procyonidae (not known from the type Uquian but certainly in South America at that time), Mustelidae, and Tayassuidae (peccaries) carried over from the Chapadmalalan, two orders, Proboscidea and Perissodactyla, and eight families, Canidae (dogs and their kin), Ursidae (bears), Felidae (cats and theirs), Gomphotheriidae (one group of mastodonts), Equidae (horses), Tapiridae (tapirs), Camelidae (camels, here llamas and their kin), and Cervidae (deer, broadly speaking), from North America appear for the first time in the known fossil record of South America.

At about the same time, in the late Blancan in terms of North American land mammal ages, there was also a definite but lesser influx of mammals into North from South America: two orders, Marsupialia (extinct in North America in the Miocene and now reappearing from South America) and Caviomorpha, the former with one family in North America, Didelphidae (opossums), and the latter with two, Erethizontidae (New World porcupines) and Hydrochoeridae (capybaras). Two South American families of Xenarthra, Dasypodidae (armadillos) and Glyptodontidae (glyptodonts), now also appeared in the known North American record.

It is convenient although arbitrary to date the boundary between Pliocene and Pleistocene by this maximal interchange, putting the Chapadmalalan in the Pliocene and the Uquian in the

MASTODON

SHREWS

HORSES

RABBITS

SQUIRRELS

MICE

TAPIRS

DOGS

PECCARIES

BEARS

CAMELS

RACCOONS

DEER

WEASELS

CATS

Fig. 39. Representatives in South America of families that spread to that continent from North America in the great American faunal interchange.

Pleistocene in South America. By the same criterion the Blancan, as now usually conceived, straddles the line in North America, with early Blancan as latest Pliocene and late Blancan as earliest Pleistocene.

In terms of South American land mammal ages the Ensenadan and Lujanian follow the Uquian. Both are undisputedly Pleistocene and have their type localities and faunas in the pampas of Buenos Aires Province, but more or less rich faunas of these ages are known from almost all South American countries. During these ages and the roughly equivalent North American land mammal ages, Irvingtonian and Rancholabrean, further interchange was relatively slight. The most distinctive change was the earliest known appearance of the South American family Megatheriidae (giant ground sloths) in North America.

In North America north of the tropics, a distinction that must now be made, the ultimate effect of the Great American Interchange—that is, the effect on the present fauna—was slight. Only three species of South American origin, our opossum (*Didelphis virginiana*), our armadillo (*Dasypus novemcinctus*), and our porcupine (*Erethizon dorsatum*), are still extant within this region. All three are still common enough, but they are a very small part of the present North American mammalian fauna. It is noteworthy that the first two of those species are now mainly southern in what is now the United States although the porcupine ranges from Mexico to Alaska and is most widespread in Canada. All the other South American migrants to nontropical North America became extinct there. The glyptodonts and ground sloths also became extinct in South America, where they had been integral in the fauna for tens of millions of years. Capybaras became extinct in North America but survive in South America.

The fact that the interchange virtually ceased after the Uquian in the south and the Blancan in the north suggests that the resulting faunas of mixed origin rather rapidly reached an equilibrium in overall composition. However, this is not literally true even for North America where the longer-term effect of the interchange was relatively slight. The North American faunas did change markedly from Blancan to Recent geological time, not only by extinction of most of the groups of South American origin but also by extinction of many not of that origin, among them the proboscideans (mammoths and mastodons), native horses, saber-toothed cats, short-faced bears, tapirs, and camels. There were also some new faunal elements coming in from Asia, most obviously the bisons.

In South America the faunal changes during and after the main interchange were more radical and more lasting. At the family level the only further new appearances were marginal and hardly involved integration into the South American fauna as a whole. However, some of the families that came from North America continued to prosper in South America. That was most notably true of the Cricetidae (field mice), which proliferated into large numbers of genera and species, a phenomenon that will be further discussed. The Canidae, Ursidae, Felidae, and Cervidae also survived on both continents and evolved new species and some new genera in South America. The proboscideans and horses became extinct on both continents. The capybaras, tapirs, and camels became extinct in the north but not in the south. However, the most striking change in South America was the complete extinction of the marsupial predators (Borhyaenidae) and of the now relatively few remaining old native ungulates.

It is tempting and indeed unavoidable to conjecture that these extinctions among old natives of the first faunal stratum were related to and somehow caused by the interchange. Placental carnivores appear; marsupial carnivores disappear. Competition in which the marsupials were the losers? Perhaps. This is a reasonable conjecture, at least, but it must be confessed that the evidence is not strong. Borhyaenids occur with a placental carnivore in the Huayquerian, but the most likely placental competitors, dogs and cats, are not known before the Uquian, in and after which borhyaenids are not known.

A stronger case can be made for extinction of the old native ungulates by competition with the newcomers. That is indeed quite likely, but it is not certain and in any case can hardly be the whole story. Remember that the old native ungulates had already been reduced to only five families long before any North Ameri-

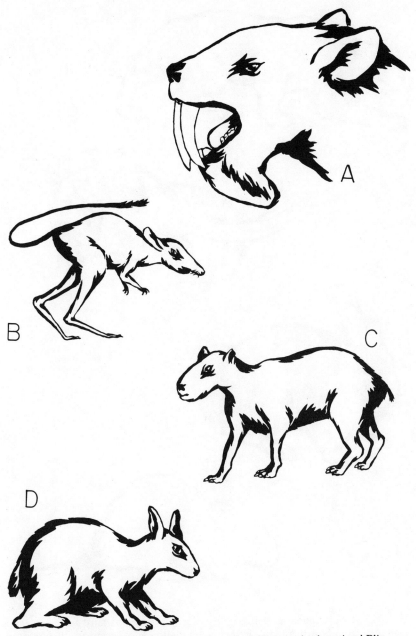

Fig. 40.   Representatives of old South American lineages in the mixed Pliocene and Pleistocene South American faunas: *A*, restoration of the head of *Thylacosmilus*, a first faunal stratum descendant sabertooth marsupial; *B*, restoration of *Argyrolagus*, a first faunal stratum bipedal, leaping marsupial; *C*, *Protohydrochoerus*, a second faunal stratum caviomorph rodent; *D*, *Paedotherium*, a first faunal stratum hegetothere notoungulate.

Fig. 41. In continuation of figure 40, representatives of third faunal stratum mammals from North America in the mixed Pleistocene-Recent South American fauna: *E*, restoration of *Smilodon*, a placental sabertooth; *F*, restoration of *Haplomastodon*, a gomphotheriid proboscidean; *G, Sylvilagus*, a living rabbit; *H, Oryzomys*, a living rice rat.

can ungulates appear in the South American record. One of those families (the Proterotheriidae, a family of litopterns) disappears before the Uquian, another (Hegetotheriidae) is last known in the Uquian, and still another (Mesotheriidae) died out in the Ensenadan, shortly after the Uquian. That all looks like gradual loss in a continuing competition, but the sequence starts before the arrival of other ungulates. And then two of the old families (Macraucheniidae and Toxodontidae) hung on for something like 2 million years *after* the other ungulates arrived from North America. Then they died out, as nearly as we can tell, at the same time as some of their supposed competitors, the horses and mastodonts.

Perhaps the lesson in this is that we don't begin to know everything, which is obviously true. The whole subject of extinction is fascinating but discouraging. Innumerable articles and several books have been written about the causes of extinction, but all that can be taken as established is a generalization so broad that it is not satisfying. Species become extinct because something in their genetic makeup, in their environment, or in their relationships with the environment becomes incompatible with continued life in an accessible environment. But exactly what went wrong in that sense as regards a particular species or larger group? Many guesses have been made, but the fact is that we simply cannot specify a definite cause of a particular case of extinction except for a few instances that happened in historic time, such as the passenger pigeon, the great auk, or Steller's sea cow—and even there we may not really have identified the whole causal complex.

In spite of this rather negative view on the subject of extinction, I have already made some suggestions on previous pages that are at worst conceivable, at best plausible, although not in any case established as adequate.

References

The references given after chapter 1 are again useful here, as throughout this book, and other references on some aspects introduced here are given after chapter 15. The Spanish language publications cited here are particularly useful as containing the most convenient and still reasonably complete faunal lists of ages considered in this chapter. These are readily consulted even by those who do not easily read Spanish.

Marshall, L. G.; R. F. Butler; R. E. Drake; G. H. Curtis; and R. H. Tedford. 1979. Calibration of the Great American Interchange. *Science,* 204: 272–279.

Pascual, R.; E. J. Ortega Hinojosa; D. Gondar; and E. Tonni. 1965. Las edades del Cenozóico mamalífero de la Argentina, con especial atención a aquellas del territorio Bonaerense. *Anales de la Comisión de Investigación Científica de Buenos Aires,* 6: 165–193.

Pascual, R., and O. E. Odreman Rivas. 1971. Evolución de las comunidades de los vertebrados del Terciario Argentino: Los aspectos paleozoogeográficos y paleoclimáticos relacionados. *Ameghiniana,* 7: 372–412.

Pascual, R., and F. Fidalgo. 1972. The problem of the Plio-Pleistocene boundary in Argentine [*sic*] (South America). [Separate from] Collection of Papers, International Colloquium on the Problem "The Boundary between Neogene and Quaternary." Moscow, USSR. 58 pages.

Reig, O. A. 1958. Notas para una actualización del conocimiento de la fauna de la formación Chapadmalal. I. Lista faunística *Acta Geológica Lilloana,* 2: 241–253.

CHAPTER 15

The Great American Interchange:
Special Aspects and Analyses

"Coming at the time it did [Montehermosan], the land connection provided the complex penis cricetines with an escape hatch as well as a gateway to a great evolutionary opportunity. With a nearly clear field before them they began an evolutionary burst in South America that has resulted in the remarkable number of species in the present fauna." Patterson and Pascual, in Keast et al. 1972 (see references, below).

"There is absolutely no evidence for the occurrence of complex-penis-type cricetines in boreal [Northern] America prior to the invasion by them in the Blancan, there is no indication that these rodents arose in Middle America prior to their appearance in South America." Hershkovitz, ibid.

"The unfounded assumption that the Isthmian channel was an effective barrier to cricetine expansion is seriously compromised by the Patterson and Pascual premise that all other Tertiary mammals of South America . . . are of waif origin." Hershkovitz, ibid.

"This is not so. The very small number of mammals that reached South America over the water gap during seventy million years is eloquent testimony to its effectiveness as a barrier." Patterson and Pascual, ibid.

"Such cricetines are unknown in Middle American fossil deposits of any age." Hershkovitz, ibid.

"Since no identifiable rodent remains at all are known from the later Tertiary of Central America this piece of negative evidence has no significance whatever." Patterson and Pascual, ibid.

"If the ancestral sigmodontine stock did not enter South America through boreal America, it could have done so by rafting from Africa." Hershkovitz, ibid.

"This is virtually impossible." Jon Baskin (1978, in reference to Hershkovitz's suggestion of African origin for South American cricetine rodents).

"The phyllotine group of South America cricetines initially evolved in North America and did not enter South America until the Panamanian land bridge was established, in the latest Pliocene or earliest Pleistocene." Baskin, ibid.

And in a paper written in 1978 for publication in 1979 that does not provide a sufficiently concise statement for similar quotation, Osvaldo Reig agrees with Baskin that the South American cricetids (or more clearly sigmodontines) did not come from Africa, agrees with Patterson and Pascual, Baskin, me, and almost everyone else except perhaps Hershkovitz that they came from North America, but agrees with Hershkovitz and differs from almost everyone else that they came in the early Miocene, while probably differing from Hershkovitz, who does not seem entirely clear on this point, that they came by waif dispersal.

What on earth is all that about? Isn't it suggestive of the scholastics who are said to have disputed on such topics as the number of angels that could perch on the point of a needle? (The answer is no.) Is it of any interest to anyone but a mouse fancier? (The answer is yes.)

As an aid to understanding what is being said, let us first clear up why the disputants seem so interested in the complexity of the penises of these members of the field mouse family (Cricetidae). Oddly enough, the male members of this family, like those of most rodents and many other mammals, have a bone in the penis. In some living North American cricetids and at least two South American genera this is a fairly simple rod with a single apex. In most South American cricetids and in most cricetids anywhere (they are almost worldwide except for Australia) and also in most of the family of true mice and rats (Muridae) the bone ends distally in three prongs, which may be bony but are generally of cartilaginous or soft tissue. The proximal bases of the bones also differ, being usually and variously expanded in the three-pronged type and a simpler nob in the others. The only reason for paying any attention to these bizarre, or perhaps merely esoteric, facts is that the specialists who study rodents often take the variants of this bone (it is called a baculum, Latin for "rod") as particularly important indications of relationships.

The field mice, Cricetidae, of the Americas are generally divided into two subfamilies, the Microtinae, which do not now occur in South America, never have done so as far as known, and so do not here concern us, and the Cricetinae, which occur all over the Americas and far and wide also in the Old World. Some of the American Cricetinae have simple and some have complex penises. The two groups thus distinguished are usually considered to be phylogenetically distinct, that is, each to descend from an ancestry different, at some time, place, or both, for the two groups. The distribution of these groups at the present time is given by Patterson and Pascual as shown, in slightly different form, in table 3.

Those are facts about known characteristics and geographic occurrences of real animals, and (with insignificant differences in the precise numbers in such a tabulation) those facts are accepted by all the disputants who disagree so strongly, even violently, about the historical background of those facts. Whether or not one is interested in just this subject for its own sake, it surely is interesting as a casebook example of methods of inference and sources of agreement or disagreement.

First, some of the questions that everyone directly involved is trying to answer: Where did the South American cricetids origi-

Table 3

Distribution of taxa of Cricetidae with different types of bacula

	Nontropical North America		Tropical North (or Central) America		South America	
	Genera	Species	Genera	Species	Genera	Species
With simple penis	5	43	1	5	2	2
With complex penis	2	5	5	33	36	183

nate as such? If not in South America, where did they come from; or if they originated in South America, where did their ancestors come from? When did this occur? In relation to that question, how long did the obviously great diversification of South American cricetids take? Why and how did it occur? Is the presence of a few closely similar genera in North America relictual, survivors there from the common ancestry; or is it by migration of originally South American lineages; or is it by back-migration from South American genera evolved from North American ancestors?

With such questions, the fossil record is an obvious possible source of further data. Another point here arises, because the minute, often incompletely ossified, and unattached penis bones are not known in any fossil cricetid or likely to be. Fossil cricetids are identified mostly by their teeth, sometimes by some characters of skull and jaws, rarely by postcranial bones. If the teeth are quite like those of members of one of the two living groups with different penis bones, it is a fair but not certain inference that the penis bones of the fossil species were also similar.

The oldest known South American cricetids are from the Montehermosan. It is thus a fact that cricetids were on that continent at that time, that is, in the middle or late Pliocene depending on just how one arbitrarily subdivides that epoch. Faunas including mammals as small and as likely to be difficult to find are well known from numerous pre-Montehermosan deposits in South America, not only in Argentina but also in other regions, notably for the Friasian of northern South America. They contain no known cricetids. Both Hershkovitz and Reig believe that cricetids reached South America in the early Miocene, which means Santacrucian at latest, but that cricetid fossils for the span of at least 10 million years between Santacrucian and Montehermosan just have not been found. Hershkovitz argues that the ancestral complex-penis cricetids were not then in tropical North America, or Middle America, because none have been found there, but he thus wholly cancels out his own argument. As Patterson and Pascual hurried to point out, *no* identifiable rodents of relevant age have been found in Central America although some were certainly there. Hundreds of identifiable Miocene rodents, none of them cricetids, have been found in South America. The evidence, being largely negative on both sides, is not conclusive, but on these grounds it indicates a later, Pliocene, date of arrival in South America as distinctly most probable.

Although there is no fossil evidence on the cricetids themselves one way or the other in Central America, there is some in non-tropical North America. Cricetids with dentitions closely resembling those of South American complex-penis cricetids are known from faunas of early Pliocene age in southwestern United States approximately equivalent in age to South American Huayquerian and hence probably somewhat older than the oldest known South American cricetids. Reig counters rather feebly to the general effect that the North American Pliocene cricetids so far described are not intermediate between certain Oligocene North American rodents and Recent South American cricetids, which is not exactly what was claimed for them. Hershkovitz, although not yet aware of the early Pliocene North American occurrences when he last wrote on this subject, countered with the hypothesis that the early North American rodents similar to the South American complex-penis cricetines were migrants *from* South America. That is not impossible, but surely what evidence there is makes it improbable.

Both Hershkovitz and Reig use as their most cogent argument the extreme diversity of the South American cricetids in numbers of genera and species and also in differences of habitats and adaptations. They believe that the time since and including the Montehermosan, not more than 6 million years, is insufficient for such proliferation. The time since the earliest Miocene is about 22 million years, and that seems to err on the other side. When the caviomorphs, with which Reig makes comparisons in this respect, had been in South America for not more than 22 million years, taking them into the Friasian, they had proliferated enormously and at the level of families, not just of tribes and genera like the South American cricetids. Reig also weakens the argument by his statement, with which every paleontologist will surely agree, that to infer the antiquity of a given taxon by comparison of its morphological and taxonomic differentiation with that of another taxon over a similar span of time is unwarranted. But only by some such comparison could one safely infer, with Reig, that the differentiation of South American cricetids requires more nearly 22 than 6 million years.

Finally, Reig argues that if the Montehermosan cricetids were in fact among the first or nearly the first to reach that continent they would also be among the most primitive, whereas in his opinion they are relatively specialized. If, however, they had been evolving rapidly in tropical America during part of the Miocene and the early Oligocene, as Patterson and Pascual (and I and others) think more probable, it would be expected that the first ones to reach South America later in the Pliocene would by then be relatively advanced, just as Reig believes them to be.

The flat, honest answer to "When?" is thus "We do not know," but in my opinion a time in the Montehermosan or not long before, geologically speaking, is more likely on what evidence we now have. That could of course be overturned at any time by further discovery in South America, or it could be essentially confirmed by discoveries in Central America. We need more direct evidence, but there is also some indirect evidence to be considered later in this chapter.

There is hardly any doubt about "Whence?" In spite of Hershkovitz's other suggestion, one feels that even he thinks the ancestors of the South American cricetids probably came from North America, and that makes it unanimous. The only real question here concerns how far along their evolution was when they reached South America, and that depends mainly on the unsettled question of timing.

There is also little doubt about the general evolutionary reasons for the great proliferation of this group. Whenever they reached South America they had "a nearly clear field," as Patterson and Pascual put it, in a whole continent with extremely varied regional and local habitats and few close or strong competitors. That last point is supported by evidence that their proliferation seems to have had little effect on the rodents already in residence, the caviomorphs.

It has already been suggested that this group of rodents in South

America merits special attention here as a case of historical inference that remains dubious and hotly disputed because, first, there
simply are not enough known facts for conclusive settling of the
questions involved and, second, the disputants have approached
these questions by different methods and with different biases. It
is further evident, however, that the data already available do
provide a definite and almost unparalleled example of a different
sort: the enormous proliferation of a single group, all within one
family or even one subfamily in taxonomic terms. There can only
have been a few species, although probably more than one, when
this group reached South America. According to Reig it now has
46 genera and 225 species on that continent. (J. R. Ellerman's
work, cited below, recognizes only 17 South American genera,
one obviously of North American origin and a marginal newcomer
in South America; Reig and incidentally also Hershkovitz have
split the classical genera by raising many subgenera or species
groups to the generic level; on the other hand, both Reig and
Hershkovitz recognize many fewer species than did Ellerman,
considering about 80 of the classical species invalid.)

I will return more briefly to the makeup and ecological roles of
this family when considering the third faunal stratum as a whole in
the next chapter. Now we turn to various analyses of the phenomenon of the Great American Interchange.

Since we know that the greater part, surely, and all, probably, of
this interchange occurred during the Pliocene, Pleistocene, and
Recent epochs, we can consider the mammals known to have lived
then in South America on one hand and North America on the
other as possible participants in the interchange. For a start, it is
clear that not all the possible participants did in fact participate.
There was a screening or filtering effect evidently imposed by
ecological conditions in southern, tropical North America, the
part now Central America plus much of southern Mexico. During
the interchange the groups of mammals spreading from North to
South America had either to be already in that region or to spread
through it on the way. A quantitative estimate of the extent of
such filtering can be obtained by counting the number of families
definitely known to have been present on each continent from

Table 4

Numbers of families known from Pliocene to Recent in relation to intercontinental spread

	Total Families Not from Other Continent	Number of Those That Did Spread to Other Continent	Percentage
Nontropical			
North America	32	16	50
South America	30	8	27

Pliocene to Recent and *not* as immigrants from the other continent. These figures can then be compared with the number of those families definitely known to have spread to the other continent. Using a somewhat conservative criterion for groups (taxa) of family rank, the data are as shown in table 4. Although the number of families potentially involved on the two continents was nearly equal, about twice as many spread from North to South America as in the other direction.

Here and throughout this chapter the numerical data and the discussions refer to land mammals only; that is, they exclude bats and aquatic mammals. Bats will be briefly considered in the next chapter, but aquatic mammals (and *Homo sapiens* as an animal species) are not among the topics of this book.

Next it will be interesting to consider any relationship between interchange and extinction. This can be estimated by seeing how many of the twenty-four families involved in the interchange from both sides have survived into the Recent and how many have not (table 5). These figures can be somewhat misleading because two of the living families from North America, Tapiridae and

Table 5

Survival of families involved in the Great America Interchange

	Still Living		Now Extinct	
Direction of Spread:	No.	%	No.	%
North to South America	13	81	3	19
South to North America	4	50	4	50

Camelidae, are extinct in nontropical North America and survive only in South America and, for the Tapiridae, tropical North America. Also, one of the living families from South America, Hydrochoeridae, did become extinct in nontropical North America. Nevertheless, it is evident that the families spreading from North to South America were not only more numerous but also less liable to extinction than those spreading in the opposite direction. It is then natural to wonder whether this was true not only of families involved in the interchange but also in general of families originally North rather than South American. The relevant data are as shown in table 6, for all Pliocene-to-Recent North American families not from South America and all Pliocene-to-Recent South American families not from North America.

It appears that South American families were indeed more liable to, or at least more affected by, extinction than North American families, but there is a catch also revealed by the tabulation. The evident greater survival of the North American families is probably due entirely to the survival of six of those families elsewhere than in North America, two of them in South America as previously stated and four (Hyaenidae, Elephantidae, Equidae, and Rhinocerotidae) in the Old World.

The possibility, or in some cases one can say probability, that the irruption of North American families into South America was itself a partial cause of extinction of South American families was discussed in the preceding chapter.

The overall changes in the South American mammalian fauna during the interchange can be well shown in terms of the three

Table 6

Survival of families known from Pliocene to Recent on each continent and not derived from the other

	Still Living on Same Continent		Still Living but Not on Same Continent		Living Total		Extinct Everywhere		Overall Total
	No.	%	No.	%	No.	%	No.	%	No.
North America	20	62.5	6	19	26	81	6	19	32
South America	18	60.0	0	0	18	60	12	40	30

faunal strata previously defined. (For these purposes the Procyonidae are assigned to the third stratum although at least one
member of that family reached South America as a precursor of
that stratum before a definite land connection existed.) The figures
for land mammal families now known from each of the South
American land mammal ages are given in table 7.

There was a progressive and apparently fairly steady decrease in
the part played by descendants of the first stratum, caused by
extinction most of which was concentrated in the Pleistocene.
When compared with the marked increase in the third stratum,
also mostly in the Pleistocene, this does look like faunal replacement, and it is tempting, but inconclusive, to see this as at least
partial cause and effect. Although the proportion of the second
stratum decreased somewhat between Pliocene and Pleistocene,
the change was not great and there was virtually no extinction at
the family level among descendants of the second stratum. The
apparent increase of the second stratum between Pleistocene and
Recent is statistically a sampling error: it indicates only that fossils
of some Recent families have not been found in the Pleistocene,
although the families certainly existed and were in South America
then. The moderate fluctuation of total number of known families
is probably also mostly sampling error, that is, incomplete discovery of families as fossils of these ages. There is, however, some
probability that the total number of families in South America did

Table 7

Stratal origin of families known from the Pliocene to Recent of South America

	Age	First Stratum		Second Stratum		Third Stratum		Total
		No.	%	No.	%	No.	%	No.
Recent		5	16	13	41	14	44	32
Pleistocene	Lujanian	9	26	11	32	14	41	34
	Ensenadan	10	30	11	33	12	37	33
	Uquian	12	34	11	31	12	34	35
Pliocene	Chapadmalalan	15	50	11	37	4	13	30
	Montehermosan	16	55	11	38	2	7	29
	Huayquerian	16	59	10	37	1	4	27

increase somewhat during the most active times of the interchange and then decreased somewhat into the Recent.

David Webb has recently (1976) analyzed some of the phenomena of the Great American Interchange in terms of genera rather than families. I have been using families for the estimates given up to this point, largely because this reduces the sampling error; that is, it is probable that we know nearly (but not quite) all the families present in both South and North America for the ages here in question, but it is certain that we know a definitely smaller fraction of the genera and also, incidentally, that we know relatively so few of the species as to make them of little significance for these uses. (Webb does not use the species in his analysis.) Furthermore, for the points hitherto made here the indications from numbers of families agree fairly well within limits of sampling error with those obtainable from genera. That is because there is usually a fairly good correlation (not, of course, equality) between numbers of families and numbers of genera.

An important further point that Webb's analysis does bring out is that within a given region of South America, and hence perhaps for the continent as a whole, the "originations" (first appearances in the known fossil record) of genera after the (Uquian) height of the interchange are mostly within families from North America in what I call the third stratum. (The faunas analyzed in this way by Webb are all from Argentina but, contrary to his statement, not from Patagonia.)

Karl Flessa (1975) related the diversity of North and South American land mammals to the areas of the continents according to a formula earlier developed by Robert MacArthur and Edward Wilson, among others. From this he calculates the number of extinctions that would have occurred if the faunas had been completely mixed during the Great American Interchange. This gave him a figure of 17 for extinctions of land mammal families, whereas he takes the actual number (also a calculated estimate) to be 10. However, as Flessa took care to note, in fact the faunas did not mix completely, far from it, and this could readily explain the apparent discrepancy. The new and I believe more reliable figures now given in this chapter differ from those used by Flessa. As indicated in table 4, the total number of land mammal families that might have taken part in the interchange was 62 by my classification, not 48 as taken by Flessa from earlier publications, and of these 62 only 24 did in fact take part. The figures given in table 8 for the present numbers of land mammal families also differ from those given by some previous authors.

Webb also discussed this matter of area and diversity and effects of the interchange and made the further point that "the theatre of effective interchange never extended far into temperate North America. The fully mingled neotropical fauna seems to have reached at most from about the northernmost latitudes of the Gulf of Mexico and Southern California southward into Patagonia. Only about 9 percent of North America was involved, that is about 2.55×10^6 km² in the narrow subtropical and tropical part of the continent." However, since as noted in table 4 only about 40 percent of the families known to have been candidates, so to speak, for intermingling are known to have intermingled in fact, one can hardly speak of a "fully mingled" fauna anywhere. Also, in North America there was no definable line where intermingling did, or now does, definitely stop. It decreases noticeably more or less along the somewhat vague boundary between tropical and temperate North America, but some mammals of South American ancestry reached boreal Alaska, and one, the northern porcupine, still does.

There are various ways of putting faunal resemblances into definite numerical terms. One that seems appropriate for the present discussion is the expression $100 (C/N_1)$, in which C is the number

Table 8

Recent numbers of land mammal families in the Nearctic
and Neotropical regions

Nearctic (Nontropical North America)		Neotropical (South America and tropical North America)		Both Nearctic and Neotropical	Total for Both Continents
Only	Total	Only	Total		
9	27	14	32	18	41

of taxa, for example families or genera, present in both of two faunas being compared and N_1 is the total number in the smaller of those two faunas. Values can range from 0 to 100. That expression is sometimes called Simpson's Index, and in another connection Flessa has coined the terser expression "simfams" for units of the index when applied to families. Table 9 gives resemblances between the Recent families of land mammals in various regions in terms of simfams. "Guiana" is used as a matter of convenience to include the three small adjacent countries Guyana, Surinam, and French Guiana.

Florida is within the subtropical marginal area considered by Webb as having had or perhaps to some extent still having a "fully mingled neotropical fauna," and these figures show its mammals as now being only slightly more like those of Costa Rica (somewhat marginally neotropical) than is the fauna of decidedly nontropical New Mexico. But the fact that the fauna of Florida is decidedly more like that of "Guiana" and even of Argentina, both decisively neotropical, than is that of New Mexico supports Webb's point of view.

It is interesting to extend the comparisons to a time in the Pleistocene when most of the interchange had occurred but most of the extinctions that later altered all the faunas had not. For this purpose we can take the Inglis fauna of Florida as listed by Webb and the Ensenadan fauna of Argentina as listed by Pascual. These are of nearly the same date: the Inglis fauna is assigned to the late Blancan land mammal age of North America, and the Argentine (pampean) Ensenadan is the type for the South American land mammal age of that name, approximately contemporaneous with latest Blancan. Table 10 shows simfams comparing those fossil

Table 9

Resemblances of land mammal faunas measured in simfams

	New Mexico	Costa Rica	"Guiana"	Argentina
Florida	100	77	69	69
New Mexico	—	74	58	58
Costa Rica	—	—	89	67
"Guiana"	—	—	—	79

Table 10

Resemblances of some Pleistocene and Recent land mammal families measured
in simfams

	Florida Recent	Argentina Ensenadan	Argentina Recent
Florida, Inglis, late Blancan	100	67	59
Florida Recent	—	62	69
Argentina, type Ensenadan	—	—	69

faunas with each other and with the recent faunas of the same
region.

As with any numerical procedures, the calculator or computer
does no thinking for us, and we must bear in mind just what the
numbers mean. Here 100 simfams for comparison of Pleistocene
and Recent in Florida does not mean that the faunas are identical.
They are quite different in some respects. The figure 100 means
that all the families of Recent Florida were present there in the
late Blancan. The difference is due almost entirely to extinction
between that age and the Recent. As might be expected, the
Florida Pleistocene is somewhat more like the Argentine Pleistocene than is the Florida Recent, but the difference is slight. On
the other hand the Florida Recent fauna is distinctly more like the
Argentine Recent than is the Florida Pleistocene. Here there is
some distortion in sampling, because several families now present
in Argentina as a whole do not now occur in the pampean region
where the known Ensenadan fauna lived. Of course that also af-
fects the comparison of Ensenadan and Recent in Argentina.

In this discussion a distinction has frequently been made between tropical and nontropical North America. The usual formal
boundary approximates the line where the Tropic of Cancer
crosses Mexico, but it does not coincide with that tropic because
some highlands south of the tropic, such as the region around
Mexico City, are not tropical in climate or other environmental
factors. Zoogeographers have long taken the environmentally
definable line as the boundary between two major divisions, "re-

gions," of lands with distinctive mammalian faunas. Thus, as regards Recent land mammals the nontropical part of North America is known as the Nearctic Region, although most of it is not arctic in the usual climatic sense of the word, and tropical North America and all of South America are the Neotropical Region, although a considerable part of South America is not climatically tropical.

The inclusion of present-day tropical North America in the Neotropical Region is justified because on the whole its Recent mammalian faunas are somewhat more like those of South America than those of nontropical North America. That is confirmed by table 9, which shows the fauna of land mammals in Costa Rica, more or less central in tropical North America, to be decidedly more like that of "Guiana," a northern but fully South American fauna, than like that of New Mexico, a southern but fully nontropical North American fauna. This is clearly a result of the great interchange. When a land connection between the two continents occurred toward the end of the Pliocene, mammals of northern South America already adapted to tropical conditions readily spread into tropical North America, but many of them, for instance the sloths and monkeys, did not spread onward into nontropical North America. Mammals already adapted or behaviorally adaptable to tropical, subtropical, or at least warm temperate environments in North America held on in tropical North America, including some like the tapirs and peccaries that became extinct or more limited in distribution in nontropical North America.

In that way the whole of Middle America can be seen as the environmental filter that caused the previously mentioned filtering of the great interchange. It can also be considered as a region of transition between the Nearctic and Neotropical regions as they are today because not all distinctive elements of the two regions reached while others not only reached but also crossed the formal line traced by zoogeographers as the boundary between the regions.

Darwin's impression that the fauna of the two regions were more alike in the Pleistocene than they now are was mentioned in chapter 2. That opinion was justified in a descriptive and impressionistic sense, and in those senses we still share it. Darwin's im-

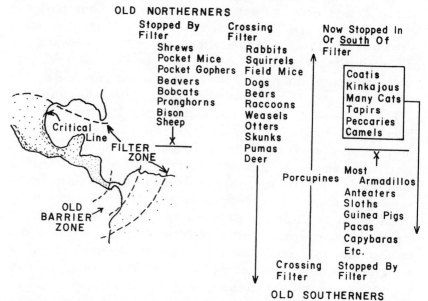

Fig. 42. Middle America as a filter zone and its effect during the great interchange on the Recent faunas of the two regions. Groups that crossed through the filter but are now extinct are not taken into account in this diagram. The "old barrier zone" represents approximately the most persistent part of the marine barrier that so long kept South America an island continent. The "critical line" approximates the (vague) boundary between temperate North America and tropical North America; the latter area became a part of a Nearctic Region during, but in all reasonable probability not before, the great interchange.

pression can be ascribed to a canny intuition of what we now call the great interchange. This impression arises from the presence in the Pleistocene on both continents of such striking creatures as giant ground sloths and some mastodonts, now extinct everywhere. There were also several groups, notably capybaras, tapirs, and camels, then common to the two regions but now surviving in only one. Nevertheless, in quantification of relative proportions of elements in the faunas as measured in simfams or other usual indices of faunal similarity there is little or no significant difference between the Pleistocene and Recent resemblances of these faunas. The indices in table 11 are relevant to the changes or lack of them in faunal similarity between nontropi-

Table 11

Indices of land mammal faunal resemblance between South America and non-tropical North America

	Late Miocene	Pleistocene	Recent
Simfams	0	56	67
Otsuka indices	0	54	61

Note: The Otsuka index is here included because it sometimes gives results different from the simfams. The formula is $100(C/\sqrt{N_1 N_2})$, C and N_1 as before, N_2 the total for the larger fauna.

cal North America and South America. In absolute numbers there were 19 known families in common in the Pleistocene and now there are 18, not a striking change, but in relative terms the similarity has increased, not decreased.

What is now tropical North America or Middle America became incorporated in the Neotropical Region with South America as a result of the great interchange. The evidence is not absolutely conclusive, but it is strongly indicative that what is now Middle America did not have much faunal resemblance to South America before the interchange and that there was then no Neotropical Region in the present sense but a southern New World region including only South America.

Stratigraphic and invertebrate faunal evidence indicates that the marine barrier that inhibited or prevented interchange of land mammals before the middle or late Pliocene was in far northwestern South America and what is now the southeastern part of tropical North America. Pleistocene mammals from tropical North America are of the mixed origins to be expected during or after the main interchange. Pre-Pleistocene land mammals from that region are poorly known as yet, but there are a few so far reported from middle Miocene beds in Panama, late Miocene beds in Oaxaca, tropical Mexico, and late Miocene to early Pliocene beds in Honduras. All these belong to families and most of them, as far as identified, to genera known also at these times from nontropical North America and not from the early Pliocene or pre-Pliocene of South America. In the absence of contrary evidence, the reasonable conclusion is that up to the early Pliocene the land mammal fauna of Middle America was with high probability entirely North American in character.

The Miocene and Pliocene faunas from northern Mexico and southern United States, especially along the Gulf of Mexico coastal plain and into Florida, are now well known. They are of North American faunal origin except for the few ground sloths that appeared before the end of the Pliocene, but their makeup in species and in a few genera differs from that of contemporaneous faunas farther north. It is a hypothesis that the mammals that spread into South America in the great interchange had already become somewhat diversified and specialized in southern North America before they spread to South America. That is most likely for the cricetids in the Miocene and early Pliocene. It might also be true of the ceboids (New World monkeys) and caviomorph rodents in the late Eocene and early Oligocene if they came from North America. I consider this the most reasonable hypothesis at present, but it has been shown earlier in this chapter that it is not unanimously supported. Further discoveries of fossils in southern North America and in the Miocene and early Pliocene of South America may well substantiate it or, less readily, falsify it.

References

Baskin, J. A. 1978. *Bensonomys, Calomys,* and the origin of the phyllotine group of neotropical cricetines (Rodentia, Cricetidae). *Journal of Mammalogy,* 59: 125–135.

Ellerman, J. R. 1941. *The families and genera of living rodents.* Vol. 2, *Family Muridae.* London: British Museum (Natural History).

Flessa, K. W. 1975. Area, continental drift, and mammalian diversity. *Paleobiology,* 1: 189–194.

Flessa, K. W.; S. G. Barnett; D. B. Cornue; M. A. Lomaga; J. M. Miyazaki; and A. S. Murer. 1979. Geological implications of the relationship between mammalian faunal similarity and geographic distance. *Geology,* 7: 15–18.

Hershkovitz, P. 1962. Evolution of neotropical cricetine rodents (Muridae) with special reference to the phyllotine group. *Fieldiana, Zoology,* 46: 1–524.

Keast, A.; F. C. Erk; and B. Glass, eds. 1972. *Evolution, mammals, and southern continents.* Albany: State University of New York Press. (The contradictory chapters by Patterson and Pascual, on one hand, and Hershkovitz, on the other, are both in this book.)

Reig, O. A. 1978. A new fossil genus of South American cricetid rodents allied to *Wiedomys*, with an assessment of the Sigmodontinae (consulted in a preprint distributed by the author).

Simpson, G. G. 1950. History of the fauna of Latin America. *American Scientist,* 38: 261–389. (This was the original publication of an article included without change in books published by others in 1951 and in 1965, sometimes cited as of those later dates. Some of the views there expressed are modified in the present volume.)

Webb, S. D. 1976. Mammalian faunal dynamics of the Great American Interchange. *Paleobiology,* 2: 220–234.

CHAPTER 16

The Newcomers and
the Living Fauna

The newcomers were those mammals that first appear in the known fossil record of South America between the early Pliocene and the present time. They were listed in chapter 4 along with all the other known South American families, and aspects of their arrival have been discussed in the two chapters on the Great American Interchange. In this chapter each family of newcomers will be discussed, and that will be followed by a summary of the present South American mammalian fauna.

In the time framework of the South American land mammal ages, the known occurrences of the newcomers are as shown in table 12. Insectivores, shrews, moles, and more or less close relatives, are common both as fossils and as living animals in North America, Europe, Asia, and Africa. It is a peculiarity of the South American fauna that insectivores are completely unknown as fossils and are rare and somewhat marginal as living animals there. The Recent shrews of South America all belong to the genus *Cryptotis,* which occurs widely in the United States (only one species) and through Mexico and Central America (numerous species). In South America it is present at considerable elevations, mostly above 3,000 meters (nearly 10,000 feet), in the mountains of Colombia, Ecuador, and Venezuela. It has also been reported from Surinam, but the locality data were probably incorrect. Cabrera recognized five South American species of this genus as valid, including the one supposedly from Surinam. The apparent failure of these shrews to range more widely in South America

Table 12

Distribution of newcomers (third faunal stratum) in South American land mammal ages

	Huayquerian	Montehermosan	Chapadmalalan	Uquian	Ensenadan	Lujanian	Recent
Insectivora							
Soricidae							X
Rodentia							
Sciuridae							X
Cricetidae		X	X	X	X	X	X
Carnivora							
Canidae				X	X	X	X
Ursidae				X	X	X	X
Procyonidae	X	X	X	X	X	X	X
Mustelidae			X	X	X	X	X
Felidae				X	X	X	X
Proboscidea							
Gomphotheriidae				X	X	X	
Perissodactyla							
Equidae				X	X	X	
Tapiridae				X	X	X	X
Artiodactyla							
Tayassuidae			X	X	X	X	X
Camelidae				X	X	X	X
Cervidae				X	X	X	X

may be related to the presence of the insectivorous caenolestid marsupials in similar habitats from Colombia down to Chile. The absence of a fossil record could be due only to the rarity of fossils from similar habitats, but the restricted range and slight diversity suggest recent spread in South America, where these may have been among the last North American immigrants.

Squirrels, Sciuridae, also lack a South American fossil record, but they are now widespread there, from Colombia to Brazil, northeastern Argentina, and Peru. Besides the very widespread genus *Sciurus,* they include one genus, *Microsciurus,* confined to Central and South America and another, *Sciurillus,* confined to South America. They are all tree squirrels and almost entirely limited to tropical forests, which probably explains the absence of known fossils, just as the tropical forest monkeys known to have been in South America in the Pleistocene have no known fossils in that epoch. The squirrels, too, probably were present in the Pleistocene, but there is no reason to think they were there earlier than that. The absence of ground squirrels, so conspicuous in the cooler regions of North America and Asia, is an understandable negative feature of the South American fauna—understandable because they would be filtered out by the tropical forest zone.

An otherwise exclusively North American family, ancient and recent, has a foothold in South America: Heteromyidae, pocket mice and kangaroo mice and rats. One genus, *Heteromys,* has three species in Colombia, Venezuela, and Ecuador and others in Central America, where the genus probably originated. Like the shrews, the spread of these animals into South America was probably one of the late events of the interchange. However, like the squirrels they are here virtually confined to tropical forests and that may explain the absence of any fossil records.

The practically ubiquitous presence of field mice, Cricetidae, their great abundance in South America, and their scanty fossil record from Montehermosan on have already been discussed. It remains here to exemplify the range of their adaptive types. All are small rodents, largely nocturnal although some may be active in the day as well as the night. They range from pastoral, eating mostly grasses and usually with high-crowned cheek teeth, grazers in their small ways, to sylvan, usually with low-crowned cheek teeth and browsers. Some of the latter are partly or mainly arboreal although usually feeding on the ground. A number of the pastoral genera and species are semiaquatic, living in marshes. The great majority are herbivorous, but *Ichthyomys* ("fish mouse") and two other genera with nine species in all have become aquatic and feed mainly or in some species even exclusively on fish. At the other extreme some have become adapted to somewhat arid, even desert, environments. A genus, *Eligmodontia,* with only one species, lives along the relatively dry eastern slopes of the southern Andes up to elevations as high as 4,575 meters (about 15,000 feet). It has long hindlegs and leaps readily but is not bipedal.

Among those South American cricetids are examples of convergent evolution such as are frequent among older groups long confined to South America and here appear again in a group that reached South America comparatively late and has relatives widely distributed over almost all continents. *Ichthyomys* closely resembles Australian *Hydromys* ("water rat"), also aquatic and carnivorous although it may eat more mollusks and crustaceans than fish. *Hydromys* belongs to the family Muridae, which evolved from ancestral cricetids. (The two groups are sometimes united in one family.) *Eligmodontia* is very like the gerbils of Africa and southern Asia, which are also cricetids, live in deserts, and have elongated hindlegs and a leaping gait. These South American genera and their Australian and Old World look-alikes and live-alikes certainly evolved their peculiarities independently.

The Canidae, dogs and their kin, were among the placental carnivores that poured into South America in the early Pleistocene. They there evolved into numerous species, ten to thirteen being recognized by different students, all but one species now confined to South America. All but two of them are rather similar, small, foxlike or coyotelike animals. Most mammalogists have placed these closely similar species in six genera. The most recent revision, however, puts them all in the typical dog genus *Canis,* but in five different subgenera, which does not greatly simplify the situation (Van Gelder 1978). One genus, or subgenus, is represented in South America by the common North American gray fox, almost always called *Urocyon cinereoargenteus* although Van Gelder calls it *Canis (Vulpes) cinereoargenteus*. It has gained a narrow foothold in northern South America, where it was probably a late arrival. The foxes common all over South America have usually been called species of the genus *Dusicyon* but Van Gelder puts them in a subgenus *Canis (Pseudalopex)*. *Dusicyon* in the narrowest sense was first applied to the now extinct fox of the Falkland Islands made famous by Darwin. Three mainland species of foxes closely related to the common mainland *Dusicyon* or *Pseudalopex* are nevertheless distinct enough to have been referred to separate genera or subgenera. Of these *Cerdocyon* or *Canis (Cerdocyon) thous* is distinguished as the crab-eating fox for no obvious reason, as like all foxes it has a mixed diet usually heaviest in small rodents.

Universally regarded as a distinct genus is *Speothos,* with a single species usually called a bush dog in English vernacular (equivalent to *cachorro do mato* in Brazilian Portuguese). It is rather distinctive, being stocky, with short legs and tail, relatively large head, and small ears. The genus was first found fossil in Pleistocene caves in Brazil, named by Lund in 1839, and later found to be living over much of South America and marginally into Panama. The name *Speothos* was coined from Greek and means literally "cave wolf," which was apt for the occurrence of the first fossil specimens, but the living bush dogs of this genus do not especially frequent caves.

The most distinctive of all South American canids is the maned wolf or *azuará-guazú* (its Paraguayan Indian name), *Chrysocyon brachyurus,* literally "short-tailed golden dog." Most of the coat is indeed golden although the exceptionally long legs are dark in color and the tail, of medium length and furry, is lighter. It has a thick mane that can be erected. The head is pointed and bears large, erect ears.

Dusicyon, in a broad sense, at least, had already become differentiated from other canids when it entered the known record in the Uquian, early Pleistocene, and *Speothos* was present near the end of that epoch. Fossils so far discovered do not fill out the origins of the other living genera. Hershkovitz suggests that the genera now present in South America first evolved in Central America, although he denies that as a possibility for the South

American cricetids. For the canids and for many cricetids that is a reasonable hypothesis, but one without evidence. Among the distinctive genera only *Speothos* ranges at all into Central America and it barely so, as an extension of its South American range. *Urocyon* is probably of nontropical North American origin.

The bears, Ursidae, are another family of placental carnivores that first appear in the known record in the Uquian, early Pleistocene. Although a number of different names have been given to the Pleistocene bears of South America, all are more soundly placed in just two rather closely related genera, *Arctodus* (often mistakenly called *Arctotherium*) and *Tremarctos*. They differ from other bears in having unusually short snouts and rounded or domed brows and are sometimes put in a subfamily of their own as Tremarctinae, the short-faced bears. They apparently originated in North America, where an older possible ancestor is known. (The only other possibility is Eurasia, where there are also numerous fossil and Recent bears but none like these.) Both genera are also common in the Pleistocene of North America, where fossil *Arctodus* is known all the way from Alaska to Mexico, but *Tremarctos,* probably significantly, is known only from what is now southern United States (southern California, Texas, Florida) and Mexico. In both North and South America *Arctodus* varied greatly in size, but the largest specimens were considerably larger than the great Alaskan and Siberian brown bears, largest of living carnivores. *Arctodus* became extinct on both continents, but *Tremarctos* survives in South America, where *Tremarctos ornatus* is the only living bear. It lives in the mountains of northern and central South America at elevations up to about 3,000 meters (about 10,000 feet). Most bears are omnivorous, happy to feed on almost anything animal or vegetable but rarely on grass or other leaves. The South American bear, however, is said to be largely herbivorous and often to eat the leaves of trees. It is called the spectacled bear because it usually has large white rings in the fur around its eyes, but these are variable and are occasionally lacking.

It has already been mentioned that the Procyonidae were the first placental carnivores known to have reached South America. This is an originally North American family dating at least from the Miocene. Its main differentiation probably took place in Miocene to Pleistocene in Central America, which, as noted, had a purely North American fauna until some time in the Pliocene. Although this is called the raccoon family, *Procyon,* the raccoon genus, being its type, six other living genera superficially quite different from raccoons are referred to it. Early occurrences in South America include at least two not yet well-known extinct genera. Six of the seven usually recognized Recent genera are present in Central America, but only five of them in South America, to which one is confined. One genus, *Procyon* itself, is widespread in what is now the United States, and two others within the United States live mainly in our southwest—*Bassariscus,* the ring-tailed cats or cacomistles, which occur as far as Central but not in South America, and *Nasua,* the coatimundis, coatis, or (in northern Mexican and Arizonan Spanish) chulos, which are also widespread in South America.

Only one raccoon, the so-called crab-eating racoon (*Procyon cancrivorus*), occurs on continental South America, where it is marginal in the north. Like all raccoons it usually lives near water and swims well. It does eat crabs where available but also makes do with almost any animal and some vegetable food. As is well known, raccoons often wash their food before eating it, which has earned them a German name "Waschbär" ("wash bear"), although raccoons are not native in any German-speaking countries.

There is only one species of coati, *Nasua nasua,* a double name that emphasizes or even overemphasizes the long, pointed, flexible snout which it sticks into every cranny seeking food—animal, vegetable, or one almost wants to add "mineral." Coatis are highly gregarious and usually go about in playful, busy groups, sometimes of several dozen individuals. The species occurs all the way from Arizona to Argentina. A distinct coatilike species occurs in the Andes of Venezuela, Colombia, and Ecuador and is now placed in a separate genus, *Nasuella,* but looks like a smaller *Nasua.*

The kinkajou, *Potos flavus,* also the only species of its genus, ranges from southern Mexico to southern Brazil. It is highly arboreal and lives mostly on fruit although it also eats insects and other small animals. As far as I know it is the only carnivore with a truly prehensile tail. Its English vernacular name has come to us via French from its name in Tupi, an Indian language that is the lingua franca, or in Brazilian terms the *lingua geral,* of the Amazon Basin. The generic name has embalmed an old mistake. In 1776 Buffon recorded that these animals were called "poto" by the natives of Jamaica. In fact the natives of Jamaica had never seen and had never even heard of a kinkajou. Buffon may have been confused by the fact that some natives of West Africa, from which Jamaican slaves came, knew a decidedly different animal, a small lemurlike primate, that they (and now we) call "potto."

In northern South America there is another animal, usually called an olingo, that looks and acts much like a kinkajou and even goes around with groups of kinkajous but that has a bushier, nonprehensile tail and other differences that have caused it usually to be put in a distinct genus, *Bassaricyon.* Although several species have been named, they are probably all local varieties of only one valid species, *B. gabbii.*

(Humans find most procyonids attractive, and some procyonids also find humans attractive, or at least interesting, and so make playful pets. They have their drawbacks as such, however, because they tend to be nocturnal and may be all too playful when their human companions prefer to sleep.)

Members of the weasel family, Mustelidae, are known in South America from the Chapadmalalan onward, later than the Procyonidae but before the other families of placental carnivores that did spread to that continent. The occurrence then of a skunk of the still extant genus *Conepatus* has already been mentioned. In the Uquian there is an extinct mustelid genus, *Stipanicicia* (Stipanicic is an eminent Argentine geologist), and a grison of the living genus *Galictis.* The grisons, with one species widespread in Central and South America and another confined to South America, owe their vernacular name to the French word for "gray-haired." In the eighteenth and nineteenth centuries knowledge of South American animals was largely due to French naturalists. The grison also has a Latin American Spanish name, "hurón," derived from the late Latin name for the European ferret, a similar animal. Grisons are built like rather large weasels, with long gray hair on back and tail and strikingly patterned heads, black on the face and white on brow and upper neck. Like weasels, they are almost entirely carnivorous and are fierce predators.

In the Ensenadan, more or less middle Pleistocene, two other still extant genera appear in the known fossil record. *Lyncodon,* known locally as "huroncito," that is, small hurón or grison, closely resembles the grisons, but the color contrast is less marked. The single living species occurs in southern South America, on the pampas of southern Argentina, especially Patagonia, and Peru. The other new mustelid record in the Ensenadan is an otter of the practically worldwide genus *Lutra* (its Latin name). This genus is represented in the Recent South American fauna by the otherwise North American species *Lutra canadensis.*

Several other South American mustelid genera are not as yet known as fossils. They include *Mustela,* the typical and widespread genus of weasels, represented in northern South America by the same species as in Canada, throughout most of the United States, Mexico, and Central America. Another weasellike Recent genus in South America is *Grammogale* with one species curiously named *africana* because E. Desmarest, an early nineteenth-century French naturalist, thought it came from Africa, whereas in fact it is confined to central South America.

The only other Recent South American species of mustelids is *Pteronura brasilensis,* usually called giant otter in English but like other South American living mammals with a plethora of vernacular names in Spanish, Portuguese, and various Indian languages. *Pteronura* means "wing tail" and was given with dubious justification because the animal's tail is not round, as in other otters, but is flattened horizontally and so expanded laterally in an unusual but not obviously winglike way. All otters are acrobatic swimmers and this one is the champion. If it wants to make a quick reverse, it rotates to its side and with a swish of its thus vertically flattened tail can turn, as the saying goes, on a dime. As R. F. ("Griff") Ewer has written, "Mammals are more playful than any other animals. . . . It is . . . only natural that carnivores should be amongst the most playful of mammals," and she goes on to

exemplify the fact that otters are among the most playful of carnivores (Ewer 1973, p. 351). In this respect no otters, and probably
no animals with the possible exception of *Homo sapiens,* outdo
Pteronura.

The other family of placental carnivores to reach South America
is that of the cats, Felidae, which, again, enters the known record
in the Uquian, early Pleistocene. By that time the felids in North
America and elsewhere had been sorted into two broadly defined adaptive types: one, that of cats in a usual sense but ranging
from house cats to Siberian tigers; the other, that of the sabertooths, quite unlike tigers in spite of their popularization as
"saber-toothed tigers." It is more likely than not that both kinds
reached South America at about the same time, but the earliest
known South American felid was a probable sabertooth, known
only from parts of the pelvis and hindleg and somewhat dubious as
to exact affinities. In any case there were certainly both kinds of
felids, cats and sabertooths, in the next land mammal age, the
Ensenadan.

It is tempting to think that the placental sabertooths replaced
the marsupial sabertooths, *Thylacosmilus* and its relatives, by competition in South America, but the last known marsupial sabertooth is distinctly earlier than the earliest known South American
placental sabertooth, so evidence for possible competition is lacking. There is, however, an overlap in the known temporal distribution of other marsupial carnivores (Borhyaenidae) and other placental carnivores (as noted in the last few pages) in South America.

Although some other names have been given to them, the definitely identified South American sabertooths are most reasonably all placed in the genus *Smilodon,* a name that appropriately
means "knife tooth." The same genus in species not surely different was abundant practically everywhere in both South and
North America. In North America it is best known by the hundreds of specimens from the tar pits of Rancho La Brea in Hollywood, California, but it also occurs at many other localities, as it
does also in South America. It became extinct at about the same
time, around the end of the Pleistocene, on both continents.
W. D. Matthew suggested that its extinction was caused by the reduc-

tion and extinction of large, tough-skinned ungulates on which it could prey more successfully than the other large (nonsabertooth) cats, a plausible idea but one that passes the explanation on to the extinction of the suitable prey.

There is fairly good agreement that there are ten (some say nine) species of native cats now living in South America, but there are differences of opinion as to how many genera should be distinguished. Some students put them all in one genus, *Felis;* others put them in six different genera. I prefer to classify them in two genera: *Felis,* with eight South American species and many others elsewhere, and *Leo,* with only one South American species but several others elsewhere. Both genera originated in the Old World and reached North America from Asia, and South America from North America. However, the South American species referred to *Felis* arose mainly from an adaptive radiation in southern North America and partly from further radiation in continental South America, while the species here referred to *Leo,* the jaguar *Leo onca* or its immediate ancestor, evolved in Asia and spread through both Americas without further radiation. Both groups of felids, in *Felis* and in *Leo,* are definitely known in South America from the Ensenadan onward.

There has been the utmost confusion about the names, both vernacular and technical, for the South American cats. It would serve no good purpose to argue or even discuss these at any length here, so I will simply list the names I choose to use and tabulate the briefest summaries of what they are like and where they live.

Small to medium-sized spotted cats
   Now or recently marginal in extreme southwestern United States and occurring thence through Mexico and Central America into South America
      Ocelot, *Felis pardalis*
      Margay, *Felis wiedii*
   Yaguarundi, *Felis yaguaroundi*
   Central America and South America, the above and also
      Little spotted cat, or little tiger ocelot, *Felis tigrina*

South America only
    Tigrillo or huiña, *Felis guigna*
    Mountain cat, *Felis jacobita*
    Geoffrey's ocelot, *Felis geoffreyi*
    Pampas cat, *Felis pajeros*
Large unspotted cat
  From southern Canada to Patagonia
    Puma or mountain lion, *Felis concolor*
Large spotted cat
    Jaguar, *Leo onca*

One point about nomenclature does require some comment. Why is the jaguar, much more like a leopard than like a lion, put in a genus called *Leo,* which obviously means "lion"? The Old World lions, tigers, and leopards are a natural group, evolved from the same ancestry. There is evidence that jaguars are especially related to those large Old World cats and evolved from the same ancestry. All these animals can be considered divergent species of one genus. That genus was for years usually called *Panthera,* the Latin name for the Old World leopards. However, although that name was in print in 1816 or earlier, it was finally decided that it did not meet some formal codified rules laid down for the naming of genera and that the oldest name for this group that does meet those rules is *Leo.* So, silly as it seems, the more commonly used name *Panthera* had to be replaced by *Leo.* Incidentally, in South America the jaguar is called *tigre,* pronounced more or less tee'-gray and meaning "tiger," and its specific name although now written *onca* is pronounced as if it were *onsa.* Further incidentally, it was suddenly discovered about forty years ago that some large fossil cats known for several generations from localities around the United States were in fact of the same species as the living jaguars. It was even later learned that the big cat called *Felis atrox* and well known from the Pleistocene of Rancho La Brea is surely a lion and possibly of the same species as the living Asiatic lion. (Yes, lions do live in Asia as well as Africa.)

The newcomers that remain to be discussed are the late-arriving ungulates, which eventually became the only remaining South American hoofed mammals. The most conspicuous although probably not the most numerous of them were great beasts collaterally related to the elephants. By Pleistocene times this whole order of ungulates, the Proboscidea, had become well differentiated into three major groups best characterized as families: Gomphotheriidae, an unwieldy name that seems to mean "bolt beast family" which in turn doesn't seem to mean anything except as a handle for this family; Mammutidae, which seems to mean "mammoth family" but means "American mastodon family" despite the probability that the family originated in Eurasia; and Elephantidae, which means just what it sounds like, given the fact that mammoths are simply extinct elephants. The first two families reached North America from Asia in the Miocene. The Elephantidae, one of the youngest of all recognized mammalian families, did not reach North America until the Pleistocene. The Mammutidae and especially the Elephantidae spread some distance into southern North America but as far as we know never reached South America. (There have been two reports of finds of tooth fragments of mammoths, hence Elephantidae, in South America, but both reports are now considered erroneous.) For unknown reasons those two abundant and widespread families were somehow screened out by the Middle American filter.

The Gomphotheriidae were not screened out. They appear in the South American record in the Uquian early Pleistocene, and toward the end of that epoch they were present and apparently quite abundant everywhere in South America with the possible exception of the highest mountaintops. They are not, however, everywhere the same. There are three well-known and well-distinguished genera: *Stegomastodon,* with a short skull and high brow, simple curved tusks without enamel, and complexly cusped molars; *Cuvieronius,* with a long skull, low brow, long, nearly straight tusks with a spiral band of enamel, and simpler molars; and *Haplomastodon,* with brow and skull intermediate in shape between the other two genera, upturned, stout tusks with a straight enamel band only in juveniles, and simple molars like those of *Cuvieronius.* These are clearly related to each other but represent three lineages diverging to a moderate degree from a common ancestor most like *Haplomastodon* among these three.

Although many supposed species have been named, extensive study by the Brazilian paleontologist Carlos de Paula Couto and me found only a single South American species clearly valid in each genus. The various local occurrences suggest some regional and ecological differences among them. Their ranges apparently overlapped, but two of them are seldom found at the same locality. *Cuvieronius,* named for Baron Georges L. C. F. D. Cuvier (1769–1832), who is often considered the father of vertebrate paleontology, is characteristic of the southern Andes and has been called the Andine mastodon, but it does also occur elsewhere. *Stegomastodon* is best known from the pampas of Argentina and is sometimes called the Pampean mastodon, but it also occurs in far northern South America. *Haplomastodon* is best known from Brazil and Ecuador and is not definitely known from Argentina or the Andean region south of Ecuador but is widespread in tropical South America. Knowledge of the detailed distribution of all these mastodonts is obscured by the eccentricities of nomenclature as used by different authors and by the fact that single, worn teeth, the commonest finds, are difficult or sometimes impossible to identify beyond doubt. For instance, those of *Cuvieronius* and *Haplomastodon* can often be more easily confused than distinguished. This point is made here because it is a somewhat extreme but by no means unique example of a kind of problem that often faces a student of South American fossils. Another problem in this case is that there is a supposed fourth genus of South American mastodonts, called *Notiomastodon* by Angel Cabrera (1879–1960), a distinguished first Spanish and later Argentinian mammalogist. This possible genus is known only by scraps from a single locality and of quite dubious status.

There is little doubt that the generic differentiation of these mastodonts took place in North America. *Stegomastodon* and *Cuvieronius* are definitely known from the late Pliocene and Pleistocene of North America, and there are less surely identifiable North American specimens representing either *Haplomastodon* or the ancestral gomphotheriid stock that gave rise to that relatively conservative genus and to the other two more advanced genera known from both North and South America. All these proboscideans on both continents were extinct by the end of the Pleistocene or shortly thereafter.

The horses, Equidae, are another group that reached South from North America and that are known on the southern continent from the earliest (Uquian) to the latest (Lujanian) Pleistocene or into the earliest Recent depending on how the upper boundary of the Pleistocene is defined. Again many genera and species have been proposed for the known South American forms. The sorting out of the valid species has never been reliably done and will be a truly Herculean or perhaps a Sisyphean task if or when it is done. Fortunately, that does not need to concern us here. The less chaotic generic nomenclature can reasonably be reduced to only three well-defined genera, although each must be rather broadly characterized: *Hippidion, Onohippidium,* and *Equus.*

Hippidion and *Onohippidium* are closely related to each other but different enough to merit generic separation. They occur widely in South America but are most completely known from Argentina and Bolivia. They share some differences from other Pleistocene horses, most obviously the fact that the long nasal bones were less supported, leaving a long slit in the side of the skull between them and the upper jaw, and that their metapodials (the cannon bone of the hindfoot and shank of the forefoot) were relatively short and wide. Other distinctive details indicate that they can hardly have evolved from the terminal genus *Equus* but probably did from *Pliohippus,* the immediate predecessor of *Equus* in North America. They are known only from South America and are there most common in the early to middle Pleistocene (Uquian and Ensenadan), but one is also reported from the late Pleistocene (Lujanian). Their divergence from *Pliohippus* and from each other might have occurred in southern North America or, more narrowly, Central America, but there is no clear, positive evidence to that effect. A species of *Pliohippus* is known from the Pliocene, probably early Pliocene, of Honduras, but it has no special resemblance to the South American genera. There were surely other Pliocene species of *Pliohippus* in Central America, but they are not yet known.

The genus *Equus* probably reached South America somewhat later than the two genera just discussed, but that is not quite certain. The South American species, one or more, differ from the North American, and also from almost all the living Old World species, in that the lower incisors lack a little enamel-lined cup or pit. (The French call it a *cornet,* pronounced about core-neh, which among other things can mean a cone as in "ice-cream cone.") There are some other equally esoteric distinctions which led the French paleontologist Hoffstetter in 1950 to propose that the South American species be placed in a different genus, *Amerhippus,* but in 1952 he decided that the distinction did not merit fully generic separation, with which I agree.

All the horses native to the Western Hemisphere became extinct at or shortly after the end of the Pleistocene. It is still sometimes claimed that some of them did survive and were still living when Europeans began to settle in the Americas, but despite long and careful investigation there is absolutely no reliable or even probable evidence for that. The so-called wild horses of the Americas are in fact feral horses, that is, horses that were formerly domesticated or had descended from such domesticated horses. It is also an unsubstantiated myth that such feral horses are largely or solely descended from Arabian or Spanish horses of early colonial times. Most or in some cases all of their heredity comes from much later horses that escaped from farms and ranches or that were turned out as useless.

Relatives of the horses, distantly related but of the same order, Perissodactyla ("even-toed"), are the tapirs, Tapiridae. That is a very old family, possibly of Old World origin but already in North America in the Oligocene. They were widespread but mainly southern in what is now the United States through the Pleistocene, but since then have been confined to Central and South America except for a southern Asiatic survivor of the Old World branch. Only one living genus, *Tapirus,* is now generally accepted, and it enters the known South American record in the early Pleistocene (Uquian). There are three living species, one almost everywhere in tropical South America, another in tropical North America to Colombia and Ecuador, and one, oddly enough for such otherwise tropical animals, well up in the northern Andes.

The remaining newcomers to be discussed are all members of the order Artiodactyla, even-toed ungulates, but of three very different families: Tayassuidae (peccaries), Camelidae (camels, but with other South American names), and Cervidae (deer).

The peccary family is old in both hemispheres, known from the early Oligocene in both North America and Europe, but most of their history has been North American. Oddly enough, a fossil peccary recently turned up in the late Miocene or early Pliocene of South Africa, the only one known from that continent which has long been occupied by hoards of similar but distinct true pigs, Suidae. The peccaries are known from the Chapadmalalan onward in South America and so apparently reached there before the climax of the great interchange. Two living genera, *Tayassu* with two species and *Catagonus* with one, are now distinguished. Both of them and another, *Platygonus,* doubtfully distinct from *Catagonus,* are recorded in Argentina in the more or less mid-Pleistocene Ensenadan. As with several other groups, these genera probably became differentiated in southern North, or Central, America although *Platygonus* ranged all over the present United States in the Pleistocene and one species of *Tayassu,* the collared peccary, still ranges into Arizona, New Mexico, and Texas. The other species of *Tayassu,* the white-lipped peccary, ranges from tropical Mexico over most of South America along with the collared peccary. The genus *Catagonus* (or *Platygonus*), long considered extinct, now occupies a restricted area around the junction of Brazil and Paraguay.

Peccaries resemble pigs and are often erroneously given that name, but they have been distinct from pigs for tens of millions of years, and true pigs have never lived in the Western Hemisphere except as introduced by European humans. The most obvious differences are that in true pigs, Suidae, there are large upper canine tusks curving outward and upward and on the hindfoot there are two small toes, one on each side of the two large, weight-bearing toes. In peccaries the upper canines are relatively small and point down, and there is only one small toe (on the inner side) besides the two weight-bearing toes of the hindfoot. There are other equally or more marked but less evident differences in the dentition and internal anatomy.

The camel family originated in the Eocene of North America, and the more familiar Old World camels were Pleistocene immigrants in the Old World. In South America the living genus *Lama* appears in the early Pleistocene, Uquian, record along with two extinct genera, *Palaeolama* and *Hemiauchenia.* In the following Ensenadan all of those are also known as well as the other living genus *Vicugna*. All of the previously mentioned genera and one other extinct genus, *Eulamaops,* occur in the late Pleistocene. *Hemiauchenia* appears in North America earlier than in South America and *Palaeolama* as early. It is probable again that generic divergence was well under way and possible that it was complete in southern North America before these animals spread to South America. No camelids now occur in North (including Central) America.

In the present South American fauna three species of *Lama* are usually recognized with the vernacular names guanaco (pronounced gwah-nah'-koh or wah-nah'-koh), llama (pronounced yah'-mah), and alpaca (pronounced ahl-pah'-kah). Two of these, however, llama and alpaca, existed only as domesticated animals when Europeans first encountered them, and there is doubt whether they had been domesticated from what were originally two distinct wild species or whether they were two domesticated breeds of guanacos. Cabrera, a good authority, believed that they had been distinct wild species. The genus *Vicugna* and its one species are wild and have the vernacular name vicuña (pronounced vee-koon'-ya; the generic name is an Italianate spelling of the same word and should be pronounced the same).

All of the four species of South American Camelidae are similar, much like the Old World camels in many respects but humpless, smaller, and shorter-legged. The domesticated forms or species have longer, woolly hair—especially the alpaca, as is well known—and vary in coloration. Although guanacos come down to

Fig. 43. Some of the mammals now typically South American and among the genera defining a Neotropical Region that are of late North American, Nearctic

sea level in Patagonia, all four South American camelids are cold-climate animals and live mainly in the high Andes.

The last family to be particularly discussed here is the Cervidae, deer. This is another of the eight families with an early Pleistocene, Uquian, to Recent known time range in South America.

Odocoileus virginianus, the well-known Virginia or white-tailed deer, ranges not only in southern Canada and over most of the United States but also through Mexico and Central America into South America. It is mainly northern in the latter continent, but its range does extend marginally as far as northern Peru and Brazil. The generic name, from Greek roots meaning "hollow tooth," was coined with an incorrect rendering from those roots by an eccentric pioneer American naturalist usually named as Constantine Rafinesque (1783–1840) although he called himself Rafinesque-Schmaltz. He based the name on a single premolar tooth found in a cave in Pennsylvania. That tooth was later found to belong to the species still common in Pennsylvania and called *Cervus virginianus* before Rafinesque. With the exception of one modern eccentric, everyone now uses Rafinesque's name for the genus.

The only other deer now occurring in both South and Central America are brockets of the genus *Mazama,* a name also coined by Rafinesque. He got it from an early Spanish rendering of a Nahuatl name for some ungulate, which could hardly have been a brocket because brockets do not range into the area where Nahuatl was spoken. The name "brocket," now always applied to these deer in vernacular English, is also peculiar in this application. It was a sixteenth-century or earlier name, derived from French, applied in England to a stag in its second year when it had antlers with single tines. The name was transferred to these small tropical

---

ancestry: *A,* a collared peccary, *Tayassu tajacu; B,* a vicuña, *Vicugna vicugna; C,* a Brazilian tapir, *Tapirus terrestris; D,* a pampas deer, *Blastoceros* (or *Ozotoceras*) *bezoarcticus.* This peccary still does occur in Nearctic North America, but it is marginal there and more characteristically Neotropical. The genus *Tapirus* still occurs in tropical North America, which became incorporated in a Neotropical Region during the great interchange, but the species there is *Tapirus bairdi,* not *terrestris. Tapirus* does not now occur in the Nearctic Region. Both the genera and species *Vicugna vicugna* and *Blastoceros bezoarcticus* live only in continental South America.

American deer because their males also have antlers with single tines, at all ages and not only in their second year. Cabrera lists four South American species ranging southward to Paraguay.

Two strictly South American genera of deer have the unfortunately similar names *Blastocerus* and *Blastoceros*. Those names are both valid under the International Code of Zoological Nomenclature, but zoologists who prize clarity more than rules sometimes use *Edocerus* in place of *Blastocerus* and *Ozotoceros* in place of *Blastoceros* to avoid confusing the two. Each genus has only one valid living species. *Blastocerus* or *Edocerus dichotomus,* the swamp deer, is the largest South American deer, reaching a shoulder height of more than a meter (about $3\frac{1}{3}$ feet) and a weight up to about 100 kilograms (about 220 pounds). The mature antlers are usually doubly forked (hence the name *dichotomus*) and so have four tines. *Blastoceros* or *Ozotoceros bezoarticus,* the pampas deer of southern South America, is somewhat smaller and its mature antlers generally have three tines.

Hippocamelus includes the two species of huemuls (pronounced way-mools'). These are mountain deer living along the Andes from Ecuador to northern Chile. They are about as large as the pampas deer and somewhat similar, but their mature antlers normally have only two tines, the longer posterior branch not divided as in the pampas deer. The strange name *Hippocamelus,* "horse-camel," was given to these animals in 1816 under the extraordinary conviction that they are intermediate between, or perhaps hybrids of, horses and llamas. More extraordinary still is the fact that even earlier a South American naturalist believed them to be strange horses and put them in the genus *Equus.* The vernacular name huemul is a genuine Araucanian Indian name for these deer.

The two species of *Pudu* are tiny deer, much the smallest of any deer in the Americas, with a maximum shoulder height of only about 415 millimeters (about $16\frac{1}{3}$ inches). The mature males have only short, spikelike antlers, and both sexes are nearly tailless. Pudu, pronounced poo'-doo, is another correctly applied Araucanian Indian name from Chile. One species ranges along practically the whole of the Pacific coast of South America and also at low elevations east of the Andes in Argentina. The other species lives well up in the Andes in Bolivia and Ecuador.

The fossil record of the Cervidae in South America is highly unsatisfactory. It does show that deer were present in some variety in the early Pleistocene Uquian, but the relationships of these earliest known South American deer are not clear. The six living genera have all been reported from the late Pleistocene, or in some cases perhaps early Recent, hither and yon in South America. Several extinct genera have been named, but sometimes on fragments of antlers of dubious significance. Some, for example *Agalmaceros* Hoffstetter from the Pleistocene of Equador, are clearly distinct from any living genus. That and some other extinct genera such as *Antifer* Ameghino in Argentina show that by the end of the Pleistocene there were more varied deer in South America than at present. The origin and diversification of the South American representatives of the family remain obscure beyond the reasonable probability that *Odocoileus,* at least, originated in North America and spread to South America relatively late.

As a summary of the present South American fauna of land mammals, table 13 names the orders and families and gives figures for the numbers of living genera and species in each family. Those numbers depend to some extent on personal opinion and cannot be taken as hard facts, but they do give an idea of the relative diversity of the various groups. When in doubt I have more often followed Cabrera than any other one authority. Cabrera's catalogue is definitely for continental South America. Other lists and counts, such as one by Hershkovitz, are later in date and also authoritative but include genera and species in the Neotropical part of North America and also, in Hershkovitz's case explicitly, taxa on various Caribbean islands that I judge should not be included in the Neotropical Region.

The tabulation further separates the living fauna into descendants of each of the three basic faunal strata, the first group discussed in chapter 6, the second in chapter 11, and the third in the present chapter.

Before leaving discussion of the present fauna and going on to

Table 13

Estimated numbers of taxa of Recent South American mammals and their stratal origins

	Estimated Numbers	
	Genera	*Species*
From Stratum 1		
Marsupialia		
Didelphidae (opossums)	12	67
Caenolestidae	3	7
Xenarthra		
Dasypodidae (armadillos)	9	16
Bradypodidae (tree sloths)	2	3
Myrmecophagidae (anteaters)	3	3
Totals and percentage for 1	29, 18%	96, 20%
From Stratum 2		
Primates		
Cebidae (monkeys)	12	26
Callithricidae (marmosets)	5	16
Rodentia		
Erethizontidae (porcupines)	3	8
Caviidae (guinea pigs, etc.)	6	9
Hydrochoeridae (capybaras)	1	1
Chinchillidae (chinchillas)	3	3
Dasyproctidae (agoutis)	2	2
Cuniculidae (pacas)	1	1
Dinomyidae (pacaranas)	1	1
Octodontidae (degus, etc.)	6	8
Abrocomidae (chinchillones)	1	2
Echimyidae (spiny rats)	16	44
Myocastoridae (nutrias or coypus)	1	1
Totals and percentage for 2	58, 36%	122, 26%
From Stratum 3		
Insectivora		
Soricidae (shrews)	1	1
Lagomorpha		
Leporidae (rabbits)	1	2
Rodentia		
Sciuridae (squirrels)	3	13

Table 13
(*Continued*)

| | Estimated Numbers | |
	Genera	Species
From Stratum 3		
Cricetidae (field mice)	38	185
Heteromyidae (pocket mice)	1	3
Carnivora		
Canidae (foxes, etc.)	6	11
Ursidae (bears)	1	1
Procyonidae (raccoons, etc.)	5	5
Mustelidae (skunks, otters, etc.)	5	6
Felidae (cats)	2	10
Perissodactyla		
Tapiridae (tapirs)	1	3
Artiodactyla		
Tayassuidae (peccaries)	2	3
Camelidae (llamas, etc)	2	4
Cervidae (deer)	6	10
Totals and percentage for 3	74, 46%	257, 54%
Grand totals	161	475

more general and more theoretical final considerations in the next chapter something should be said briefly about the South American bats, the order Chiroptera. The theme of this book has explicitly omitted the flying and the wholly aquatic mammals of the continent. The flying bats, the only truly flying mammals, were excluded not because their phylogenetic relationships and zoogeographic history cannot be analyzed but because they must be analyzed in quite different ways and because their history, even if it were well known (which it is not), would not distort that of the nonflying land mammals or add significantly to our knowledge of the latter.

The fossil record of bats in South America is almost nil. Only one fossil genus, from the Friasian, middle Miocene, of Colombia is known, and this, *Notonycteris,* is closely related to a living South

American genus, *Vampyrum,* which incidentally is not a vampire bat despite its name. Known Pleistocene bats belong to living genera and species as far as identified. Bats can cross quite extensive marine barriers even though they do not do so frequently, and they have colonized not only all continents but also all but the most isolated of oceanic islands. Once they do reach a new land area, they diversify there with probable rapidity and at levels from new subspecies to new families. It is probable that bats have been colonizing South America off and on through the Cenozoic and that these somewhat randomly distributed arrivals cannot be recognized as distinct fossil strata on the evidence of living bats, which is all we have.

South America now has the richest bat fauna of any region on earth. It has nine to eleven families, depending on the classification adopted, and about 65 genera in recent classifications. (Hershkovitz has 80, but that is for his Neotropical Region and includes about 15 genera not present in continental South America.) In distribution the genera vary from one (*Depanycteris*) known only from a single locality in Brazil to another (*Myotis*) that is practically worldwide. The history is surely rich and complex, but it has not been well worked out and cannot be further pursued here. It is interesting that the other flying vertebrates, the birds, are similar in their ability to cross oceanic barriers at long but geologically frequent random intervals, in their rapid local diversification when they do reach new lands, and in the fact that South America is richer in their various taxa than any other region. For them some essentials of the South American history have been worked out almost entirely on the evidence of the Recent fauna by Ernst Mayr.

References

Most of the compilations and reviews again relevant for this chapter have been cited with earlier chapters. There are few recent detailed studies of late Cenozoic South American faunas as a whole, but some classics of that sort are here cited as well as a monograph on one Pleistocene group and a book on carnivores that has been cited in this chapter.

Boule, M., and A. Thevenin. 1920. *Mammifères fossiles de Tarija*. Paris: Imprimerie Nationale. (The Tarija fauna is in the Pleistocene of Bolivia.)

Cabrera, A. 1957, 1960. Catálogo de los mamíferos de America del Sur. *Revista, Museo Argentine de Ciencias Naturales "Bernardino Rivadavia,"* vol. 4, nos. 1 and 2.

Cabrera, A., and J. Yepes. 1940. *Mamíferos Sud-Americanos (vida, costumbres, y descripción)*. Buenos Aires: Historia Natural Ediar.

Ewer, R. F. 1973. The carnivores. Ithaca: Cornell University Press.

Hoffstetter, R. 1952. Les mammifères pleistocènes de la République de l'Equateur. *Mémoires de la Société Géologique de France*, n. s., 31: 1–391.

Kraglievich, L. 1934. *La antigüedad pliocena de las faunas de Monte Hermoso y Chapadmalal, deducidas de su comparición con las que le procedieron y sucedieron*. Montevideo: Imprenta El Siglo Ilustrado.

Simpson, G. G., and C. de Paula Couto. 1957. The mastodonts of Brazil. *Bulletin of the American Museum of Natural History*, 112: 125–190.

Van Gelder, R. G. 1978. A review of canid classification. *Amer. Mus. Novitates*, no. 2646, pp. 1–10.

Walker, E. P., et al. 1975. *Mammals of the world*. (Contains illustrations of all the South American living genera.)

CHAPTER 17

This History as Experiment and Evidence

At this point no reader will have failed to see this history as a story. Indeed the words "history" and "story" have a common origin. This story is none the worse for having an element of mystery and for the fact that the mystery is not yet entirely solved. The history is worthwhile for its own sake, but its interest would be less if it had no other significance. It does have such significance in abundance and variety. In the preceding chapters something of the broader meaning and insight has been mentioned where appropriate. Now, in this terminal chapter, various more or less theoretical aspects will be reviewed and some special points made.

The history of South American mammals can be considered as an experiment without a laboratory, fortuitously provided by nature. It is a grand experiment in population biology, ecology, biogeography, and other subjects, and as such it provides not only an unparalleled number and variety of populations and events with corresponding complexity but also a time scale incomparably longer than that of any experiment in a laboratory. This is the scope and this is the time scale in which evolution has really occurred. No one doubts that the laboratory experiments, as by population biologists, geneticists, and the other organismic evolutionary biologists, are also pertinent to interpretation of the larger scene, but the way to full understanding of their implications must include what is known in that larger scene. The field observations of ecologists, ethologists, biogeographers, and others are also relevant and are less limited in space and complexity, but their time scale is as restricted as that of a laboratory and equally needs to be supplemented as far as possible by histories of from millions to billions of years.

The amplification and clarification afforded by this particular history are especially valuable as a natural experiment because it has good (although far from complete) documentation under particularly enlightening and to some extent simplifying conditions. A first point has been rather fully discussed in previous chapters but may here be summarized and somewhat broadened. In this history in three different time periods groups of mammals appear somehow on a continent where there are varied ecological niches open to them and their descendants. That happened first at a time not objectively specifiable but probably in the late Cretaceous. The evidence available indicates that the oldest ancestral faunas closely relevant to those of the Cenozoic, Age of Mammals, as a whole were highly peculiar both in composition and in scope. Their origin is still largely mysterious. They included only marsupials, xenarthrans, and ungulates. By the early Eocene, in the Casamayoran land mammal age, all of these groups had undergone an adaptive radiation resulting in at least twenty families and about a hundred genera. We do not know how long that remarkable proliferation took, but even the maximum estimate of possibly available time—on the order of 15 to at most 20 million years—indicates an episode of unusually rapid evolutionary divergence and splitting of lineages (cladogenesis). The probability that rates of evolution were not steady during the whole of that time span emphasizes all the more that they must have been extraordinarily high at some time or times.

The next episode relevant to this discussion of large-scale diversification of faunas can be more closely dated. The first primates and rodents evidently reached South America in the latest Eocene or earliest Oligocene, more or less 37 to 40 million years ago. The known fossil record of the primates is so poor that we do not know any details of their expansion, but we do know from its results in the Recent fauna that it did occur on a large scale. For the rodents descending from this appearance of aliens, the caviomorphs, there is a good fossil record, and it shows that their basic radiation into families, with correspondingly greater diversification of genera and species, was so rapid as to seem practically instantaneous in geological terms. Obviously the diversification and specialization of the still older groups had not extended to all ways of life possible in the existing environments but left open a large number of ecological niches that were rapidly occupied by the caviomorph rodents. Even in the Recent fauna they still hold on to most of those niches or adaptive zones.

The last and most complex episode in this series of one sort of natural experiments was of course the Great American Interchange. For the most part this is well documented. We know that it began by waif dispersal from Central America not later than the Huayquerian, began to trickle over a closer connection of the two continents in the Montehermosan, and reached its acme in the Uquian, thus occurring for the most part within a time span of less than 10 million years. Here again there is clear evidence that evolution was occurring at unusually rapid rates during some parts of this long episode, but we are impeded from making good numerical estimates of those rates, especially by the fact that we have practically no hard data on how much of the diversification and specialization occurred in Central America before the hordes of previously North American animals reached South America. It has been shown that the most remarkable single episode in the rapid occupation of South America by formerly North American mammals was the enormous expansion of the cricetid rodents. If the strictly South American part of that expansion took place since the middle Pliocene, as I and most other students of the subject think probable, its evolutionary rate was indeed spectacular but not, as some opponents have maintained, faster than is credible by considerations of population genetics and speciation in general. If at the other extreme this expansion started in South America in the early Miocene, the event would still be remarkable, but the rates of speciation involved would be rather slower than might be expected under the circumstances. The circumstances were that we here again have a case where the previous inhabitants of South America had not occupied all ecological niches, some of which had probably been created by the interchange itself and by Pleistocene topographic and climatic changes.

Up to this point I have been considering these phenomena in terms of changes of populations within lines of descent, a process now usually called anagenesis, although Bernhard Rensch, cited as author of the term, gave it a subtly but distinctly different meaning, and of change in the numbers of such lines of descent, basically involving speciation in the sense of separation of one lineage into two or more, a process often called cladogenesis. There is, however, another quite different kind of evolutionary change: change in the makeup of communities. This is certainly affected by both anagenesis and cladogenesis, but it is another kind of phenomenon and in theory does not necessarily require either of those two processes in all particular cases although they are usually also involved.

Changes in the makeup of communities are readily described in terms of the taxa—species, genera, families, and so on—present in a given area or region at successive times. Most of this book has been devoted to such a description in broad terms, especially of families, for South America as a whole. There are other ways to go into this matter of community evolution in more quantitative and more theoretical terms, and some of them will now be briefly discussed. Their application to South American mammals is still limited but is already suggestive and promising.

Given the taxonomic faunal lists for a place or region, what is wanted is an idea, preferably in numerical terms, of the turnover of the taxa from one time to another. One simple and useful method has already been exemplified in chapter 15. An index such as $(100C)/N_1$ can measure faunal resemblance not only between contemporaneous faunas in different places but also between successive faunas in the same locality or region. It is then a measure of faunal turnover—the lower the index, the more the turnover.

In a paper cited at the end of this chapter, Björn Kurtén has shown, on the assumptions that successive faunas have a constant number of taxa, that rates of evolution and migration were also constant, and that sampling is virtually complete or unbiased, that one can then obtain an index that is in theory proportional to absolute age. If there is a year date for any one fauna, for instance by radiometric methods, one can estimate faunal half-life, the length of time in which half the taxa of a fauna will become extinct, and that in turn can be used to estimate the ages of the other faunas involved. That was Kurtén's main object, but his basic data also are a measure of faunal turnover. That works quite well for species in the European Pleistocene, where most of the species and their sequence are well known. Kurtén gave figures for both mollusks and mammals. His figures for mammals have quite different half-lifes for middle and late Pleistocene: 84,000 years and 343,000 years, respectively. That indicates much more rapid turnover for the middle than for the late Pleistocene. His average figure for the whole Neogene (later half of the Age of Mammals), 1,800,000 years, indicates still lower average turnover.

Knowledge, or regional sampling, of species of fossil mammals in South America is not nearly good enough to give comparably good estimates of faunal turnover. For the continent as a whole the sampling of genera, although better than for species, is also not good enough, but it can give some idea of turnover for limited spans of time in particular regions. David Webb has used a different method of estimating faunal turnover among mammals in Argentina during the late Miocene to Pleistocene. He estimated the lengths of each of the relevant ages in millions of years and counted the first known appearances and last known appearances of genera in them. He then calculated the number of first and of last known appearances per million years and averaged the two as a mean rate of change in genera, and hence of faunal turnover in those terms, for each time unit used. He gave the following mean rates for the stated ages, here listed from youngest (late Pleistocene) to oldest (early Pliocene):

Ensenadan and Lujanian (together)	38
Uquian	12.7
Chapadmalalan and Montehermosan	16.3 (24.5)
Huayquerian	3.2 (4.1)
Chasicoan	3.2 (2.5)

I believe that these figures are interestingly indicative in some respects but dubious in others. The durations used are questionable. The Ensenadan and Lujanian may have been twice as long as estimated, and the mean turnover rate hence half that given. The shorter alternatives for Chapadmalalan plus Montehermosan and for Huayquerian may be better estimates, making the figures in parentheses more probable. The sampling is almost certainly better for some intervals than for others. It is hard to understand why the middle or late Pliocene turnover appears to be higher than that in the Uquian, when the interchange was certainly at its height. The high Ensenadan-Lujanian figure is also a surprise but is probably not an artifact. It is largely influenced by the heavy extinction rate around the end of the Lujanian. These doubts are raised not in criticism of Webb but to emphasize that the data now in hand are not entirely adequate for detailed analysis in this way, largely because of variations in sampling and inadequacy of dating. What the data and this analysis do show beyond reasonable doubt is that turnover of genera was much slower in the late Miocene and early Pliocene than in the later Pliocene and the Pleistocene, another sidelight on the great interchange.

I have made similar analyses for the faunas of a number of earlier land mammal ages, but I do not include them here because the data are even less adequate than for the later ages analyzed by Webb. They do, however, suggest that the turnover for genera in Argentina was higher through the Eocene and Oligocene into the early Miocene than in the late Miocene and early Pliocene. (Webb's data are all from Argentina but only in small part from Patagonia; the early data are largely for Patagonia.)

The fact that faunal turnover was continuous and considerable even during long periods of isolation and of relatively static physical environments has already been brought out. The thoroughgoing and multiple instances of convergent evolution have also been exemplified and emphasized. The point made here is that these potentialities of evolution are quite general. They are just especially obvious and clear in the South American history.

Another general principle of evolutionary history that is well exemplified in South America is that of ecological replacement.

The old native ungulate herbivores of the continent were first partly replaced by rodents and finally entirely replaced by late immigrant ungulates from North America. One group may be replaced in its community and ecological functions by another quite distant in biological and geographical origin. There was also a noteworthy sequence of partial and total replacements among the omnivores and carnivores. These were at first exclusively marsupials of various families. One family, Didelphidae, the opossums, never was replaced and is now flourishing. In fact, it has replaced some of the smaller members of another marsupial family, the Borhyaenidae. That family is now wholly extinct, and various of its other branches have been replaced by members of the dog (Canidae), raccoon (Procyonidae), and cat (Felidae) families. It is a peculiar complication that some of the large, cursorial, predaceous borhyaenid marsupial mammals were for a long time in competition with large, cursorial, predaceous birds which probably also preyed on small ungulate mammals. Those birds are also extinct and were replaced by dogs and cats. The replacement of borhyaenids is graphically shown by Marshall in his study cited below. There were and still are also numerous carnivorous reptiles, some of great size, among the South American crocodilians and snakes, many also competing for mammalian prey. Concentration on the history of land mammals must not make us overlook that they lived throughout that history in communities in which they necessarily interacted with many other kinds of animals and also with many kinds of plants.

Harry Jerison has written extensively on Neotropical herbivores (meaning South American ones only, as he does not include Central American or West Indian forms) as "an evolutionary experiment" in the evolution of the brain and intelligence. This special topic has wide interest, and some comment is necessary here. Jerison's studies are based largely on endocasts of fossil animals, casts of the interior of the brain cavity, which in mammals closely represent the bulk and overall form but not always the true detail of the surface of the brain. From them he has obtained figures for the endocast volume and from that estimates of brain weight. He has also estimated the body weight for the same animals, in many cases extinct animals in which the postcranial skeleton is unknown and its size and weight are loosely estimated from the size of the skull. From these data he calculates what he calls an encephalization quotient or EQ for short.

It has long been known that small mammals have larger brains as a fraction of total body weight than do large mammals, and it is postulated that this is simply a result of size and not of the efficiency or other functional characteristics of the brain. Thus for an expected brain size independent of absolute body size Jerison and others use an equation of the form $E = kP^{2/3}$, in which E is the expected brain size, k is a constant derived as an average over a considerable number of relevant animals, and P is the body weight of any given individual. Relying on a considerable series of observations of Recent mammals, Jerison uses the value 0.12 for the constant k. Having an estimate of the body weight of an extinct mammal, it is thus possible to calculate an "expected brain size" as 0.12 times the body weight raised to the 2/3 power. (That computation may seem complex, but it is simple and quick even with a pocket calculator.) Jerison then takes the ratio of his estimate of the brain weight of the extinct animal to its "expected brain weight" and that ratio is his EQ. In ourselves the average EQ is more than 7; that is, our brains are more than seven times as large as would be "expected" from our body size, if we take $0.12P^{2/3}$ as a valid "expectation." Being constitutionally conceited, humans are not surprised to hear that they have much the largest encephalization quotients known.

Jerison's reason for calculating EQs for extinct South American ungulates from the first faunal stratum (he does not use that term), and the reason for discussing it here, is that he predicted that the (old native) South American ungulates would show little progression in EQs in contrast to his figures for North American ungulates. He made this prediction on the hypothesis that the South American ungulates were unprogressive in intelligence because they were preyed on by supposedly unprogressive marsupial carnivores while the North American ungulates were progressive in intelligence because they were preyed on by more progressive placental carnivores. His figures, put in different form and their presentation simplified, show comparisons in EQs as given in table 14.

It is not solidly established that EQ does measure something that can be called "intelligence." The term "encephalization" is neutral in that respect although Jerison tends to correlate it with intelligence. For that matter, there is no firm consensus as to what intelligence is and whether or how it can be measured. Yet it is reasonable to think of EQ as having something to do with brain power in a broad, colloquial sense. The figures from the natural experiment in South America agree with Jerison's prediction, but I do not think that they necessarily support his hypothesis. The data, scanty as they are, tell us something about the South American ungulates, but I see no reason to think that they are explained by the nature of the contemporaneous predators.

The South American ungulates involved all belong to the first faunal stratum; that is, their ancestors had probably been in South America since sometime in the late Cretaceous and during most of the subsequent time had been isolated there. As far as they go, the data and analyses here available suggest: first, that encephalization was highly variable among these ungulates as a whole; second, that its average among them did not change much; and third, that it tended to be around the average level of the less "archaic" Eocene and Oligocene ungulates of North America. Jerison's sample of what he calls "Paleogene ungulates" in North America does not differ from his "Archaic ungulates" so much in age as in origin. None of the "Paleogene ungulates" had ancestors or close relatives among the "Archaic ungulates." They were a new wave in a fauna that unlike that of South America was *not* isolated in the early Eocene. Also, in the North American ungulates dated as Neogene there are ungulates without previous North American ancestors, and they or their influence are probable contributors to the increased encephalization of the ungulate fauna as a whole. The differences of origin, of history, and of ecological adjustment are at least as likely (I think more likely) to explain the apparent differences in encephalization as the hypothetical influence of less or more progressive predators.

Table 14

Jerison's EQ (see text) for some North and South American ungulates
(rearranged from Jerison 1973)

	Number of Genera Correctly Included	EQ Range	EQ Mean
North American			
"Archaic ungulates" [mostly Eocene]	12	0.11–0.37	0.20
"Paleogene ungulates" [Eocene and Oligocene]	19	0.19–0.92	0.43
"Neogene ungulates" [Miocene and Pleistocene]	13	0.26–0.98	0.64
South American			
"Paleogene" [Casamayoran to Deseadan]	8	0.20–0.91	0.48
"Neogene" [Colhuehuapian to Lujanian]	11	0.26–0.82	0.48

Note: These figures are based on small samples drawn from large faunas and representing a number of quite distinct lineages, not progression in any one. There are, however, some included genera that are related and do come close to being ancestral and descendant at a generic level. For North America, in temporal sequence from oldest to youngest:

Genus	EQ
Mesohippus	0.88
Merychippus	0.98
Pliohippus	0.62

—which looks as if something retrogressed. For South America:

Proadinotherium	0.48
Adinotherium	0.38
Toxodon	0.45

Toxodon belongs to the same family as Adinotherium but was not a descendant of the latter: the change from Proadinotherium to Adinotherium also looks regressive.

Two other predictions for testing in this natural experiment may be made: that overall mammalian faunal encephalization increased in the Deseadan with the introduction of groups without earlier South American ancestors even though there was no change in the kinds of predators present; and that there was a marked overall increase in the Pleistocene with the introduction of both new ungulates and new predators. The necessary data are not now in hand for really testing either prediction, but Jerison's figures do give an inconclusive but suggestive idea about the first prediction. He has five EQs for pre-Deseadan ungulates, observed range 0.20–0.51, mean 0.37, and five for Deseadan ungulates, observed range 0.28–0.91, mean 0.46, which at least is in the direction of the prediction. Further testing would have to involve the newcomers themselves, but at present there are no data on encephalization in Deseadan rodents and primates. For the Neogene ungulates of Jerison's analysis he gives EQs for only two Pleistocene genera, and these are remarkably low, 0.26 and 0.45. It might be expected that if encephalization had survival value the last survivors of an ancient group would have higher EQs, but the sample is too small. There are no figures for South American Pleistocene ungulates as a whole, and among these were newcomers of groups with very high EQs elsewhere, for example horses with EQs around 1, mastodonts around 2.

Inconclusive as these considerations must be until much more information is in hand, I believe that what they suggest is of such interest as to warrant what would otherwise be an undue amount of space devoted to this special subject.

A more general aspect inherent in the preceding history is its bearing on biogeography. Throughout the narrative there has been a geographic background. That a fossil was found at a given place is a fact, and the observed characteristics of the fossil are also facts. Beyond those facts are inferences as to their interpretation and significance, inferences the probability of which ranges from near (but not quite) certainty to mere guessing. It is nearly certain that a species represented by a fossil lived at or near the place where the fossil was found. It is usually highly probable, with exceptions to be watched out for, that the species lived at a point in geological time determined with varying precision by the recognized methods of geochronology. Such are some paleobiogeographical facts and strong probabilities. Some of the broader inferences from them may also be quite probable but can become less clear and less probable.

It is reasonably probable that South America has existed as a discrete continental unit ever since some time in the late Cretaceous, at latest. It is further probable on both paleontological and geological grounds that South America was completely surrounded by marine barriers by the end of the Cretaceous and remained so until some time in the Pliocene when it was united by isthmian land with North America. Still probable on present evidence but with less confidence is the inference that some spread of terrestrial organisms was possible, in one direction or both, between South America and Australia at an early, probably Cretaceous date. It is improbable that this involved a continuous land connection, but if the inference is correct it does involve a situation of Australia near Antarctica at the time and consequent drift from there to its present position far from Antarctica. That is the most probable, or even the only probable, inference as to the involvement of continental drift in the biogeography of known South American mammals. South America may then also have been closer to Antarctica than at present, but that is not made necessary or even clearly probable by any known fact. It is probable on other grounds that the oceanic gap between South America and Africa was narrower in the early Cenozoic than at present, but it still must have been a formidable barrier. There was almost certainly some waif dispersal between North and South America in the late Cretaceous and Paleocene. There was possibly some between South America and Africa, but no known fact requires that interpretation or makes it more probable than any other.

It is extremely probable that rodents and primates evolved somewhere else and reached South America by waif dispersal around the end of the Eocene. It is not clear whether they came from North America or from Africa. They evolved independently in South America. It is virtually certain that the families of land mammals that first appear in the South American fossil record from the Huayquerian age onward were of North American origin. Some of them, at least, also evolved further after spreading to South America, but it is still almost wholly uncertain to what extent they had already become differentiated in southern North America. Some of them probably had evolved there as far as genera, at least. Tropical North America became incorporated in a statically defined Neotropical Region because in the Pliocene to Recent its mammalian fauna became a mixture of mammals of northern South American and southern North American elements, a mixture more similar to that of South America as a whole than to the residual post-Pleistocene fauna of nontropical North America.

That summarizes what I think can now be said with reasonable confidence about the broad aspects of the historical biogeography of land mammals of South America on the basis of the data given in previous chapters. Recently there has been some conflict of opinion about the general principles of biogeography. I shall state supposedly contrasting views in extreme forms. In one view, when related groups of land organisms occur in different regions their common ancestry originally occupied both regions and continuous land between them and then became separated by some barrier and evolved as distinct descendant groups. No dispersal is involved, and especially no waif dispersal across a barrier. Enthusiasts for this process as the primary or basic principle of biogeography call the process "vicariance," which seems and is sometimes said by them to be a synonym of the well-established term "allopatry," which means simply that related species evolved in geographically separate areas. The other process sometimes claimed to be a general principle involves the origin of new species from small populations in restricted areas, their subsequent expansion in numbers and in area, and eventual dispersal into distant regions, sometimes by waif dispersal over barriers.

It is absurd that these two principles or ways of looking at biogeography should be considered as mutually exclusive alternatives, one or the other but not both. Yet some few enthusiasts have maintained that absurdity so emotionally as even to descend to personal vituperation, outside any acceptable discussion of scientific principles. Almost all biogeographers, even some of the few hotheads, know perfectly well that both processes can and do occur singly or in combination, that there are intermediate cases, and that some cases do not clearly fit either model or both. Some adherents of vicariance involve it in other special procedures and concepts that do not need review here, but vicariance itself is defined as allopatry and as such has long been held by most systematists and biogeographers to be the usual, but not the only, way in which new species arise. That has no restriction on the possibilities that dispersal may or may not be involved before, during, or after the speciation occurs. A reasonable biogeographer is neither a vicarist nor a dispersalist but an eclecticist. What is known and reasonably inferred about the history of South American mammals supports and illustrates this point of view.

A passion for rationality should not make this book end on a downbeat with a mildly objurgatory comment on schools of biogeography. Another current dispute, this one on principles of classification, that also calls for some objurgation should and does receive it elsewhere and need not do so here. A more suitable envoi here is on an upbeat: on the grandeur of this history; on the light that the great natural experiment throws on so many things that even transcend the story itself; on its helping us to understand more about the processes of evolution that have produced ourselves and all the other wonders of organic nature. This summary book is evidence that the labors of many devoted people over a great many years have indeed produced much knowledge and comprehension. It is a hopeful prospect that further discoveries and further study will continue to advance these plainly desirable ends.

References

For further consideration of the principles of evolution and of biogeography I have included an excellent recent treatise on evolution and one on biogeography that is now out of date but better than most of the recent works on that subject.

Darlington, P. J. 1957. *Zoogeography: The geographical distribution of animals.* New York: John Wiley and Sons.

Dobzhansky, Th.; F. J. Ayala; B. L. Stebbins; and J. W. Valentine. 1977. *Evolution.* San Francisco: W. H. Freeman.

Jerison, H. J. 1973. *Evolution of the brain and intelligence.* New York and London: Academic Press.

Kurtén, B. 1960. Faunal turnover dates for the Pleistocene and late Pliocene. Soc. Sci. Fennica, *Commentationes Biologicae,* 22: 14 p.

Marshall, L. G. 1978. Evolution of the Borhyaenidae, extinct South American predaceous marsupials. *University of California Publications in Geological Science,* 117: i–vi, 1–89.

Webb, S. D. 1976. Mammalian faunal dynamics of the great American interchange. *Paleobiology,* 2: 220–234.

Note on the Restoration of Extinct Animals

The idea that paleontologists reconstruct whole animals from a single tooth or bone still persists among many nonpaleontologists. Writers find it a useful simile for comparison with other real or supposed instances of drawing wide conclusions from limited clues. In fact it is untrue, and it may be useful here to explain how paleontologists and artists working with them do restore approximations, at least, of what extinct animals looked like when alive.

Any paleontologist can recognize a single tooth of a horse, *Equus caballus*. In spite of the differences among breeds and the one still barely surviving wild species, all horses do look much alike. An artist then can draw a reasonable picture of the animal represented by that single tooth, even though he will not know how long its hair was or how it was colored. That does not really involve "reconstructing" or "restoring" the animal. It simply results from identification of the tooth as belonging to a well-known group still extant.

Mammoths, unlike horses, are extinct. Their teeth resemble those of elephants, and it is a reasonable inference from that fact that mammoths looked something like elephants. A portrait based on that resemblance of a single tooth nevertheless would probably be rather wide of the mark. In the case of the best known of several species of mammoths, the woolly mammoth, the restorer does not have to depend on such dubious evidence. Woolly mammoths frozen whole have been found in Siberia and Alaska, and in Europe Stone Age men, who knew woolly mammoths when they were alive, painted excellent portraits of them on the walls of caves. The "restorations" of them made by modern artists are not true restorations from a single tooth or bone but are portraits of the whole animals based on their frozen remains and on contemporaneous pictures of them.

Obviously the case of the woolly mammoth is quite special, and that method of portrayal is not applicable to the vast majority of extinct mammals, in which, with extremely rare exceptions, only bones and teeth are preserved. Restoring an extinct animal on the basis of its apparent resemblance to one still living is inapplicable when, as in many instances, there is no fairly close resemblance. Experience has further shown that when there is some resemblance it may be superficial or grossly misleading. This is shown by the case of another member of the horse family (Equidae). In 1840 Richard Owen, a famous British anatomist and paleontologist, described the fossil skull and jaw of a small animal that he named *Hyracotherium leporinum*. *Hyracotherium* means "a mammal resembling a hyrax" or cony, small, hoofed, but somewhat rabbitlike animals living in Africa and southeastern Asia. *Leporinum* means "of or among the hares" (and rabbits). In fact the resemblances to hyraxes or rabbits eventually proved to be entirely superficial. *Hyracotherium* did not really look at all like either one of those two groups of living animals.

Later in the nineteenth century, in 1876 to be exact, the likewise famous American paleontologist O. C. Marsh named some fossils of a small animal *Eohippus*, which means "dawn horse." Marsh recognized this creature as a member of the horse family near or, probably, in the direct ancestry of our living horses. That conclusion would have been impossible if Marsh had not also had several other fossil members of the family intermediate between *Eohippus* and *Equus* both in geological age and in anatomical structure. It then was observed that *Hyracotherium* was closely similar to *Eohippus*, indeed that the two supposed genera are identical. Finally, the whole skeleton of eohippus, a term that has now become a popular name for the genus technically called *Hyracotherium*, was found and put together. Only then could it be restored with fair probability. It turned out not to look much like *Equus* and hardly at all like hyraxes or rabbits.

Even from the first specimen ever discovered and described, it would have been possible to make a reasonable life restoration of the head of *Hyracotherium*. When it was learned that *Hyracotherium* belongs to the horse family, reasonable restoration of the whole animal still was not possible until its whole skeleton was known. It could be concluded that it must have had from one to five toes on each foot, but not just how many it really had. (It turned out to have four toes on each front foot, three on each hindfoot.) The length and posture of the limbs, the length of the tail, the extent of the back and rib cage, and other features necessary to make a fair likeness could not even be guessed at when only the teeth and head were known.

The usual first requisite for making a life restoration of a fossil animal is thus to know the structure of the skeleton in the parts to be restored. If only the skull and jaws are known, only the head can be reliably restored. Except for some fossils closely related and similar to living animals, the whole animal cannot be reliably restored unless the whole skeleton is known. In the restorations for this book, we have strictly adhered to those rules. This is especially desirable in the present case because most of the fossil mammals of South America are not closely related to any living mammals.

The great majority of fossil mammals everywhere are not known from complete skeletons, and that is decidedly true for South America. Most of the extinct species are based on teeth or bits of jaws. These are distinctive and recognizable in themselves and also are usually good evidence of relationships, but they are not safe guides to what the living animals looked like. Fortunately, however, complete or nearly complete skeletons have been found for at least one member of many of the families of extinct South American mammals. Only one skeleton is yet adequately known for the whole of the Paleocene and Eocene, first two epochs of the Age of Mammals in South America, but a fair sampling of later genera are known from skeletons and are thus scientifically restorable as whole animals.

It should be understood that some characteristics of the once living animals cannot be really determined from the fossil remains and may require some technical imagination and artistic license.

From the skull and jaws the form of the head can be readily restored along with the placement of the ears, the position and relative size of the eyes, the position of the nose and mouth, and the presence of such things as gnawing front teeth or tusks. The shape and size of the external ears, which have no bones, have to be guessed at. Some of the extinct South American mammals had a proboscis, also boneless, the existence of which can be determined by the shape of the bones around the nasal region, but there is some guesswork as to whether the proboscis was short as in tapirs or longer, perhaps (but we think probably not) even as long as in elephants. Since almost all living rodents have vibrissae, the long sensitive hairs on the snout, it is fair enough to put them on restorations of extinct rodents even though they leave no trace on the skull.

The proportions of body, legs, and tail are readily determined from the skeleton, and so is the presence of hooves or claws on the toes. Apart from the bones, the external shape of the body is largely determined by the muscles that move bones, and educated judgment about them can be based on the bones, as can probable postures and locomotion. *Argyrolagus* has no close living relatives, but it does have close analogies with some of the ricochetal placental rodents and it has here been restored with that convergence of function as a partial guide. Convergence in general can help in restoration but must be judiciously considered.

It is safe to conclude that the nonburrowing and unarmored fossil land mammals were mostly covered with hair, but the length and exact distribution of the hair or the possible presence of such things as manes or of wool is not determinable. As a rule it seems best to restore land mammals as if the hair, where it occurred, was short and did not significantly affect the overall contour. The color and possible patterning, as in spots or stripes, of an extinct animal are absolutely undeterminable. Some artists have enjoyed giving their fancy free play in that respect. The style of drawing that is used in our restorations here avoids that temptation.